The Gluten-free Gourmet
Makes Dessert

B E T T E   H A G M A N

The Gluten-free Gourmet Makes Dessert

AN OWL BOOK

Henry Holt and Company | New York

Henry Holt and Company, LLC
Publishers since 1866
115 West 18th Street
New York, New York 10011

Henry Holt® is a registered trademark of
Henry Holt and Company, LLC.

Library of Congress Cataloging-in-Publication Data

Hagman, Bette.
    The gluten-free gourmet makes dessert/Bette Hagman.
        p.   cm.
    Includes index.
    ISBN 0-8050-7276-4 (pbk.)
        1. Gluten-free diet—Recipes.   2. Desserts.   I. Title.

RM237.86 .H3383 2002
641.5'63—dc21   2001039309

Henry Holt books are available for special promotions and
premiums. For details contact: Director, Special Markets.

First published in hardcover in 2002 by
Henry Holt and Company

First Owl Books Edition 2003

Designed by Kelly S. Too

Printed in the United States of America

1 3 5 7 9 10 8 6 4 2

This book is dedicated to my sister, Eva Jean Purdum,
a great travel companion who is willing to walk that extra
block or more to find a place where a celiac can eat well,
or if none is nearby, is equally content to stay in the
hotel room and share my soup and crackers.

Contents

Foreword

According to a new study by the University of Maryland School of Medicine, as many as one out of every 150 Americans lives with celiac disease, making it the most common inherited genetic illness in the country. It is estimated, therefore, that as many as two million Americans may have celiac disease and, of course, a vast majority have no idea they have it. I have often referred to this condition as the "mystery illness," since symptoms vary greatly from patient to patient, ranging from a difficulty gaining or losing weight to diarrhea, constipation, or heartburn. In my experience, the most common complaint shared by all tends to be fatigue.

Celiac disease is an inherited disorder, which may become unmasked at any age, in childhood or adulthood. If one is genetically predisposed, it is thought that a "trigger" is needed to initiate the illness. I often think of it as a lock and key: The lock is the individual's predisposition to celiac disease, but a key—such as an infection, surgery, stress, overindulgence in gluten, possibly even overuse of antibiotics—is necessary to "turn on" the condition. I strongly believe that all patients with gastrointestinal symptoms should be screened with appropriate blood testing since celiac disease is so common and difficult to diagnose, as well as potentially quite serious.

In this country, because celiac disease is not usually suspected, some patients present first with another associated autoimmune illness, such as diabetes, lupus, Addison's disease, or rheumatoid arthritis, to name just a few. At the University of Maryland, Dr. Alessio Fasano has done serologic testing on more than ten thousand individuals as part of a study and found that first-degree relatives of a celiac patient have a one in twelve likelihood of having the disease as well, even though some may be virtually asymptomatic. I hope studies such as this will help increase physicians' awareness of the condition. Serologic testing should also be considered in all individuals with autoimmune diseases, chronic fatigue syndrome, or fibromyalgia. Appropriate blood testing should include antigliadin antibodies, antiendomysial antibodies, tissue transglutaminase, and a serum IgA level. But it is important to remember that blood testing alone does not guarantee an accurate diagnosis. A biopsy of the small intestine has to be taken for a conclusive result.

If you have celiac disease, ingesting gluten, which is found in wheat, rye, barley, and possibly oats, will not only exacerbate these symptoms, but may also lead to inflammation and damage to the microscopic villi in the small intestine. These tiny, fingerlike projections are important in vitamin and mineral absorption, including bone-making calcium. In fact, undiagnosed celiac disease and osteoporosis often go hand-in-hand. However, a gluten-free diet may help prevent osteoporosis, as well as other autoimmune diseases associated with celiac disease, and can greatly improve the quality of life of people living with this condition.

One of the greatest concerns and biggest challenges for celiacs is how to manage a healthy diet without sacrificing one's quality of life. The prospect of a diet without traditional breads, pastas, puddings, cakes, cookies, and other flour-based goodies may seem challenging to some people. Fortunately, there are wonderful, healthy alternatives that can help you live a happier, healthier life.

Bette Hagman's delightful books provide these alternatives. Not only are her recipes completely gluten-free and easy to make, they are exciting and delicious. In this new dessert cookbook, you will find an answer to almost every imaginable craving. What's more, they are healthy and delicious goodies that at a family picnic, a dinner party, a birthday, or even a wedding everyone, not just the celiac, can enjoy and feel good about. Recently, I had the pleasure of attending the Ninth International Symposium on Celiac Disease held in Baltimore, and one of the presentations suggested that celiacs who follow and strictly adhere to a gluten-free diet live years longer than the general population!

My practice is devoted to screening and treating individuals with celiac disease, and Bette Hagman's wonderful books are a cornerstone in my program for patient education and wellness. She has shown the celiac community that delicious meals are certainly possible and how varied the gluten-free diet can be. As I tell my patients upon hearing their diagnosis, "This is wonderful news! You have a genetically inherited illness that is potentially reversible by total gluten elimination. Your body may heal in as soon as six weeks (longer for severely damaged celiacs), and you don't have to take any medications to be cured!" Celiac or not, everyone will enjoy Bette's Chocolate Mousse Cake as well as her other wonderful desserts. A gluten-free diet can be a healthy and delicious diet for everyone.

Cynthia S. Rudert, M.D., F.A.C.P.
Board Certified Gastroenterologist
Medical Director, Gluten Sensitive Support Group of Atlanta
Medical Advisor, Celiac Disease Foundation
Medical Advisor, Gluten Intolerance Group of North America
Member, Celiac Standardization Group
Founder and President, Atlanta Women's Medical Alliance

Acknowledgments

A book is like a suit of clothes, made up of many parts, molded to fit a certain type of person. So also are these gluten-free cookbooks. They are of special material and created to fit a need. For much of this material I have to thank my loyal readers who not only send recipes, suggestions, and their stories, but inspire me to keep searching for more recipes with different flours.

I owe the greatest debt to the wonderful set of testers who've worked (sometimes for the third time) on the recipes, helping to perfect them: Katherine Barkley, Bert Garman, Catherine Gayton, Marlene Keier, Vicki Lyles, Karen Meyers, Jean Nichols, Alicia Paley, Wendy Percival, Genevieve Potts, Virginia Schmuck, Deb Souder, and Mary Lou Thomas. Without these loyal cooks, I could never have finished the recipes in this book.

I also have to thank the suppliers who not only furnish many of the flours but also teach me how to use them. I am especially indebted to Steve Rice of Authentic Foods, Sam Wylde II and Sam Wylde III of Ener-G Foods, and Jay Berger of Miss Roben's. Without their help I would still be blending flours without any idea of the outcome. Between them, they furnished most of the answers to the section "What Did I Do Wrong?"

I thank Cynthia Kupper, M.S., R.D., for the medical review of the manuscript and Cynthia Rudert, M.D., for reading the manuscript and writing the Foreword.

And finally I want to thank my agent, Dominick Abel, for his continued support and faith in my writing.

The Gluten-free Gourmet
Makes Dessert

Introduction

*T*o my new readers and old friends, welcome to a world without gluten. To some of you this will, at first, appear bewildering, upsetting, and frustrating. But once you get the hang of it, stepping into this world should be the gateway to better health. Whether you are living gluten-free because of a wheat allergy, a diagnosis of celiac disease (gluten-sensitive enteropathy), or because you simply feel better without wheat or gluten, you've probably already discovered that practicing this takes a surprising amount of discipline and some sacrifices.

Eating out socially will take planning ahead. A business luncheon might be pure business with a salad on the side, travel planning may include an extra suitcase for your food, while grocery shopping will require much reading of ingredient lists—and probably a magnifying glass. Be thankful for those lists; we didn't have these until the 1990s.

But cheer up! Eating gluten free is getting simpler every day. The number of suppliers has multiplied and their offerings now include pasta, pizza, and other main dishes as well as mixes for baking (see pages 325–32). Now, with this book, you can indulge in desserts we only dreamed of twenty-five years ago.

When I started writing the *Gluten-free Gourmet* series my most elegant sweet was a puffed rice cracker slathered with jam—and the designation for adult celiac disease was nontropical sprue, as it was thought that only children had celiac disease.

Did I say, When I started writing the series? Oops! I mean, When I started putting the collection of recipes my students and I had exchanged into a book. I never dreamed of a series and neither, I'm sure, did my publisher. After all, the celiac condition was considered rare at the time. The list of those with wheat allergies was far longer, but they, I presumed, were satisfied with foods made with oats, barley, and rye—grains that were wheat-free but not gluten-free.

It seems I was wrong; when I went looking for recipes written for those with wheat allergies, I found very few, and most of them were no tastier than my rice cracker and jam. They'd been suffering deprivations as well as those estimated one out of approximately three thousand in the United States who had been diagnosed with celiac disease at the time.

In England in the late 1970s, although the rate of celiacs in the population was thought to be much higher than in the United States, there still was little attention given to feeding the patient. There seemed to be more information about the medical aspects of celiac disease than there was about food. The recipes I could find—rice droppies and potato flatties—did little to satisfy my apple pie and coffee cake yearnings. For open-faced sandwiches one author suggested spreading thin slices of liver loaf or headcheese with cucumber and peanut butter. And nowhere could I find any recipe for yeast breads or exciting desserts. One can only eat so many baked apples!

While nutritionists insist we don't have to have much fat and sugar (desserts) in our diet, the idea of that little sweet at the end of the meal is inherent in most of us. I wasn't diagnosed until I was fifty, but I must have been a celiac all my life for I avoided most obvious glutens such as bread, pancakes, cakes, and cookies because they gave me a stomachache. I can remember as a child that while others were eating the cake or pie my mother had prepared as dessert, I would trot down to the cellar and bring back a jar of home-canned fruit (picked at the peak of perfection and sweetened in heavy syrup) as my treat. I'd still be content to end a meal with some wonderfully sweet—one celiac child calls it "slippery"—fruit if any canning company would go back to putting enough sugar in their syrup. Do you notice how most of it now tastes flat since it's often picked before it's ripe and canned without sugar? I'd like to have my peach taste like the ones we picked from the tree and the juice ran down the arm as one nibbled.

This need for food that tastes like I remember may have been a contributing factor to my quitting my job as a writing instructor in a local technical college and gambling on my first cookbook, *The Gluten-free Gourmet*. I was not a cook and had never made a cake "from scratch," so my first attempts at baking were dismal failures. I could have built a cabin from the number of "bricks" I turned out, and could have landscaped a beachfront from the crumbs that resulted from the rest of my attempts.

At that time rice flour was the only nonwheat baking starch used extensively and if any of you have eaten any gluten-free product made with only rice flour, you know that it's gritty tasting, heavy, and often unappealing since it doesn't brown well. So, being both frustrated and persistent—and ignorant—I added other flours such as soy, potato starch, cornstarch, and tapioca starch, the most common ones available at the time. My baked goods improved in taste and texture. Years later, when I discovered bean flour and sorghum, I included them, thus adding more nutritional value as well as great taste to the baked products. There are still a lot more nutritional gluten-free flours to be experimented with: amaranth, buckwheat, millet, quinoa, and teff, and I'm looking forward to working with them.

There are no recipes for those exotic flours in this book but there is one exciting chapter—"No Special Ingredients" (page 271). Every ingredient can be found in your local grocery store. No sending away for odd items like xanthan gum or a special flour. If any flour is used it will be cornstarch, sweet rice flour, or potato starch, which can be found in small boxes in the baking section of any grocery. These are practical for the beginning baker or for someone who is cooking for a celiac relative or friend so doesn't want to store much flour, but impractical for someone baking constantly for the gluten-free diet.

I've included desserts in all four of the previous books in the *Gluten-free Gourmet* series, so you may wonder if we need a whole book of desserts. Yes, we do! Although sugars and fats are only the tip of the nutrition pyramid, anyone deprived of being able to stop in at Dunkin' Donuts, pick up a cake at the local bakery, or even buy a bag of cookies while grocery shopping needs the emotional lift of the assurance that he/she can go home to a gluten-free dessert treat either in the cookie jar or hidden away in the freezer marked with a GF label so others don't nibble.

Although now that our desserts can taste as good or better than wheat-filled ones, even labels don't keep kids and spouses from enjoying them. It wasn't hard in the 1970s to warn a would-be snitcher off with "You won't like that." My husband, one of my best supporters, then agreed that "Yes, it could taste better." I remember when I had to warn anyone eating my pie that it was the filling that counted and forget the crust. Those days are past. Now most of the celiacs who enjoy baking find that friends and family play critic by asking them to "bring the dessert." And they can proudly comply with cake, pie, cheesecake, or cookies that rival any wheat-based sweet.

With this, the fifth book in the *Gluten-free Gourmet* series, it is easy to see that both my publisher and I were wrong about the need for this kind of book. I had no idea that some doctors would be suggesting the gluten-free diet for their arthritis patients or that mothers of autistic children would embrace the idea of a gluten-free–casein- (milk protein) free diet as a possible solution for helping their child to better health. And definitely the medical field had miscalculated the number who would later be diagnosed with celiac disease. Little did they suspect that by the middle of 2000, it would be estimated that of the number of celiacs had grown from 1:3000 to (possibly as great as) 1:150. The sad thing is that although there may be so many out there, most of them are still unaware of the disease for they have few or no symptoms and are not seeking help from any medical authority.

Another and sadder fact is that often those who are diagnosed are not aware of how much help is available. The diagnosis of wheat intolerance, wheat allergy, celiac disease, or gluten enteropathy is just the beginning. Learning to understand how to ferret out the hidden glutens (such as gluten in toothpaste, pills, mouthwash, lipstick, and so on), learning how to find gluten-free foods and supplies, attempting to eat gluten free in restaurants, and trying to explain the need for the diet to relatives and friends is going to be an ongoing reminder that this condition, to keep it in complete remission, calls for help. And the best help now comes from others who have been through it all—the sympathetic and knowledgeable members of a support group. If you can find one locally, you can attend meetings; but if there isn't one, there are national groups that offer help by newsletters, printed materials, phone calls, Web sites, and yearly educational conferences. Don't be afraid to ask for help whether it is for you, a spouse, your child, or a friend or relative. Following is a list of the national groups. Call one of them to find a local group near you.

American Celiac Society Dietary Support Coalition, 59 Crystal Avenue, West Orange, NJ 07052-3570; phone: (973) 325-8837.

Canadian Celiac Association, 5170 Dixie Road, Suite 204, Mississau 1E3, Canada; phone: (905) 507-6208; fax: (905) 507-4673; toll free: (800) 363-7296.

Celiac Disease Foundation, 13251 Ventura Blvd., Suite 1, Studio City, CA 91604-1838; phone: (818) 990-2354; fax: (818) 990-2397; e-mail: cdf@celiac.org; Web site: www.celiac.org.

Celiac Sprue Association/United States of America (CSA/USA), P.O. Box 31700, Omaha, NE 68131-0700; phone: (402) 558-0600.

Gluten Intolerance Group (GIG), 15110 10th Avenue, SW, Suite A, Seattle, WA 98166; phone: (206) 246-6652; fax: (206) 246-6531; e-mail: info@gluten.net; Web site: www.gluten.net.

Internet: http://cekuac@maelstrom.stjohns.edu
http://rdz.acor.org/lists/celiac/index.html

REFERENCES

Alessio Fasano, M.D., "Evolution of Diagnostic Tools of Celiac Disease." Paper presented at the Ninth International Symposium on Celiac Disease, August 2000, Hunt Valley, Maryland.

Joseph Murray, M.D., "Current Serological Screening in U.S.: Tools and Results." Paper presented at the Ninth International Symposium on Celiac Disease, August 2000, Hunt Valley, Maryland.

The Gluten-free Lifestyle

*A*ctually this is a chapter about the gluten-free diet and how to live it. If you think of it as a lifestyle and not a diet, it may not sound so dire.

Diets are rigid; our lifestyle as a celiac can be anything we make it. If we look at the bright side, we can now make or buy almost anything we crave to eat; the downside is that we have to plan ahead for our meals whether at home or eating out. And we are going to spend more time ordering food by mail, shopping at health food stores, or cooking.

When my doctor's nurse handed me two crumpled, mimeographed sheets instead of a prescription when I was diagnosed, I figured this was going to be easy. When I carried the sheets into the grocery on my way home, I received the same shock you probably did—there was nothing on the dry cereal shelf that didn't contain gluten. And naturally the breads, cookies, and crackers were off-limits—as were the pancake and waffle mixes. I went home with rice cakes and jam. After a few of those for breakfast, it didn't take me long to figure out a way of making muffins from some of the gluten-free flours.

That was my approach to **the diet—don't let it intimidate you!**

There's a lot to learn. What foods contain gluten? Where can I shop? What happens if I get some gluten? How long do I have to be on the diet?

Let's start with the last. This will have to be a lifetime change, or until the scientists who are working on the problem either find a vaccine or learn to genetically change our faulty immune systems, or the cereal chemists create a wheat without the gliadin fraction of the gluten that irritates our guts.

As for the foods that contain gluten, that's much harder to answer. It's simple to recognize that most of the breads, cakes, cookies, and crackers on the grocery shelf are made with (wheat) flour. For many it's hard to remember that pastas and the batters on fried foods are also. But not many of us realized when we first read the list that our biggest problem would not be the obvious but the hidden glutens that go into the ingredient lists of soups, custards, ice creams, and so on as modified food starch, which can be potato, corn, tapioca, or wheat.

If you're starting to panic, hold it!

Don't expect to learn it all at once. **Start with the basics.** Eliminate the obvious wheat products and substitute gluten-free ones either from your own baking or purchased from mail-order suppliers or health food stores. Remember: you can have any plain fruit or vegetable and plain cuts of any meat. (You'll have to read labels on blended meats such as hot dogs and sausages and avoid turkey or ham that has been injected with HVP [hydrolyzed vegetable protein]).

In time, you'll learn to question the pharmacist to see if your prescriptions or over-the-counter drugs contain gluten, and you may question such things as vitamins, toothpaste, and mouthwash.

But, **relax. No one can learn it all the first day.**

I realize that it sounds frightening to have to change a way of living if you're used to picking up a doughnut on your way to work and grabbing a sandwich for lunch. The new gluten-free muffins replaced the doughnut for me, and salads took the place of sandwiches until xanthan gum was introduced and I learned to make bread. It's sandwiches for lunch for me again.

Now there are plenty of recipes, muffin mixes you can order, and even ready-baked muffins, cinnamon rolls, and other breakfast breads, as long as you're willing to order ahead and keep your freezer full. I told you it takes planning.

Once you have mastered the basics and know you are eating gluten free, you should be free of the symptoms (diarrhea, constipation, irritable bowel, mental haze, or just lethargy) that led you to the doctor and diagnosis. If you are not, it's time to look for either **contamination** somewhere in your food or note **other sensitivities or allergies** you may have.

Let's take contamination first. One of the major sources of contamination is in the home itself. A toaster may sprinkle crumbs from the wheat bread to yours. The kids mixing up their pancakes will pollute the air and workplaces with wheat dust that can linger for twenty-four hours or until wiped up. If possible, to avoid the latter, it's sensible to bake gluten free for the whole family. This doesn't mean you have to deprive them of their own favorite gluten-filled cereal or bread. These can be purchased and don't shed gluten into the air; you can also buy their cookies and cakes rather than contaminating your kitchen. But you may find, as many do, that the gluten-free desserts in this book will be enjoyed by the entire family. And most celiacs who cook for their family try as much as possible to make the main dishes, side dishes and vegetables gluten free so only one meal has to be cooked. Now that we have great pastas to make or buy, the Four Flour Mix for a breading that's better than wheat flour, and GF Mix for thickening gravies and soup, it's easy to tempt the others into joining the celiac in this healthy lifestyle.

Other sources of contamination can be in the way the gluten-free flours are marketed. Open bins in a health food store may be contaminated by customers unthinkingly using wrong scoops or returning unwanted flour to a wrong bin, thus mixing gluten flours with gluten-free ones. To avoid this, try to buy all your flours prepackaged.

Now for **sensitivities and allergies**: This is a whole new can of worms. Remember when I said I had apple pie and coffee cake cravings? When I baked my first gluten-free apple pie, I knew the crumbly crust needed more work, but I never realized that the pie would bring on my old celiac symptoms. I thought that my flour was contaminated so I made another pie with newly purchased flours. Again the stomach distress! I tried eating cooked apples without the crust. Same symptoms!

I discovered that I am sensitive to apples. Since apples contain aspartame, one of the ingredients in diet sodas, I realized why I couldn't tolerate diet soda and, now, apples.

This was a plus for me—to know another of my sensitivities. I already had and continue to have intolerance to all dairy products (lactose, whey, casein), so I added apples and aspartame to my sensitivities list—and discovered that, alarmingly, almost all mixed-fruit drinks have an apple juice base. No mixed-fruit drinks for me. Warning: If you, too, find an allergy to a common food, remember to check ingredient lists for all forms of this food as well as gluten. No, these foods do not damage the gut as gluten does, but no one wants to be sick when they can avoid it.

Once they've eliminated gluten, others find sensitivities to simple things like chocolate, eggs, nuts, soy, oranges, potatoes, and many other foods. I've heard of some who cannot tolerate rice. So don't blame all your upsets on "gluten poisoning." It's not uncommon for celiacs, with their already sensitive gut, to find other allergies. Recognizing them will save you from embarrassment by crying "Gluten! gluten!" only to be proven that you've cried out falsely.

Living gluten free will, at times, be frustrating (like having to order a hamburger "without the bun" when you'd rather dig into the featured pasta entree), annoying (trying to explain that you have a condition that limits your choice of food), or downright embarrassing (refusing that cookie your best friend baked). But the good health that results will offset these infrequent occasions. **Don't compromise this by cheating.**

You certainly will feel like it and, at times, it would be far easier. But in the long run you will have to pay for the cheating. Your symptoms will return, and the effect of constant irritation to the small intestine every time you cheat can, in the end, damage your health. It has been shown that a celiac who stays gluten free over a period of five years has reduced the chance of cancer of the small bowel to that of someone without celiac disease. Who wants to gamble on cancer when you can help to avoid it? Other complications of long-term damage can be osteoporosis or pancreatic insufficiency, or both.

Naturally, you may not always be able to avoid accidents. My very worst was when a kitchen helper added some imitation crab (made with wheat) to my fresh crab salad because "We'd run out of real crab and the salad looked skimpy." If you have an accident, treat it as such and figure you've learned a lesson. I did. I now ask several times if all the crab is "real."

Accidents are accidents but cheating should be unforgivable.

It's not easy, is it? But there are several ways we can **make this new lifestyle as easy as possible.**

1. To save time and trouble, **try to make as much of the meal gluten free as possible.** The celiac will appreciate not feeling different and the cook will not have to make two meals. And there will be less risk of contamination. Using gluten-free condiments is one easy and painless way. Using the GF Mix for thickening and gravies is another. Many casseroles and main dishes can easily be converted to being gluten free. And, definitely, gluten-free desserts, as I've shown in this book, will please anyone. That is—if the celiac will share.

2. **Learn to bake.** There are now many gluten-free main dishes and treats that can be ordered, as well as mixes for breads, cakes, cookies, and pizza crusts. But

these take time and trouble to order. You can buy a few in health food stores, and some even in our regular groceries.

But even more and better breads and desserts can be made from scratch at home. And they are far less expensive. One of the best perfumes in the world is the scent of fresh baked bread filling the house.

3. **Make good use of your freezer.** Always have some treats frozen so the celiac will not feel deprived when others are eating a gluten-filled dessert. Freeze single portions of main dishes for the time the family dinner is off limits to the celiac. Mark these with large letters: GF. Or buy red dot stickers to warn others that the package is reserved for the celiac.

4. Get into the habit of **carry**ing some bagged **treat in your purse or pocket** for emergencies. A small plastic bag of Fritos along with coffee or a soda might get a celiac through the noon hour. Cookies or a granola bar can be eaten on a bus ride or tour. And always carry something for a celiac child who can't wait to get home to eat.

As I go into my twenty-seventh year living gluten free I'm thankful for my diagnosis and the years of active good health it has given me. I hope you, too, will feel the same and consider this diet not a restriction but the beginning of a new, healthy lifestyle.

It's almost impossible to write a gluten-free diet that will suit everyone because of the many sensitivities, preferences, and lifestyles. There has been much discussion among the various celiac groups in the United States about certain foods such as distilled grain alcohols and vinegars and natural flavorings. I've added the controversial grains of amaranth, buckwheat, millet, quinoa, and teff, which have always been allowed in Canada. There is also a difference between the zero tolerance allowed in the United States, Canada, and Australia to that of most European countries (.003). In the following pages I've simply listed the foods that are gluten free and those that aren't according to the diet list compiled in 2000 by two of the groups in the United States and representatives of the Canadian Dietetic Association and the Canadian Celiac Association, which was later published in the American Dietetic Association Diet Manual.

If you feel that any items I've listed as acceptable in this list are not for your diet, don't hesitate to leave them out. Our diet is a judgment choice and we are free to make it using the best and latest information we have.

	FOODS ALLOWED	FOODS TO AVOID
BEVERAGES	Coffee, tea, cocoa (Baker's, Hershey's, Nestle's), some carbonated beverages, rum, tequila, wine, vodka (if made from potatoes, grapes, or plums), spirits from distilled grains (use your own judgment).	Postum, Ovaltine, beer, ale, gin, some flavored and instant coffees, some herbal teas. Some carbonated beverages (root beer), spirits from distilled grains (use your own judgment).
BREADS	Breads made with gluten-free flours only (rice, potato starch, soy, corn, bean, sorghum) baked at home or purchased from companies that produce GF products. Rice crackers or cakes, corn tortillas.	All breads made with wheat, oat, rye, and barley flours. All purchased crackers, croutons, bread crumbs, wafers, biscuits, and doughnuts containing any gluten flours. Graham, soda, or snack crackers, tortillas containing wheat.
CEREALS	Cornmeal, hot rice cereals, hominy grits, gluten-free cold rice, corn cereals (those without malt), and cereals cooked from the grains of teff, buckwheat, or quinoa.	All cereals containing wheat, rye, oats, or barley (both as grain and in flavoring, such as malt flavoring, malt syrup).
DAIRY PRODUCTS	Milk (fresh, dry, evaporated, or condensed), buttermilk, cream, sour cream, butter, cheese (except those that contain oat gum), whipped cream, yogurt (plain and flavored if GF), ice cream (if GF), artificial cream (if GF).	Malted milk, artificial cream (if not GF), some chocolate milk drinks, some commercial ice creams, some processed cheese spreads, flavored yogurt (containing gluten), some light or fat-free dairy products (containing gluten).
DESSERTS	Any pie, cake, cookie, or other desserts made with GF flours and flavorings. Gelatins, custards, homemade puddings (rice, corn-starch, tapioca). Prepared cake or cookie mixes (if GF).	All pies, cakes, cookies, and so on that contain any wheat, oat, rye, or barley flour or flavoring. Most commercial pudding mixes, ice cream cones, prepared cake mixes using wheat flour.
FATS	Margarine, vegetable oil, nuts, GF mayonnaise, shortening, lard, some salad dressings.	Some commercial salad dressings, some mayonnaise (watch for modified food starch).
FLOURS	Rice flour (brown and white), soy flour, potato flour, tapioca flour, corn flour, cornmeal, cornstarch, rice bran, rice polish, arrowroot,	All flours or baking mixes containing wheat, rye, barley, or oats. And triticale.

	nut flours, legume, buckwheat, and sorghum flours. Millet, teff, amaranth, and quinoa flours.	
FRUITS AND JUICES	All fruit, fresh, frozen, canned (if GF), and dried (if not dusted with wheat flour to prevent sticking).	Any commercially canned fruit with gluten thickening.
MEAT, FISH, POULTRY, AND EGGS	Any eggs (plain or in cooking), all fresh meats, fish, poultry, other seafood; fish canned in oil, water, or brine. GF prepared meats such as luncheon meats, tofu, GF imitation seafood.	Eggs in gluten-based sauce, prepared meats containing gluten, some fish canned in HVP, self-basting turkeys injected with HVP, imitation seafood containing wheat flour.
PASTAS	GF homemade noodles, spaghetti, or other pastas, oriental rice noodles, bean threads, purchased GF pasta made with corn, rice, tapioca, quinoa, and potato flours.	Noodles, spaghetti, macaroni, or other pastas made with gluten flours. Any canned pasta product.
SOUPS AND CHOWDERS	Homemade broth and soups made with GF ingredients, some canned soups, some powdered soup bases, some GF dehydrated soups.	Most canned soups, most dehydrated soup mixes, bouillon and bouillon cubes containing HVP.
VEGETABLES	All plain fresh, frozen, or canned vegetables; dried peas, beans, and lentils.	All creamed, breaded, and scalloped vegetables. Some canned baked beans, some prepared salad mixes.
SWEETS	Jellies, jams, honey, sugar, molasses, corn syrup, other syrups, some commercial candies.	Some commercial candies, some cake decorations. Note: icing sugar in Canada may contain wheat.
CONDIMENTS	Salt, pepper, herbs, food coloring, pure spices; rice, cider, and wine vinegars; yeast, GF soy sauce, GF curry powder, baking powder, baking soda.	Some curry powder, some mixed spices, some ketchup, some prepared mustards, most soy sauces. Some pepper with wheat flour added (often found ouside the United States).

This is just a general list for your information. Always remember to read the full ingredients list when purchasing any product that might contain any form of gluten.

Gluten-free Flours

*I*f you are a recently diagnosed celiac or have just discovered that you have to eliminate wheat from your diet, or if you are cooking for someone like this, most of the flours in this book will seem strange to you. And the recipes may call for odd-sounding ingredients.

If you haven't worked with these flours before, it's easiest to start with simple recipes but it won't be long before you can turn out baked products that rival any made with wheat. As for thickening gravy, use the GF Mix, substitute potato starch and sweet rice flour in cream sauces and soups, tapioca and cornstarch in pies and fruit dishes.

You've probably used few of these flours before so here's a short explanation of what they are and how best to cook with and store them. I've also added some of our unusual baking additives.

ARROWROOT

This white flour is ground from the root of a West Indian plant and can be exchanged measure for measure with cornstarch in recipes and mixes if you are allergic to corn. I do not call for this in any recipe in this book.

GARBANZO BEAN FLOUR

Ground from garbanzo beans (often called chickpea or cici beans), this flour may be used in combination with Romano bean flour (equal parts) to make a flour similar to the Garfava flour. Do this if you are allergic to fava beans.

GARFAVA FLOUR

This is the registered tradename of a smooth combination of garbanzo and fava beans, produced by Authentic Foods (see page 326). It is a staple in many of my recipes. High in protein and nutrients, it makes a better-textured baked product than rice flour. The flour is very stable and may be stored in the pantry. See "Garbanzo Bean Flour" above if you are sensitive to fava beans.

Warning: There are some flours now being sold that claim to be compounded like this but often are not the same formula. They may not produce equally good results in these recipes.

ROMANO BEAN FLOUR

A dark, strong-tasting bean flour, this is milled from the Romano or cranberry bean. The flour is high in fiber and protein and can be used in combination with garbanzo bean flour to make up a flour similar to Garfava flour (see Garbanzo Bean Flour above). It can be purchased in health food stores in Canada and by mail-order suppliers in the United States.

BUCKWHEAT FLOUR

Canada has always allowed this flour in the GF diet. Only recently have most of the U.S. organizations agreed that, in spite of its unfortunate name, the flour is not related to wheat but to rhubarb. Because of its strong taste, it is more easily accepted when used in small amounts to give flavor to other bland flours. To start to use it, try a tablespoon or two in pancakes or waffles if you wish to include it in the diet.

CORNSTARCH

This refined starch from corn is used in combination with other flours to make one of my baking mixes. If allergic to corn, replace this with arrowroot in mixes and recipes.

CORNMEAL

This meal, ground from corn, may be obtained in yellow and white forms. Combine this with other flours for baking or use it alone in Mexican dishes.

CORN FLOUR

A flour milled from corn, this can be blended with cornmeal when making corn breads and corn muffins.

NUT FLOURS

Chestnut, almond, and other nut flours can be used in small quantities, replacing a small portion of other flours to enhance the taste of homemade pasta, puddings, and cookies. I haven't given any recipes in the book, but chestnut flour can be added to your pasta mix and to plain cake mixes. Since they are high in proteins, nut flours are a great addition to the diet if you have the opportunity to experiment. These are expensive flours and need to be either refrigerated or frozen.

POTATO STARCH FLOUR

Made from potatoes, this fine white flour is used in the Gluten-free Mix. This keeps well and can be bought in quantity.

POTATO FLOUR

Do not confuse this with potato starch. This is a heavy flour. Buy it in small quantities because you will need very little of it. Store this in the refrigerator.

WHITE RICE FLOUR

This very bland (and not very nutritious) flour milled from polished white rice doesn't distort the taste of any flavorings used. It has long been a basic in gluten-free baking, but the more nutritious bean flours are now gaining popularity. This can be stored in the pantry and has a long shelf life.

There are several blends of this flour: fine (found in Asian groceries and some suppliers), medium (some suppliers), and coarse (home milled). My recipes are based on the fine grind and may take slightly more liquid than the other blends.

BROWN RICE FLOUR

This flour, milled from unpolished brown rice, contains bran and is higher in nutrient value than white rice flour. Use it for breads, muffins, and cookies where a bran (or nutty) taste is desired. Because there are oils in the bran, it has a much shorter shelf life and tends to become stronger tasting as it ages. Purchase fresh flour and store it in the refrigerator or freezer for longer life.

SWEET RICE FLOUR

This flour, made from a glutinous rice often called "sticky rice," is an excellent thickening agent. It is especially good for sauces that are to be refrigerated or frozen, as it inhibits separation of the liquids. I also use it by the tablespoon to add to breads when the dough is too thin or to batters when they seem too runny. I've found this in many grocery stores under the label Mochiko Sweet Rice Flour, but it can be ordered from several of the suppliers or found in some Asian markets. Do not confuse it with plain white rice flour.

RICE POLISH

This is a soft, fluffy, cream-colored flour made from the hulls of brown rice. Like rice bran, it has a high concentration of minerals and B vitamins. And like rice bran, it has a short shelf life. Buy this at a health food store and keep it in the freezer or refrigerator.

SORGHUM FLOUR

This new flour, ground from specially bred sorghum grain, is available from several suppliers and should soon be on the shelves of some health food stores. This combines with the bean flours to make my Four Flour Bean Mix, which is used in a lot of recipes in this book. Sorghum flour is seldom used alone. It stores well on the pantry shelf. Sorghum is distantly related to sugarcane.

SOY FLOUR

A yellow flour with high protein and fat content, this has a nutty flavor and is most successful when used in combination with other flours in baked products that contain fruit, nuts, or chocolate. Purchase it in small quantities and store in the freezer or refrigerator as it, too, has a short shelf life. Some celiacs may be sensitive to this flour. Bean flour can be substituted in many recipes that call for soy.

TAPIOCA FLOUR

Made from the root of the cassava plant, this light, velvety white flour imparts "chew" to our baked goods. I use it in all my mixes. It can be stored at room temperature for a long time.

SOME FLOURS THAT HAVE BEEN QUESTIONED

Amaranth, Quinoa, Millet, and Teff

These four flours, more exotic and less well known, have been accepted in Canada for years as gluten free. Most of the U.S. groups are coming to accept the fact that botanically they are not related to the gluten-containing grains but all emphasize that one should watch out for contamination that can occur in growing, shipping, and handling. As with all flours, there is always the chance that a person will be allergic or sensitive to one or another. Since these have not been a staple of the diet here, introduction of any of these grains is best made slowly. An understanding of their botanical relatives may help to determine whether you want to try these flours, which have a nutritive value far surpassing that of rice.

Amaranth flour is ground from the seed of a plant related to pigweed.

Quinoa seeds come from the plant in a family related to spinach and beets. These grow with a bitter coating, so always buy debittered flour.

Millet and *Teff* are grains in the same grass family as corn, rice, and sorghum.

FLOURS ON THE RESTRICTED LIST

Spelt, Kamut, Club, Durum, Bulgur, Einkorn, and Semolina

These are all different species of wheat and should be eliminated in any form from the gluten-free diet.

Triticale

This is a hybrid of rye and wheat. Not for a gluten-free diet!

Oats

The question of whether people on a gluten-free diet can safely eat oat products remains the subject of scientific debate. Some medical experts are now listing oats as only "possibly" containing toxic gluten but most doctors in the United States admit that they don't want to commit their patients to oats in the diet at this time. Difficulties in identifying the precise amino acids responsible for the immune response and the chemical differences between wheat and oats have contributed to the controversy.

OTHER BAKING SUPPLIES

Xanthan Gum

This is a powder milled from the dried cell coat of a microorganism called *Xanthomonas campestris* grown under laboratory conditions. It replaces the gluten in yeast breads and other baking with our flours. It is available in some health food stores and by order from some of the suppliers listed on pages 326–32. Recently I've noticed that some companies are putting out a xanthan gum that is lighter in weight, more granular, and less powdery. Because of its lighter weight, I find that it takes about one fourth more in a recipe to achieve the same texture of batter. If you find your batter too thin, check the xanthan gum and try adding slightly more.

Guar Gum

A powder derived from the seed of the plant *Cyamopsis tetragonoloba*, this powder can be purchased in health food stores or ordered from suppliers. Because it has a high fiber content and is usually sold as a laxative, it can cause distress to people whose digestive systems are sensitive. This can be used in place of xanthan gum in baking.

Dry Milk Powder

I used to call for nonfat, noninstant milk powder in my recipes until some readers complained that they were sensitive to so much milk powder. Now I suggest that you can use the regular powder from your grocery. This will still turn out excellent bread and baked products.

Nondairy Powdered Milk Substitutes

For the lactose intolerant, substitute either Lacto-Free, Tofu White (both contain soy), or NutQuik (made from almonds), or almond meal for the dairy milk powder. Another choice could be one of the powdered baby formulas from the supermarket or drugstore: some are soy based and others corn based.

Liquid Egg Substitutes

These cholesterol-free liquid substitutes for whole eggs are made from the egg whites plus other ingredients. They may be found in the dairy section and freezer cases of most grocery stores. *Always read the ingredient label to be sure the one you choose doesn't contain gluten or some other ingredient to which you are allergic.*

Egg Replacer

This powdered substitute for eggs in cooking contains no egg product and is also free of dairy, corn, soy, and gluten. I use a little of this for extra leavening in many recipes. Egg replacer can be ordered from Ener-G Foods or found in most health food stores. A similar product is also available in Canada.

Dough Enhancers

These powdered products are used in bread making to substitute for the vinegar that balances the pH in most waters. They also tend to make the bread stay fresh longer. They are put out by many companies and can be found in baking supply stores and some health food stores. *Always read the ingredient labels to find one that's gluten free and doesn't contain anything else to which you may be sensitive.* Several suppliers listed on pages 326–32 carry dough enhancer.

High-Altitude Baking

I'm jealous! One of my testers can get three loaves of bread out of a two-loaf recipe and the bread she turns out is so light it practically floats off the table. Her secret? She lives at approximately 5,000 feet of altitude while my oven sits barely 10 feet above sea level. Of course, this tester has baked all her life at her high altitude and thinks nothing of making the adjustments that have to be made to assure the best results.

High altitudes do present challenges when baking. Leavened products using yeast, baking powder, baking soda, or egg whites rise more rapidly and often collapse, while anything cooked with moist heat, such as vegetables and stews, take much longer to prepare. This is because the atmospheric pressure is lower and water will boil at a lower temperature while your cakes and breads rise higher, often overflowing the pan.

Since I've lived at sea level all my life, I didn't understand this principle when I first tried to bake in my tester's kitchen. First, the buns I was making proofed faster (the principle was that fermentation of sugar is faster at higher altitudes so bread rises faster) and the dough I had put on the sheet in small bun shapes (in typical sea-level fashion) spread all over the sheet, as she had warned me it might.

Most cake recipes for sea level need no changes up to the altitude of 3,000 feet. Above that, it is often necessary to adjust recipes slightly. Usually a decrease in leavening or sugar (or both) and a change in liquid are all that is needed (although my high-altitude tester tells me that she often just adds a tablespoon or so of flour if the batter seems too thin). Any of these adjustments may require a different balance of ingredients.

Repeated experiments with a recipe will give the cook the most successful proportions to use. Anyone who has cooked for years at their altitude usually has discovered the best ratio of changes to make.

A few rules of thumb for high-altitude baking:

Cookies usually need no changes.

For cakes that contain a large amount of fat or chocolate (a cup or more) you may need to reduce the shortening by one to two tablespoons to prevent the cake from falling. You may also have to adjust the leavening, sugar, and liquid according to the chart below.

For cakes using eggs for most of the leavening (such as angel food or sponge), beat the eggs to only soft peaks. Otherwise your cake may expand too much.

For cakes, try the temperature suggested on the recipe but be sure to test the cake before the end of baking time. Adjust baking time or temperature on the next try, if needed.

HIGH-ALTITUDE ADJUSTMENTS

Ingredients	3,000 feet	5,000 feet	7,000 feet
Decrease sugar for each cup	0–1 tablespoon	0–2 tablespoons	1–3 tablespoons
Reduce baking powder for each teaspoon	⅛ teaspoon	⅛–¼ teaspoon	¼ teaspoon

Even though our flours are different, the principles of baking remain the same for high altitudes. The best suggestion that my high-altitude testers give is that anyone living above 3,000 feet having trouble with the recipes should call their own county extension agent for the best information on baking in their region.

The Secret to Success in Gluten-free Baking

When someone in the family has been diagnosed with celiac disease or a wheat allergy, you'll soon find the bakery off-limits and the cookies on the grocery shelf all full of wheat. If you decide to make your own desserts, when you open that first cookbook you may recoil in shock. I'm sure you didn't expect to be faced with weird products you've never heard of—bean and sorghum flours, xanthan gum, Lacto-Free—to name a few—plus an arm-long list of ingredients in every recipe. If you wonder why you can't just replace the wheat base with rice flour and forget the odd ingredients, you're not the only one.

I got this question from one man who wrote objecting to my recipes: "I recently had the opportunity to peruse [you notice he didn't say 'purchase'] your latest book and I have a couple of comments. I'm wondering if you've ever encountered the K-I-S-S formula which is: 'Keep It Simple S_____,' inserting the S word of your choice for the second S." I inserted the Stupid which he probably thought me. He went on: "I currently purchase a commercially produced rice bread that is quite good and contains only the following ingredients: rice flour, water, honey, soya oil, natural gum, salt, and yeast. Most of your recipes are fairly complex."

Yes. I'm afraid they are complex. But it's because of this rice bread he refers to that I developed my more complicated, but far tastier, recipes. Some of you may have been diagnosed long enough to remember when *that* was our only bread. It was a pretty tasteless one-size-fits-all type of bread developed originally for patients with PKU or on dialysis machines. It was all we could find twenty-five years ago when I was diagnosed.

Not satisfied with this, I resolved to improve the taste of my muffins, cakes, cookies, and bread. I knew nothing about cooking but I did know about taste. Starting with Mr. KISS's rice, I added tapioca, potato starch, potato flour, cornstarch, corn flour, and soy at first. About five years ago, I added bean flour, which required the addition of molasses and/or brown or maple sugar to cut the bitterness. After I discovered sorghum, which mates with bean flours with fantastic results, I added that.

When I started baking, I figured, like Mr. KISS, that since all the flours looked the same they should act the same, so I just dumped and mixed and guessed—and turned out many a pan of crumbs, or the reverse, pounds of doorstops. I wasn't at all scientific but I did discover that a lot of other flours could combine with the original gritty-on-the-tongue rice flour to create a lighter and tastier product. I added eggs, mayonnaise, milk, and soy powders to make the finished product more palatable, smoother, and to increase the shelf life. I just grabbed and guessed while my kitchen resembled the laboratory of a mad scientist.

I realize now I should have started with the scientific equivalent of all the ingredient properties. But I wasn't a scientist; I was a celiac hungry for food that tasted like my old wheat-laced favorites. I had no idea that a scientific approach would save me from a lot of failures. I didn't realize that knowing the properties of the different flours would help me understand what additions would make the gluten-free ones act like wheat in baking. But thanks to the patience of the cereal chemists at Ener-G and Authentic Foods who took hours explaining the factors involved in their baking, I realized I'd have to do more research on my part to understand the composition of the various flours. To do this I developed Table 1.

TABLE 1: A COMPARISON OF GLUTEN-FREE FLOURS TO WHEAT

| | Food Value | | | |
Flour	Carbohydrates %	Protein %	Fat %	Fiber %
Amaranth	66	13	6	0
Bean Flour (Authentic Foods)	59	23	6.5	7.5
Bean Flour (Romano)	64	18.2	1.27	23.5

Buckwheat	72	11.5	0	1.6
Corn Flour	76	7	1	14
Cornmeal	77	8	3	10
Cornstarch	88	Trace	0	Trace
Garbanzo	60	20	4	12
Millet	73	10	3	3
Potato Flour	80	8	.05	3.5
Potato Starch	77	.05	0	0
Quinoa	66	12	5	7
Rice (brown)	79	6	1	2
Rice (sweet)	80	6	0	0
Rice (white)	76	6	0	0
Sorghum	75	10	4	2
Soy Flour	30	36	20	2.5
Tapioca	99	1	0	0
Teff	71	11	4	3
Wheat Flour	76	10	1	3

It's not overly scientific so even I, with my literary but unscientific mind, can understand it. For instance, look at the properties of wheat flour: 76 percent carbohydrates and 10 percent protein. Compare this to a combination of rice with tapioca to lighten, which will have much more carbohydrate and perhaps only 3 or 4 percent protein. Wheat flour and any combination of our flours may look alike in the mixing bowl, but they aren't going to act the same in that cake or cookie.

So why blend flours? you ask.

If you're like me, when you did bake before diagnosis, you probably only used the all-purpose wheat flour standard on grocery shelves. Did you realize that the little extra on the label that says "enriched" in many cases meant that it had some barley flour added? So even your common ordinary wheat flour may be a blend.

While we do have flours like tapioca, which is mostly carbohydrates, we also have bean flours, running almost double as high in protein as wheat flour. Sorghum is closer to wheat flour in almost all factors. And if you run your eye down the list of fats in the flours, you'll again see a wide variation. Soy has five times as much fat as wheat so it's best used where fat is a plus, such as in crisp cookies.

But what does this mean in baking? I combined tapioca flour with rice flour as one of my first experiments because it helped soften the gritty taste of rice and added some lightness to the finished baked product. Recently I've created four different mixes of flours in different proportions.

TABLE 2: FLOUR MIXES		
FORMULAS	FOR 9 CUPS	FOR 12 CUPS
GLUTEN-FREE MIX (called GF Mix in recipes)		
Rice flour (2 parts)	6 cups	8 cups
Potato starch (⅔ part)	2 cups	2⅔ cups
Tapioca flour (⅓ part)	1 cup	1⅓ cups
FEATHERLIGHT RICE FLOUR MIX (called Featherlight Mix in recipes)		
Rice flour (1 part)	3 cups	4 cups
Tapioca flour (1 part)	3 cups	4 cups
Cornstarch (1 part)	3 cups	4 cups
Potato flour* (1 teaspoon per cup)	3 tablespoons	4 tablespoons
LIGHT BEAN FLOUR MIX (for breads only)		
Garfava bean flour† (1 part)	3 cups	4 cups
Tapioca flour (1 part)	3 cups	4 cups
Cornstarch (1 part)	3 cups	4 cups
FOUR FLOUR BEAN MIX		
Garfava bean flour† (⅔ part)	2 cups	2⅔ cups
Sorghum flour‡ (⅓ part)	1 cup	1⅓ cups
Tapioca flour (1 part)	3 cups	4 cups
Cornstarch (1 part)	3 cups	4 cups

*This is potato flour, not potato starch.
†Garfava flour is from Authentic Foods.
‡Sorghum flour can be obtained from Red River Milling.

Mr. KISS probably cannot imagine why I have even one mix. But, with the recent addition of bean and sorghum to our list of available and extra tasty GF flours, this leads to many wonderful variations providing more tastes and textures. Just as wheat flour comes in varieties suitable for different products (all purpose, semolina for pasta, durum for bread, and a specially blended cake flour), we now have several GF mixes. Good cooks who like to experiment can use these as a base for creating their own variations. For most of you, these mixes should fill your baking needs for now.

Now that we have the mixes, the next problem is considering the makeup of each and adding to a recipe the leavening, proteins, and fat required to bring the taste, consistency, and flavor as close to wheat as possible. First we look at the proteins in the flours, for it's the proteins in wheat that cause the problem for celiacs. I'm not sure if they are the allergen factor in wheat allergies, but they certainly will have to be replaced to get a decent baked product. When I first started, I learned from others that a lot of eggs made a GF baked product hold together better but I never knew why. Now I realize that it was the egg whites that added the lacking protein.

I've added the proteins in the mixes and have figured that

GF Mix has 4.3 percent protein, about half of what wheat has

Featherlight has only 2 percent protein, one fifth of what wheat has

Light Bean Flour Mix has 8 percent protein, close to what wheat has, which may be why it makes such a great bread loaf

Four Flour Bean Mix has about 6 percent protein; we'll need to add more protein when baking with this mix, but not as much as the rice mixes

So where do we get these proteins? Some of these are probably what Mr. KISS is complaining about: those added ingredients that make the recipe seem complicated. But these are what makes the baking turn out with great texture.

PROTEIN ADDITIVES

- Unflavored gelatin—the easiest and least allergenic or texture changing
- Extra egg whites—these are also leavening agents and texture-changing elements
- Milk or milk powder—okay if one isn't lactose intolerant
- Buttermilk or buttermilk powder—the same objection as above

- Yogurt—not for the lactose intolerant, and this requires some changes to the liquid measurements
- Soy flour along with the mix—this requires a lot of testing since soy is very high in fat and creates a different texture; works best in cookies that need fat
- Lacto-Free (a powder available from Ener-G Foods)
- Soy-Quik (a powder available from Ener-G Foods)
- Isomil, Nestlé's Follow-Up Soy (baby formula powders)
- Ensure (adult nutrition powder)
- Flax meal—may have slight laxative effect
- NutQuik (a nut-based powder available from Ener-G Foods)
- Nut flours or meal—almond meal may be substituted for milk powder

At this point you may begin to understand why my recipes call for strange ingredients, but so far it's no help when you want to make up your own recipe or convert an old favorite. Wait! Don't toss out your old cookbooks yet.

I'd be remiss if I failed to mention that in almost all baked products you will have to add xanthan gum or guar gum. I call this the "stretch" factor to keep the baked goods from being too crumbly. Some cookies may be the exception for they are based on a lot of sugar and fats and you want a crisp texture to many of them. Cakelike ones, such as brownies, will definitely still need the gum. Here's a simple rule when using xanthan gum.

For breads use: 1 scant teaspoon per cup of flour
For cakes use: ½ teaspoon per cup of flour
For cookies use: ¼ teaspoon per cup of flour

If you feel that your eyes are beginning to cross and you wonder why you need all this information, just hang in there. I'm going to show you how to use this to remake your old favorites into gluten-free delights, how to create new recipes, and how to surprise your family. All the work my friendly cereal chemists did to teach me will not be in vain.

One of my testers picked up a box of Hershey's cocoa and on the back saw a cake recipe that contained only a few ingredients. From working with my recipes, she made her own changes to make it gluten free. The recipe seemed to have plenty of leavening and called for mayonnaise as both the oil and the eggs. If she changed the water to a carbonated drink she would get more leavening. She reduced the flour amount slightly, figuring that would save on adjusting the liquid. And, of course, she added the necessary xanthan gum.

Original Recipe*	Changes
2 cups flour (wheat)	Use GF Mix minus 2 tablespoons
	Add 1 teaspoon xanthan gum
1 cup sugar	Leave as written
3 tablespoons baking cocoa	Leave as written
2 teaspoons baking soda	Leave as written
1 cup water	Change to carbonated drink (citrus-flavored or cola)
1 cup mayonnaise	Be sure this is gluten-free
1 teaspoon vanilla	Leave as written

When adjusting recipes, you'll have to check the cake with a tester to determine the exact baking time. This took slightly longer than called for in the original recipe. The cake took only a few simple changes that worked well, but more complicated ones can be effected once you know the properties of the flours and want to experiment.

The following recipe was taken from *Family Circle* magazine (June 1996) and you'll find my revision complete on page 41 as Master White Cake.

Original Recipe†	Changes
3 cups all-purpose flour (wheat)	Use 3 cups GF Mix and add ¼ cup tapioca flour for lightness
	Add 1½ teaspoons xanthan gum
2 teaspoons baking powder	Increase baking powder by about half again—3 teaspoons baking powder
	For extra leavening use 3 teaspoons Egg Replacer (this is a leavening agent, not an egg product)
¾ teaspoon salt	Increase slightly to 1 teaspoon to make up for the salt in the butter

*Recipe courtesy of the Hershey Kitchens and reprinted with permission of © Hershey Foods Corporation.
†Reprinted with permission of *Family Circle* magazine. © 1996 by Gruner + Jahr USA Publishing.

Original Recipe	Changes
1 cup butter	I've used 1 cup shortening (Butter Flavor Crisco), which is better for the lactose intolerant
1⅔ cups sugar	I cut the sugar to 1½ cups to lighten the batter
3 eggs	Increase to 4 eggs for added protein
1 teaspoon vanilla	Increase to 1½ teaspoons, for more flavor
1½ cups milk	1½ cups citrus-flavored carbonated beverage, for everyone—this adds lightness, leavening, and some flavor, and for the lactose intolerant eliminates the milk

You certainly don't have to make all the changes I did. This is just to show that you can take any recipe and make it work when you understand your ingredients. Most of my baking friends take a cake and merely change the flour, add xanthan gum, and slightly increase the leavening either by adding eggs, Egg Replacer, more baking powder, or baking soda. Cake recipes with lots of eggs, such as for chiffon or sponge cakes, are the easiest to convert. Layer cakes, such as the one above, are the hardest.

Cookie recipes are easier to change because they don't have to rise and be tender. Of course, you may find them spreading all over the pan sometimes, and you will have to add more flour, but that can be remedied easily as soon as the first cookie sheet is out of the oven.

Bread is a whole different story. Our breads are batter breads and the recipes are formulated carefully, in a different way from wheat-bread recipes. The day may come when we can pound out our frustrations on the dough, but for now we have to be content to let the mixer whirl or our bread machine mix.

If I haven't answered Mr. KISS's question about the number of ingredients in gluten-free recipes, I hope I have answered yours and that you, too, are ready to pull out your old family recipes and start converting them.

Help! What Did I Do Wrong?

*O*nce a person on the gluten-free diet makes up his/her mind to bake, other difficulties seem to arise. It's often time-consuming to find the gluten-free supplies, which are always more expensive than the familiar wheat flour on the grocery shelf. This can lead to frustration even before an egg is cracked. When the baked result turns out lopsided, sunken, heavy, or inedible, the frustration doubles. The questions and answers below may help relieve some of the novice gluten-free cook's exasperation.

Q. My cake looked great in the oven but fell as it cooled. Help! What did I do wrong?

A. I can remember my mother yelling at my lead-footed brothers, "Don't stomp around so hard. I have a cake in the oven! And for goodness' sake, don't slam the door."

Teenage boys and door slamming might be enough to make cakes fall, but it's more likely caused by another reason. The cake was probably not fully cooked in the center. There could be several reasons for that:

1. The cake was too moist and needed a longer time in the oven in spite of the time given in the recipe. Always test a cake with a tester; a clean, dry tester is a sign the cake is done. Was the batter too thin as you spooned it into the pan? Our batters for many cakes are slightly thinner than wheat-flour cakes but they can be too thin.

2. Were your eggs too big? Jumbo rather than large? (Recipes always imply large eggs unless otherwise specified.)

3. Rice flours come in several textures and call for slight differences in the amount of liquid needed. Always save a bit of the liquid to add, if needed, at the end of mixing. Or if you've used all the liquid, you might have to add a bit more flour. Try adding a small bit of sweet rice flour if you don't have any more of the rice or bean mix.

Q. The top of my cake came out lumpy and gnarled looking. How can I prevent this?

A. This is probably a case of the batter being too thick. As I said before, our batters might be slightly thinner than wheat-flour batters. They should smooth as they are spooned into the pan.

Solution: Add slightly more liquid, or next time reduce the flour amount. Whisk the flour before you spoon it gently into the cup to measure. Don't pack it in by shaking the cup or tapping it on the table.

Q. The texture of my cake is dry and crumbly. What causes that?

A. Our rice-flour baked goods used to come out a bit drier than wheat cakes but they don't have to anymore. There could be several reasons:

1. You didn't have enough liquid or fat in the batter. Some of our flours will take more liquid than others, as I mentioned above. Perhaps you used a thicker liquid (replacing sour cream with a nondairy substitute will call for added liquid. I do this by thinning down the nondairy sour cream with a bit of nondairy milk). Also, using nonfat or 1% milk will cut the fat. All recipes are based on using 4% milk. Or add one to two tablespoons extra fat.

2. Perhaps you overbaked the cake. Try a slightly shorter cooking time. Did you use a larger pan than the recipe called for? This would spread the cake too thin so it dried while baking.

3. Did you use the correct amount of xanthan gum? I've just discovered that some xanthan gums seem as if they are exploded and lighter than others. It may be necessary to use slightly more of this kind. How to tell? The number of ounces on the package is the same but the amount of gum in the package is more.

4. The flour you used can be a factor. Bean flour cakes are usually far moister than the rice flour ones.

Q. I like the looks of a bundt cake so I used that pan instead of the one called for, but the inside didn't cook. How can I correct that if I still want to use a bundt pan?

A. It's tricky to answer if I don't know what cake you used. I have done the same as you but always cook the bundt cake much longer. You could try testing the cake every so often and then mark down the time, as I do when testing. Plain cream cakes do not work as well in a bundt pan as those filled with fruit or nuts.

Q. My cake turned out gummy on the inside. Why?

A. There can be many causes for gummy cakes: too much liquid, too short a baking time, or the wrong size pan. Or it could be that in some substitution, you had a thinner liquid than called for, so it resulted in too much liquid; for example, by using vinegar or lemon to sour milk, you'll end up with a slightly thinner liquid.

Q. My cake never rises like a wheat flour one. Does anyone else have this trouble?

A. I used to have problems like this part of the time. Now I understand that the old GF Flour Mix was more difficult to work with than the Featherlight Mix or the Four Flour Bean Mix. You definitely will have to add either more protein or leavening to our gluten-free batters, whether in extra egg whites, baking powder, baking soda, or in using Egg Replacer or carbonated soft drinks. These are usually written into the recipes. If you use a nondairy substitute instead of milk, be sure it has the same protein value as milk (the amount of protein will be marked on the carton).

If it's a problem with spongelike cakes, it could be that your separately beaten egg whites didn't have enough "lift" because there were traces of fat in the bowl when they were whipped.

Q. My "cut out" cookies come out tough. What causes this?

A. Usually it's a case of too much flour on the board when rolled out. Rather than roll them out immediately, using flour to thicken the dough, try putting the mixing bowl in the refrigerator for one hour to stiffen up the shortening used so the dough will roll out easier.

Q. Why did my cookies turn into crumbs when I took them from the baking sheet?

A. Oops! You may need more xanthan gum or an additional egg white in the mix next time. You might add a bit more flour (use sweet rice flour) and see if you can rescue the rest of the batch.

Q. My cookies didn't spread out on the baking sheet but stayed in lumps the way I dropped them. How come?

A. Not very appealing, were they? Thank goodness with drop cookies, we have a chance to correct errors at the beginning of the baking. Just add more liquid to the batter and watch the next pan turn out as you expected.

Q. My cookies spread out too thin when they baked. Can I correct that?

A. For the next panful try adding some sweet rice flour to the batter. The next time you bake these cookies, cut the liquid slightly. While you are baking, be sure to cool the pan between batches.

Q. My cookies have a tendency to burn on the bottom before they are browned on the top.

A. The placement in the oven may be the cause. Place the rack higher from the bottom element. If you are using a dark pan, line it with foil and see if that helps.

I know this isn't going to solve all the problems. There'll be more when you use substitutions such as honey for some of the sugar; Egg Replacer and water for egg whites; liquid egg substitute for whole eggs. In many cases, I have written recipes using these or have suggested their use. If the recipe doesn't suggest a substitution, don't expect it to come out perfectly. For this dessert book, I tried to make the best-tasting dessert possible without usually considering calories or fat.

You can, though, prevent problems if you use liquid egg substitute rather than the whole egg, replacing the missing fat with 1 tablespoon fat for each ¼ cup liquid used. This doesn't completely solve the problem of fat but you can substitute margarine or vegetable oil in place of the high-cholesterol egg fat.

Cakes

*I*magine trying to celebrate a birthday, anniversary, or wedding without a cake. Where can you place the candles or the bride and groom on a bowl of Jell-O? Don't worry. You'll find the perfect cake for any occasion among the wide selection in this section, ranging from a basic Master White Cake to one for that peanut butter and jelly freak.

For years I struggled to make our GF cakes as tasty and light as the wheat ones. With the recipes in this chapter I feel that we who have to eat GF can have cakes that rival any others. Use the Master White Cake at the beginning of the chapter for white, chocolate, spice, or an upside-down cake. Or try one of the special cakes like the rich Coconutty Layer Cake and surprise the guests at the next party or club luncheon.

But cakes aren't just for special occasions. Now that we know how to make great cakes with gluten-free flours, a cake can be just the sweet you need at the end of the meal. For the family, make one of the easy ones in this chapter and top it with fruit and/or whipped cream.

These cakes are made with several different mixes: Featherlight, Four Flour Bean Mix, or the original GF Mix, so you have a wide choice of flours as you look through the recipes. But don't try to substitute a different flour mix for the one called for in the recipe: I tested all the cakes with each flour mix and ended up with the one (or two) that turned out best.

If you don't want to bake your cakes from scratch, I'm happy to be able to announce that several suppliers of gluten-free products sell mixes by mail or phone order, and a few have placed them on the shelves of health food or specialty stores.

I have included some cake recipes in almost every cookbook I've written, so I didn't repeat them here. Turn to the end of the chapter to learn where you can find those recipes.

Master White Cake

Wonderfully versatile, this tender, springy cake is perfect for eating plain, with fruit or berries, frosted, or topped with whipped cream. For special occasions, make it into a wedding, birthday, or other party centerpiece or bake it as a homey upside-down cake.

With a change of flavorings or additional ingredients, the easy basic recipe can be adapted to make a chocolate, mocha, or spice cake.

Small cake suitable for a 9" square pan

1½ cups GF Mix

2 tablespoons tapioca flour

¾ teaspoon xanthan gum

1½ teaspoons baking powder

1 teaspoon Egg Replacer

½ teaspoon salt

½ cup Butter Flavor Crisco

¾ cup sugar

2 eggs

¾ teaspoon vanilla or favorite flavoring

¾ cup plus 1 tablespoon citrus-flavored carbonated beverage

Large cake suitable for a 9" × 13" pan or three 8" round pans

3 cups GF Mix

¼ cup tapioca flour

1½ teaspoons xanthan gum

2 teaspoons baking powder

2 teaspoons Egg Replacer

1 teaspoon salt

1 cup Butter Flavor Crisco

1½ cups sugar

4 eggs

1½ teaspoons vanilla or favorite flavoring

1½ cups plus 2 tablespoons citrus-flavored carbonated beverage

Preheat oven to 350°. Spray pan suitable for your recipe with vegetable oil.

In a medium bowl, whisk together the flour mix, tapioca flour, xanthan gum, baking powder, Egg Replacer, and salt.

In the bowl of your mixer, beat the Crisco and sugar until fluffy. Beat in the eggs, one at a time, before adding the vanilla. Alternately stir in the dry ingredients and carbonated beverage until just blended. Pour the batter into the prepared pan(s) and bake for 25–30 minutes for the round pans, 35–40 minutes for the 9" square pan, and 45–50 minutes for the 9" × 13" pan.

VARIATIONS:

CHOCOLATE: Stir 6 squares (one ounce each) of melted semisweet chocolate into the egg mixture for the large cake; 3 squares for the smaller cake.

SPICE CAKE: Add 2 teaspoons apple pie spice to the flour for the large cake; 1 teaspoon for the smaller one. Replace 1 cup of the sugar with brown sugar for the large cake; ½ cup for the smaller cake. Add ½ cup chopped walnuts or pecans to the batter of the larger cake; ¼ cup for the smaller cake.

UPSIDE-DOWN CAKE: For 9" pan, melt ⅓ cup margarine or butter in the ungreased baking pan. Scatter on ½ cup (or less) brown sugar. Arrange canned pineapple slices or peach halves (cut side down) over the sugar mix, using one 28-ounce can. Pour cake batter over the fruit and bake, adding 4 to 5 extra minutes' baking time. Serve warm or cold topped with whipped cream or nondairy whipped topping if desired.

For 9" × 13" pan, melt ½ cup margarine or butter and increase the sugar slightly. For the fruit, you will need 2 cans. *Small cake makes 9–12 servings; large cake makes 16–20 servings.*

Nutrients per serving: Calories 290, Fat 13g, Cholesterol 45mg, Sodium 210mg, Carbohydrates 42g, Protein 2g.

Always let baked goods cool completely before slicing, frosting, or storing in a plastic bag or airtight container.

Marbled Butterscotch Cake

Since I love butterscotch, this is a cake I choose when I want to stir up a cake in a hurry. It tastes great while warm but it keeps several days and still tastes good. I serve the pieces with a dab of whipped topping so it needs no frosting.

Note: There are both butterscotch and caramel sauces to be used over ice cream that are gluten free. Be sure to read the labels.

2 cups GF Mix	1½ cups brown sugar
½ cup tapioca flour	3 eggs
1½ teaspoons xanthan gum	1 tablespoon vanilla
1 teaspoon baking soda	2 tablespoons milk or nondairy
1 teaspoon Egg Replacer (optional)	liquid
1 teaspoon baking powder	½ cup purchased butterscotch sauce
1 cup (2 sticks) butter or margarine	½ cup chopped pecans, toasted

Preheat oven to 325°. Grease a 9" × 13" pan and dust lightly with rice flour.

In a medium bowl, whisk together the flour mix, tapioca flour, xanthan gum, baking soda, Egg Replacer (if used), and baking powder. Set aside.

In the bowl of your mixer, cream the butter and brown sugar. Beat in the eggs, one at a time. Add the vanilla. Add the dry ingredients, beating in the first half on low. Then stir in the rest with the milk. Pour into the prepared pan.

If the caramel sauce is too thick to spoon easily, warm it in a saucepan and add the chopped nuts. Spoon this over the cake batter. With a knife, swirl it gently into the batter for a marble effect. Bake for 25–30 minutes, or until the top tests a bit soft but firm. Serve warm or cold topped with whipped cream or nondairy whipped topping if desired. *Makes 16–20 servings.*

Nutrients per serving: Calories 350, Fat 17g, Cholesterol 75mg, Sodium 260mg, Carbohydrates 48g, Protein 2g.

German Chocolate Cake 350°

My testers and tasters were excited about this cake for it tasted just like the wheat ones they remembered. And it stays moist.

For an 8" square pan

2 ounces German sweet chocolate
¼ cup water
1¼ cups Four Flour Bean Mix
½ teaspoon xanthan gum
¼ teaspoon salt
1 teaspoon baking soda

1 teaspoon Egg Replacer
½ cup (1 stick) margarine or butter
1 cup sugar
2 eggs, separated
½ teaspoon vanilla
½ cup buttermilk

For a 9" × 13" pan or two 8" round pans

4 ounces German sweet chocolate
½ cup water
2½ cups Four Flour Bean Mix
1 teaspoon xanthan gum
½ teaspoon salt
2 teaspoons baking soda

1 teaspoon Egg Replacer
1 cup (2 sticks) margarine or butter
2 cups sugar
4 eggs, separated
1 teaspoon vanilla
1 cup buttermilk

Preheat oven to 350°. Grease your chosen pan(s).

Combine the chocolate and water in a microwaveable bowl. Microwave on defrost until a smooth sauce forms, testing every 2 minutes. Cool. If you don't have a microwave, heat water and chocolate in a pan on the stove over low heat.

In a medium bowl, blend the flour mix, xanthan gum, salt, baking soda, and Egg Replacer. Set aside.

In the bowl of your mixer, cream the butter and sugar. Add the egg yolks, one at a time, beating well after each addition. Add the cooled chocolate mixture and vanilla. Mix well. Add the dry ingredients alternately with the buttermilk until well blended. In another bowl, beat the egg whites until stiff peaks form. Fold into the batter.

Spoon the batter into the prepared pan and spread evenly. Bake for 40–45 minutes or until a tester comes out clean and the cake has pulled away from the sides of the pan. Cool before frosting. Choose any frosting your family likes, but for a true German chocolate cake taste use the Coconut-Pecan Frosting on page 133. *Makes 20–24 servings.*

Nutrients per serving: Calories 503, Fat 29g, Cholesterol 145mg, Sodium 480mg, Carbohydrates 62g, Protein 6g.

*T*o create sour milk as a substitute for buttermilk in a recipe, place 1 tablespoon lemon juice or vinegar per cup in a measuring cup and add enough milk to reach the amount called for in the recipe. Let the mixture stand 5 minutes before using.

Italian Creme Cake

Rich and moist and elegant in three tiers or simple in a flat sheet, this cake can be made ahead and served with no apologies to any guest at your party. I used the Baker's Secret Icing (page 131) with Butter Flavor Crisco, but the Fluffy Cream Cheese Frosting (page 126) would work well also.

2 cups Featherlight Mix	½ cup shortening
1 teaspoon xanthan gum	2 cups flaked coconut
2 teaspoons Egg Replacer	5 eggs, separated
1 teaspoon unflavored gelatin	1 teaspoon vanilla
2 teaspoons baking soda	1¼ cups buttermilk
2 cups sugar	1 cup chopped pecans or walnuts
½ cup margarine	

Preheat oven to 350°. Grease three 8" round cake pans or one 9" × 13" pan and dust with rice flour.

In a medium bowl, whisk together the flour mix, xanthan gum, Egg Replacer, gelatin, and baking soda. Set aside.

In the bowl of your mixer, cream the sugar, margarine, and shortening until light. Add the coconut. Separate the eggs, placing the whites in a metal or glass bowl and adding the yolks, one at a time, to the batter, beating after each addition. Add the vanilla. Add the flour and the buttermilk in 3 parts, beating just until incorporated. Stir in the nuts.

Beat the egg whites until soft peaks form. Fold gently into the batter. Spoon into the prepared pan(s) and bake for 30–35 minutes for the round pans, 45–50 minutes for the 9" × 13" pan. Cool before frosting. *Makes 16–20 servings.*

Nutrients per serving: Calories 310, Fat 17g, Cholesterol 55mg, Sodium 160mg, Carbohydrates 36g, Protein 4g.

Orange-Almond Cake

A full-flavored cake that can be made as a sheet cake and topped with whipped topping for a family dinner or as a layer cake and filled and frosted for special occasions. The orange rind peeled and finely processed with the sugar helps give the intense flavor.

Small cake for 8" square pan or 9" round pan

1 cup plus 2 tablespoons Featherlight Mix or Four Flour Bean Mix

½ rounded teaspoon xanthan gum

1 teaspoon Egg Replacer

⅓ cup almond meal

1½ teaspoons baking powder

½ teaspoon baking soda

¼ teaspoon salt

½ cup (1 stick) butter or margarine

1 large orange

1 cup sugar

2 eggs

½ cup milk or citrus-flavored carbonated drink

½ teaspoon almond flavoring

Large cake for one 9" × 13" pan or two 9" round pans

2¼ cups Featherlight Mix or Four Flour Bean Mix

1¼ teaspoons xanthan gum

2 teaspoons Egg Replacer

⅔ cup almond meal

3 teaspoons baking powder

1 teaspoon baking soda

½ teaspoon salt

1 cup (2 sticks) butter or margarine

2 large oranges

2 cups sugar

4 eggs

1 cup milk or citrus-flavored carbonated drink

1 teaspoon almond flavoring

Preheat oven to 350°. Grease your chosen pan(s) and dust with rice flour.

In a medium bowl, whisk together the flour mix, xanthan gum, Egg Replacer, almond meal, baking powder, baking soda, and salt. Set aside.

With a vegetable peeler, remove the colored part of the peel from the orange(s) and chop into about 1" lengths. Place in a food processor with the sugar and blend until the peel is finely ground.

In the bowl of your mixer, beat butter and the orange peel-sugar combination until fluffy. Beat in the eggs, one at a time. Add the flavoring to the milk or carbonated drink and, with the mixer on low, blend this into the batter alternately with the flour mix in 3 additions. Do not overbeat! Spoon into the prepared pan(s). Bake for 30–35 minutes or until the tester comes out clean and the sides pull slightly from the pan. If using layers, cool about 5 minutes and turn from the pan to cool completely before frosting with your favorite icing. A Lemon or Orange Filling (page 132) with my Lighter Cream Cheese Frosting (page 128) is excellent with this cake. *Small cake makes 9–12 servings; large cake makes 16–20 servings.*

Nutrients per serving: Calories 300, Fat 14g, Cholesterol 75mg, Sodium 320mg, Carbohydrates 40g, Protein 3g.

---

*F*or easy removal of any cake, line the pan with greased waxed or parchment paper. Remove from the bottom of the cake while still warm.

Viennese Memory Cake

Tender and full flavored, this light chocolate cake with its hint of almond, coffee, and apricots brings back memories of the Sachertorte at the Sacher Hotel in old Vienna.

2 cups Four Flour Bean Mix	1 teaspoon Egg Replacer
1 teaspoon xanthan gum	½ cup Butter Flavor Crisco
½ teaspoon salt	1¼ cups sugar
⅓ cup cocoa powder	2 eggs plus 1 egg white
2 teaspoons freeze-dried coffee	1 teaspoon almond flavoring
2 teaspoons baking powder	One 6-ounce jar junior apricots
1 rounded teaspoon baking soda	1 cup cherry cola

Preheat oven to 350°. Grease a 9" square pan and dust with rice flour.

In a medium bowl, whisk together the flour mix, xanthan gum, salt, cocoa, coffee crystals, baking powder, baking soda, and Egg Replacer.

In the bowl of your mixer, beat the Crisco and sugar until light. Beat in the eggs, one at a time. Add the flavoring. Add the dry ingredients and cola in 3 parts, beating just until blended after each addition. Pour into the prepared pan and bake for 50 minutes or until a tester inserted into the center of the cake comes out clean. Cool before frosting with your favorite icing. *Makes 12 servings.*

Nutrients per serving: Calories 280, Fat 17g, Cholesterol 35mg, Sodium 290mg, Carbohydrates 45g, Protein 4g.

---

*T*o test a creamed cake for doneness, insert a tester or toothpick into the center. If it comes out clean, the cake is done; if wet, bake a few minutes longer and test again.

Blue Ribbon Chocolate Cake

A winner! Light, fluffy, and deliciously chocolatey. The secret is in the unusual liquids. If you don't have green tomatoes, use firm, unripe, red ones.

2½ cups GF Mix

1 teaspoon xanthan gum

½ cup cocoa

2 rounded teaspoons baking powder

2 teaspoons baking soda

2 teaspoons Egg Replacer

¼ teaspoon salt

⅔ cup margarine or butter

1¾ cups sugar

4 ounces unsweetened chocolate, melted

2 eggs plus 2 egg whites

1 teaspoon almond flavoring or vanilla

1 cup cherry-flavored cola

1 cup pureed green tomatoes (about 2 medium)

Extra water, if needed, to make the batter a cakelike consistency

Preheat oven to 350°. Grease one 9" × 13" oblong pan or three 8" round pans and dust lightly with rice flour.

In a medium bowl, whisk together the flour mix, xanthan gum, cocoa, baking powder, baking soda, Egg Replacer, and salt. Set aside.

In the bowl of your mixer, cream the margarine and sugar; add the melted chocolate. Beat in the eggs, one at a time, and add the flavoring.

Combine the cola and tomato puree and add alternately with the dry ingredients in the bowl of your mixer. Beat on medium. Do not overbeat. The batter should be thick but not stiff. Add water 1 tablespoon at a time to get a smooth consistency. Pour into the prepared pan(s). Bake for about 35 minutes for large pan, about 25 minutes for the 8" round ones, or until a tester comes out clean and the cake pulls away from the edges of the baking pan(s). Frost as desired or serve topped with whipped cream. *Makes 16–20 servings.*

Nutrients per serving: Calories 400, Fat 12g, Cholesterol 25mg, Sodium 300mg, Carbohydrates 68g, Protein 8g.

Southern Living Cake

What could be easier than this cake, filled with pecans, pineapple, and bananas, using one bowl for mixing, and being beaten by hand? Over twenty years ago, Southern Living published a cake recipe that sounded wonderful. At the time I could only dream about the flavor. But with the new flours, I was finally able to adapt it. And even with our flours, it still tastes so delicious that I can believe their claim that it's been their most requested recipe.

For an 8" square pan

1½ cups Four Flour Bean Mix
½ teaspoon xanthan gum
¾ cup sugar
1 teaspoon baking soda
½ teaspoon baking powder
¾ teaspoon apple pie spice
¼ teaspoon salt
2 eggs, lightly beaten

⅓ cup vegetable oil
¾ teaspoon pineapple or vanilla
   flavoring
½ cup canned crushed pineapple
   with juice
½ cup chopped pecans
⅞ cup mashed ripe bananas

For three 8" round pans or one 9" × 13" pan

3 cups Four Flour Bean Mix
1 teaspoon xanthan gum
1½ cups sugar
2 teaspoons baking soda
1 teaspoon baking powder
1½ teaspoons apple pie spice
½ teaspoon salt
4 eggs, lightly beaten

⅔ cup vegetable oil
1½ teaspoons pineapple or vanilla
   flavoring
1 cup (8-ounce can) crushed
   pineapple
   with juice
1 cup chopped pecans
1½ cups mashed ripe bananas

Preheat oven to 350°. Grease your desired pan(s) or spray with vegetable oil spray. Dust with rice flour.

In a large mixing bowl, whisk together the flour mix, xanthan gum, sugar, baking soda, baking powder, apple pie spice, and salt. Stir in the beaten eggs and oil until the dry ingredients are moist. Stir in the flavoring, crushed pineapple, pecans, and mashed bananas.

Pour the batter into the prepared pan(s). Bake for about 25 minutes for the 8" square pan or the three 8" round pans, and slightly longer for the 9" × 13" pan, or until a tester comes out clean. Frost with a cream cheese frosting or another favorite. *Small cake makes 9–12 servings; large cake makes 16–24 servings.*

Nutrients per serving: Calories 290, Fat 14g, Cholesterol 45mg, Sodium 240mg, Carbohydrates 40g, Protein 4g.

Apple Cake

350°

Can you believe a cake so delicious that my nonceliac guests wouldn't leave me a scrap to see how well it keeps? If your family is like mine, you won't have to worry about keeping it, but it does stay moist and tasty for days.

For a 9" round springform pan or 8" square cake pan

1½ cups GF Mix
¾ teaspoon xanthan gum
1 teaspoon baking soda
1½ teaspoons baking powder
1¼ teaspoons apple pie spice
2 teaspoons powdered vanilla
  (if liquid, add to the butter-
  sugar mix)
½ cup (1 stick) butter or margarine

¾ cup white sugar
3 tablespoons brown sugar
2 eggs
3 tablespoons nondairy creamer
1½ cups apples, peeled, cored, and
  shredded (about 2 apples)
Confectioners' sugar for dusting
  (optional)

For a 12-cup bundt pan

3 cups GF Mix
1½ teaspoons xanthan gum
2 teaspoons baking soda
3 teaspoons baking powder
2½ teaspoons apple pie spice
3 teaspoons powdered vanilla
  (if liquid, add to the butter-sugar
  mix)
1 cup (2 sticks) butter or margarine

1½ cups white sugar
⅓ cup brown sugar
4 eggs
⅓ cup nondairy creamer
3 cups apples, peeled, cored, and
  shredded (about 4 apples)
Confectioners' sugar glaze if
  desired (see below)

Preheat oven to 350°. Grease your preferred pan, and dust with rice flour.

Cakes 53

In a medium bowl, whisk together the flour mix, xanthan gum, baking soda, baking powder, apple pie spice, and powdered vanilla (if liquid, add to the butter-sugar mix). Set aside.

In the bowl of your mixer, cream the butter for about 1 minute or until softened. Add both sugars and beat for about 2 minutes. Add the eggs, one at a time, and beat until well incorporated. Blend in the creamer. Turn mixer to low and add the dry ingredients half at a time, beating after each addition, until they are well absorbed.

Remove the bowl from the stand and gently fold in the apples. Spoon the batter into the prepared pan and bake for 40–45 minutes for the smaller pans, 55 to 60 minutes for the bundt pan, or until the tester comes out clean and the cake pulls away from the edges of the pan. If serving from the pan, cool at least 10 minutes before removing the springform ring. For the bundt pan, let cool 5 minutes before turning onto a cake plate. Dust lightly with confectioners' sugar, if desired. Or drizzle the bundt cake while warm with a thin glaze of confectioners' sugar mixed to a thin paste with fruit juice. *Small cake makes 9–12 servings; large cake makes 16–20 servings.*

Nutrients per serving: Calories 310, Fat 12g, Cholesterol 75mg, Sodium 330mg, Carbohydrates 51g, Protein 3g.

Apple-Walnut Cake
(Rice Free)

350°

Another delicious, moist cake my guests all loved. I didn't tell them it was made with bean flour with a dash of sorghum. Try it in the bundt size for a picnic or potluck or use the smaller size for the family. Either one will bring raves.

For a 9" round pan or an 8" square cake pan

1½ cups Four Flour Bean Mix

¾ teaspoon xanthan gum

½ teaspoon salt

1 teaspoon baking powder

1 teaspoon baking soda

1 teaspoon apple pie spice

1 teaspoon Egg Replacer (optional)

½ cup Butter Flavor Crisco

1 cup brown sugar, loosely packed

2 eggs

1 teaspoon flavoring (vanilla or Vanilla, Butter, & Nut)

1 cup finely chopped apple (1 large apple)

2 tablespoons apple (or other fruit) juice

½ cup chopped walnuts

For a 12-cup bundt pan

3 cups Four Flour Bean Mix

1½ teaspoons xanthan gum

1 teaspoon salt

2 teaspoons baking powder

2 teaspoons baking soda

2 teaspoons apple pie spice

2 teaspoons Egg Replacer (optional)

1 cup Butter Flavor Crisco

1¾ cups brown sugar

4 eggs

2 teaspoons flavoring (vanilla or Vanilla, Butter, & Nut)

2 cups finely chopped apple (2 large apples)

¼ cup apple (or other fruit) juice

½ cup chopped walnuts

Preheat oven to 350°. Grease the pan selected and dust with rice flour.

In a medium bowl, whisk together the flour mix, xanthan gum, salt, baking powder, baking soda, apple pie spice, and Egg Replacer (if used). Set aside.

In the bowl of your mixer, cream the Crisco and brown sugar. Beat in the eggs, one at a time. Add the flavoring and chopped apple. Beat for about 30 seconds or until most of the apple is chopped into the batter. With a spoon, stir in the chopped walnuts.

Spoon into the prepared pan and bake for 40 minutes for the smaller cake, 60 minutes for the bundt pan. The cake is done if it pulls from the sides and a tester comes out clean. For the bundt cake, cool slightly before turning upside down onto a cake plate.

This cake doesn't really need an icing, but for the bundt cake I drizzle the warm cake with a glaze of confectioners' sugar mixed to a thin paste with fruit juice. I often serve the smaller cake with a dab of whipped topping. *Small cake makes 8 or 9 servings; large cake makes 16–20 servings.*

Nutrients per serving: Calories 280, Fat 12g, Cholesterol 35mg, Sodium 260mg, Carbohydrates 42g, Protein 4g.

---

*M*ake a quick and easy frosting for a cake by heating a jar of apricot preserves, pouring it onto the cooled cake, and topping it with chopped nuts.

Sweet Potato Cake with Toasted Walnuts

A real party cake! This is moist and flavorful and stays fresh for days. Make it in the three layers for a celebration cake or spoon it into a 9" × 13" oblong cake pan for a special dessert for family.

Note: *To toast walnuts, place them in a 350° oven for 5 minutes.*

2 cups Featherlight Mix	½ cup maple syrup
1 teaspoon xanthan gum	2 eggs
3 teaspoons baking powder	One 16-ounce can sweet potatoes
1 teaspoon baking soda	in syrup
1 teaspoon cinnamon	½ teaspoon maple flavoring
½ cup (1 stick) margarine or butter	¾ cup chopped walnuts, toasted
¾ cup sugar	

Preheat oven to 350°. Line three 8" round cake pans or one 9" × 13" pan with wax paper and grease thoroughly. Dust with rice flour.

In a medium bowl, whisk together the flour mix, xanthan gum, baking powder, baking soda, and cinnamon. Set aside.

In the bowl of your mixer, beat the butter until smooth. Add the sugar and maple syrup and beat until creamy. Add the eggs, one at a time, beating after each addition.

Drain the sweet potatoes, reserving the syrup. Puree in a food processor or mash with a fork, adding 3 tablespoons of the syrup. Add the potato puree and maple flavoring to the butter mix, beating until smooth. Turn mixer to low and beat in the flour mix until incorporated. Fold in the walnuts. Spoon into the cake pans, dividing evenly.

Bake for 25–30 minutes for the 8" round pans, 35–40 minutes for the oblong pan or until a tester comes out clean. Cool slightly before removing from the 3 pans. Allow to cool completely before frosting. Suggested icing: Special Cream Cheese Frosting (page 127). You may use this for both filling and frosting. *Makes 16–20 servings.*

*Nutrients per serving: Calories 200, Fat 8g, Cholesterol 25mg,
Sodium 330mg, Carbohydrates 32g, Protein 2g.*

Toasted Walnut Cake

The surprise in this cake comes from the use of grated sweet potato, which not only keeps it tender and moist but adds to the depth of flavor. I call for a bundt pan and a simple drizzle of icing, but you can make a cake fit for any company by using three 9" round pans and a flavorful filling and icing.

Note: *To toast the walnuts, spread in pan and bake at 350° for 5 minutes.*

2½ cups Four Flour Bean Mix or Featherlight Mix

1½ teaspoons xanthan gum

2 teaspoons Egg Replacer

4 teaspoons baking powder

1 teaspoon baking soda

1 teaspoon cinnamon

1 teaspoon nutmeg

1 teaspoon dried orange peel (optional)

½ teaspoon salt

1½ cups vegetable oil

2 cups sugar

4 eggs, separated

⅓ cup orange juice

1½ cups grated raw sweet potatoes

1 cup chopped walnuts, toasted

1 teaspoon flavoring (black walnut, Vanilla, Butter, & Nut, or vanilla)

Preheat the oven to 350°. Grease a 10–12-cup bundt pan or three 9" round cake pans with vegetable oil spray and dust with rice flour.

In a medium bowl, whisk together the flour mix, xanthan gum, Egg Replacer, baking powder, baking soda, cinnamon, nutmeg, dried orange peel (if used), and salt. Set aside.

In the bowl of your mixer, combine the oil and sugar and beat until smooth. Add the egg yolks and beat well. Beat in the orange juice. With the mixer on low, blend in the dry ingredients. Beat well for about 1 minute. Remove bowl from mixer and stir in the potatoes, nuts, and flavoring.

Beat the egg whites until stiff and fold into the batter. Spoon into the prepared pan(s) and bake for 50–60 minutes for the bundt pan, 25–30 minutes for the round pans or until a tester comes out clean. Let the cakes cool slightly before turning out. For the bundt cake, when cool drizzle with a thin glaze of confectioners' sugar mixed to drizzle consistency with orange juice. For the round cake use your favorite icing and filling. *Makes 12–16 servings.*

Nutrients per serving: Calories 300, Fat 17g, Cholesterol 35mg,
Sodium 180mg, Carbohydrates 35g, Protein 3g.

When measuring liquids, use a clear glass measuring cup, and place on a level surface to read the markings at eye level.

Walnut Cake with Caramel Apple Topping   350°

The ultimate upside-down cake! This easy-to-make, walnut-filled cake with its own rich topping should please any guest, for no one would guess it's gluten free. Whether you top it with a dab of whipped cream or nondairy topping or serve it plain, your guests will agree that eating on this diet is great eating!

TOPPING:
4 tablespoons (½ stick) margarine
   or butter
1 cup brown sugar
¼ cup chopped walnuts
2 apples, peeled, cored, and
   sliced

BATTER:
1½ cups Featherlight Mix
2 tablespoons potato flakes
½ teaspoon xanthan gum

2 teaspoons baking powder
½ teaspoon baking soda
½ teaspoon salt
½ teaspoon vanilla
1 teaspoon apple pie spice
2 eggs
⅔ cup sugar
⅓ cup mayonnaise
⅔ cup sour cream or nondairy
   substitute
¾ cup chopped walnuts

Preheat oven to 350°. Place a 9" square pan on the stove burner and melt the margarine or butter in it. Sprinkle on the brown sugar and walnuts. Arrange the apple slices in a flat layer. Set aside.

In a medium bowl, whisk together the flour mix, potato flakes, xanthan gum, baking powder, baking soda, salt, and apple pie spice. Set aside.

In a large mixing bowl, beat the eggs and sugar until light and foamy. Add the vanilla here. With the mixer on low, blend in the flour mix, beating until smooth.

Stir in the mayonnaise and sour cream until well blended. Add the nuts. Do not beat. Pour the batter gently over the topping and bake for 35–40 minutes. The cake should be pulling away from the edges when done. Turn out while still hot onto a cake plate or 12" cardboard square covered well with aluminum foil. Serve warm or at room temperature, topped (if desired) with whipped topping, yogurt, or ice cream. *Makes 9 servings.*

Nutrients per serving: Calories 440, Fat 22g, Cholesterol 70mg, Sodium 400mg, Carbohydrates 58g, Protein 5g.

Banana Cake 350°

There's a time of the year when all the bakeries seem to be featuring banana cakes so the store smells of bananas. But you don't have to wait for your banana cake. Any time you have 2 large ripe bananas, you can stir one up.

Note: *For a lighter cake, separate the eggs and add yolks to creamed mix. Beat whites to soft peaks and fold in gently after the flour and liquids are mixed.*

2 cups Four Flour Bean Mix	1 tablespoon lemon juice
1 teaspoon xanthan gum	½ cup (one stick) margarine
2 teaspoons baking powder	1⅓ cups sugar
1 teaspoon baking soda	3 eggs (see note)
2 teaspoons Egg Replacer	1½ teaspoons Vanilla, Butter,
½ teaspoon salt	& Nut flavoring or vanilla
⅓ cup buttermilk	2 tablespoons finely chopped
1 cup mashed bananas	pecans or walnuts

Preheat oven to 350°. Grease a 9" × 13" oblong cake pan or two 8" round pans and dust lightly with rice flour.

In a medium bowl, whisk together the flour mix, xanthan gum, baking powder, baking soda, Egg Replacer, and salt. Set aside.

In a smaller bowl, stir together the buttermilk, mashed bananas, and lemon juice.

In the bowl of your mixer, cream the margarine and sugar until creamy. Add the eggs, one at a time, beating until smooth and fluffy. Add the flavoring. Add half the dry ingredients and half the banana mixture. Beat just until smooth. Repeat with the second half. Beat about 1 minute (don't overbeat). Stir in the nuts and spoon into the prepared pan(s). Bake for approximately 40 minutes for the 9" × 13" pan, 30 minutes for the 8" round pans, or until a tester comes out clean and the edges of the cake separate slightly from the pan.

Cool before serving. You may cut the cake in the oblong pan into squares and top with whipped cream (with a couple of fresh banana slices for decoration) or frost it or the 2-layer cake with a favorite cream or cream cheese icing and top with 2 tablespoons of finely chopped nuts. *Makes 16–20 servings.*

Nutrients per serving: Calories 220, Fat 6g, Cholesterol 30mg, Sodium 200mg, Carbohydrates 33g, Protein 2g.

Banana Cake with Dates

My favorite banana cake! Before I tried this cake I thought the dates would over-shadow the banana taste. Instead, they enhance it.

Note: *Buy pitted whole dates, and not the small pieces; the latter may be dusted with wheat. Cut the dates and use about 1 tablespoon each rice flour and sugar to dust the dates so they won't clump together in the batter.*

2 cups Four Flour Bean Mix	1⅓ cups sugar
1 teaspoon xanthan gum	2 eggs plus 1 egg white
3 teaspoons baking powder	¼ cup rum
1 teaspoon baking soda	1 cup mashed ripe bananas
2 teaspoons Egg Replacer	1 tablespoon lemon juice
¼ teaspoon salt	¼ cup milk or nondairy substitute
½ cup (1 stick) margarine or butter	1 cup chopped dates (see note)

Preheat oven to 350°. Grease a 9" × 13" pan and dust with rice flour.

In a medium bowl, whisk together the flour mix, xanthan gum, baking powder, baking soda, Egg Replacer, and salt. Set aside.

In the bowl of your mixer, beat the margarine and sugar until creamy. Add the eggs, rum, and mashed bananas (into which you've stirred the lemon juice). Beat on medium until smooth (do not overbeat). Blend in the dry ingredients and milk in 2 additions. Fold in the dates.

Spoon into the prepared pan and bake for 35–40 minutes or until a tester comes out clean and the cake starts to pull from the edges of the pan. Cool before frosting with a creamy vanilla or cream cheese icing. Or serve as dessert squares topped with whipped cream or nondairy whipped topping. *Makes 12 servings.*

Nutrients per serving: Calories 220, Fat 6g, Cholesterol 40mg,
Sodium 230mg, Carbohydrates 38g, Protein 3g.

Pumpkin Cake

Very moist and slightly spiced, this low-fat cake tastes wonderful and keeps well. Make it up in the 8" square pan for the family or treat your guests to a layer cake with a Fluffy Cream Cheese Frosting (page 126).

Note: For a change in taste, replace the dried orange peel with 1 tablespoon finely diced candied orange peel.

For an 8" or 9" square pan

1¼ cups Four Flour Bean Mix

½ teaspoon xanthan gum

1 teaspoon baking powder

½ teaspoon baking soda

2 teaspoons Egg Replacer

2 teaspoons pumpkin pie spice

½ cup white sugar

¼ cup brown sugar

¼ cup (½ stick) margarine or butter

½ cup canned pumpkin

¼ cup orange juice

1 egg yolk

½ teaspoon vanilla

½ teaspoon dried orange peel

3 egg whites

¼ teaspoon salt

For three 8" round pans

2½ cups Four Flour Bean Mix

1 teaspoon xanthan gum

2 teaspoons baking powder

1 teaspoon baking soda

1 teaspoon Egg Replacer

1 rounded tablespoon pumpkin
  pie spice

1 cup white sugar

½ cup brown sugar

½ cup (1 stick) margarine or butter

1 cup canned pumpkin

½ cup orange juice

2 egg yolks

1 teaspoon vanilla

1 teaspoon dried orange peel

6 egg whites

½ teaspoon salt

Preheat oven to 350°. Grease your pan(s) and dust with rice flour.

In a medium bowl, whisk together the flour mix, xanthan gum, baking powder, baking soda, Egg Replacer, and pumpkin pie spice. Set aside.

In the bowl of your mixer, cream both sugars with the margarine. Beat in the pumpkin, orange juice, egg yolk(s), vanilla, and orange peel. With the mixer on low, add the flour mix until just combined.

In a clean bowl, beat the egg whites until foamy. Add the salt and continue beating until soft peaks form. Gently fold half of the whites into the batter, then add the last half and fold in. Spoon the batter into the prepared pan(s). Bake for 20–25 minutes or until edges of cake pull away from pan sides. Cool before frosting. *Small cake makes 9–12 servings; large cake makes 18–20 servings.*

Nutrients per serving: Calories 200, Fat 6g, Cholesterol 40mg, Sodium 325mg, Carbohydrates 35g, Protein 3g.

Double Ginger Cake

A wonderfully different spice cake! This started out to be a gingerbread cake, but since I added apricot nectar as a liquid and crystallized ginger for tang, my tasters insist it deserves a better name.

1½ cups Four Flour Bean Mix	½ cup (1 stick) margarine or butter
¾ teaspoon xanthan gum	½ cup brown sugar
1 teaspoon baking soda	¼ cup molasses
1 teaspoon baking powder	½ cup liquid egg substitute or
1 teaspoon Egg Replacer	2 eggs
½ teaspoon salt	⅓ cup apricot nectar (or water)
1 teaspoon pumpkin pie spice	¼ cup chopped crystallized ginger

Preheat oven to 350°. Grease an 8" or 9" square pan.

In a medium bowl, whisk together the flour mix, xanthan gum, baking soda, baking powder, Egg Replacer, salt, and pumpkin pie spice. Set aside.

In the bowl of your mixer, cream the margarine and brown sugar. Add the molasses, liquid egg substitute, and apricot nectar. Blend. With the mixer on low, blend in the dry ingredients. Beat until well incorporated (but do not overbeat). Stir in the chopped ginger and spoon the batter into the prepared pan.

Bake for about 35 minutes or until a tester comes out clean. Cool before frosting with a cream cheese frosting. Or serve hot or cold with whipped cream sweetened with brown sugar. *Makes 9 servings.*

*Nutrients per serving: Calories 200, Fat 9g, Cholesterol 55mg,
Sodium 330mg, Carbohydrates 29g, Protein 3g.*

Ginger Carrot Cake

350°

A very light carrot cake with terrific flavor. This is my favorite.

Note: *To toast walnuts, place in a baking pan and bake in a 350° oven for 5 minutes, stirring once.*

1¼ cups Featherlight Mix	¼ teaspoon salt
¼ cup soy flour	1 teaspoon dried lemon peel
¾ teaspoon xanthan gum	¾ cup olive oil
1 rounded teaspoon Egg Replacer	1⅓ cups sugar
2 teaspoons cinnamon	3 eggs
1 tablespoon finely chopped candied ginger	1½ cups grated carrots
1½ teaspoons baking soda	¾ cup chopped walnuts, toasted (see note)

Preheat oven to 350°. Grease a 9" square pan.

In a medium bowl, whisk together the flour mix, soy flour, xanthan gum, Egg Replacer, cinnamon, candied ginger, baking soda, salt, and dried lemon peel. Set aside.

In the bowl of your mixer, beat the oil, sugar, and eggs until light and fluffy (about 5 minutes). Add the dry ingredients and beat just until blended. Fold in the carrots and walnuts.

Spoon batter into the prepared pan and bake for 45–50 minutes or until a tester inserted near the center comes out clean. When cool, frost with Lighter Cream Cheese Frosting (page 128) or serve the cake topped with whipped cream or nondairy topping. *Makes 9–12 servings.*

Nutrients per serving: Calories 330, Fat 18g, Cholesterol 55mg, Sodium 270mg, Carbohydrates 33g, Protein 4g.

Carrot-Cranberry Bundt Cake

350°

Cranberry sauce gives this carrot cake a deliciously unique flavor. It's easy to stir up in one pan, stays moist for days, and no one will guess it's gluten free. This is a small recipe. Doubled it can serve a crowd. Increase the baking time by at least 10 minutes.

CAKE:
1½ cups Four Flour Bean Mix
¾ teaspoon xanthan gum
1½ teaspoons baking powder
1 teaspoon baking soda
1 teaspoon Egg Replacer
½ teaspoon salt
1½ teaspoons cinnamon
½ teaspoon nutmeg
1 cup grated carrots

½ cup whole cranberry sauce
   (canned or fresh)
1 cup sugar
⅔ cup vegetable oil
2 eggs, beaten lightly

GLAZE:
½ cup confectioners' sugar
1 to 2 tablespoons fruit juice

Preheat oven to 350°. Spray a 10–12-cup bundt pan with cooking spray and dust with rice flour.

In a large mixing bowl or the bowl of your mixer, blend the flour mix, xanthan gum, baking powder, baking soda, Egg Replacer, salt, cinnamon, and nutmeg. Add the carrots, cranberry sauce, sugar, oil, and beaten eggs. Beat until well blended. Spoon into the prepared pan. Bake for 40–50 minutes. Cool slightly and turn from pan onto a cake plate.

For glaze, combine the confectioners' sugar and enough of the fruit juice to make a consistency that will drizzle from the spoon. Drizzle over the cake in thin lines. *Makes 12–16 servings.*

Nutrients per serving: Calories 290, Fat 13g, Cholesterol 35mg, Sodium 160mg, Carbohydrates 42g, Protein 3g.

Chocolate Carrot Cake

A new and exciting carrot cake and a very good keeper. This is as moist and tender as the others but made especially for chocolate lovers. It can be made in a bundt pan and drizzled with a simple icing of powdered sugar and orange juice. Or make the large 2-layer cake and create a masterpiece by filling and topping with either a cream cheese frosting or my Baker's Secret Icing (page 131).

2½ cups Four Flour Bean Mix

1¼ teaspoons xanthan gum

2 teaspoons Egg Replacer

2½ teaspoons baking soda

1 teaspoon salt

½ cup unsweetened cocoa powder

2¼ cups sugar

1½ cups vegetable oil

4 eggs

2 cups finely grated carrots

1 cup chopped pecans or walnuts

1½ teaspoons grated orange peel

One 11-ounce can mandarin
   oranges drained, cut into
   ½" sections

Preheat oven to 375° for a bundt pan, 350° for two 8" or 9" round cake pans. Spray chosen pan(s) with vegetable oil spray and dust lightly with rice flour.

In a large bowl, whisk together the flour mix, xanthan gum, Egg Replacer, baking soda, salt, cocoa, and sugar. Set aside.

In the bowl of your mixer, beat the oil and eggs on medium high until well blended and thick (about 2 minutes). Add the dry ingredients and beat on low to blend. Increase the speed and beat 1 minute longer (the batter will seem very thick). With a spoon, stir in the carrots, nuts, and orange peel. Stir in the orange pieces.

Spoon into the pan(s). Bake the bundt cake at 375° for approximately 40 minutes. Reduce the heat to 350° and bake for 15 minutes longer or until a tester inserted into the center of the pan comes out clean. If using the round cake pans, bake at 350° for approximately 40 minutes.

Cool 5 minutes before turning out. For the bundt cake, drizzle on an icing of confectioners' sugar and orange juice mixed to a drizzling consistency. Ice the layer cake as desired. *Makes 20–24 servings.*

*Nutrients per serving: Calories 340, Fat 20g, Cholesterol 40mg,
Sodium 300mg, Carbohydrates 40g, Protein 3g.*

Carrot Bundt Cake   375°–350°

This is not just "another carrot cake." With the new Four Flour Bean Mix and the added coconut and orange juice in the batter, it makes a very special bundt cake that will keep moist for days. You can top this with a drizzle of confectioners' sugar and orange juice or brush on the Rum Sauce from the Christmas Rum Cake (page 83).

3 cups Four Flour Bean Mix
1½ teaspoons xanthan gum
1 cup dark brown sugar
¾ cup white sugar
1 tablespoon baking powder
1 teaspoon baking soda
2½ teaspoons pumpkin pie spice
½ teaspoon salt
4 eggs

1¼ cups vegetable oil
¼ cup orange juice
1 tablespoon Vanilla, Butter,
  & Nut flavoring or vanilla
3 cups grated carrot
1 cup flaked coconut
1 cup chopped pecans or walnuts
½ cup dried cranberries or raisins

Preheat oven to 375°. Grease a 10–12-cup bundt pan and dust with rice flour.

In the bowl of your mixer, combine the flour mix, xanthan gum, brown sugar, white sugar, baking powder, baking soda, pumpkin pie spice, and salt. Whisk well or blend with your mixer for 30 seconds.

In a small bowl, beat the eggs and stir in the oil, orange juice, and flavoring. Make a well in the center of the dry ingredients and pour in the egg mix. Beat with a spoon until well mixed. Then with your mixer on medium, beat for 3 minutes.

Stir in the carrots, coconut, pecans, and cranberries. Pour into the prepared pan and bake for 45 minutes at 375°. Lower the heat to 350° and bake for 15 minutes longer or until cake tests done. Let cool about 5 minutes before turning out onto a cake plate. Brush on the Rum Sauce while still warm. Let it cool longer if using the confectioners' sugar and orange juice drizzle. *Makes 20–24 servings.*

Nutrients per serving: Calories 300, Fat 17g, Cholesterol 35mg, Sodium 170mg, Carbohydrates 35g, Protein 3g.

Lighter Carrot Cake

350°

This old favorite has a leaner look but none of the flavor appeal is lost as apricot sauce replaces much of the oil or mayonnaise of my former recipes—the amount of nuts was cut to be replaced by optional raisins.

For an 8" square pan

1½ cups Four Flour Bean Mix

¾ teaspoon xanthan gum

1 teaspoon cinnamon

⅛ teaspoon ginger

1 teaspoon baking powder

¾ teaspoon baking soda

1 teaspoon Egg Replacer

¼ teaspoon salt

1 tablespoon almond meal or NutQuik

½ cup white sugar

⅓ cup brown sugar

⅓ cup junior apricot baby food

3 tablespoons oil

2 eggs

1½ cups grated carrots

¼ cup chopped walnuts

¼ cup golden raisins (optional)

For a 9" × 13" pan

3 cups Four Flour Bean Mix

1½ teaspoons xanthan gum

2 teaspoons cinnamon

¼ teaspoon ginger

2 teaspoons baking powder

1½ teaspoons baking soda

2 teaspoons Egg Replacer

½ teaspoon salt

2 tablespoons almond meal or NutQuik

1 cup white sugar

⅔ cup brown sugar

⅔ cup (1 jar) junior apricot baby food

⅓ cup oil

4 eggs

3 cups grated carrots

½ cup chopped walnuts

½ cup golden raisins (optional)

Preheat oven to 350°. Grease your chosen pan and dust with rice flour.

In a medium bowl, whisk together the flour mix, xanthan gum, cinnamon, ginger, baking powder, baking soda, Egg Replacer, salt, and almond meal. Set aside.

In the bowl of your mixer, place both sugars, apricot sauce, and oil. Beat for about 1 minute. Add the eggs, beating after each addition. Stir in the dry ingredients. Add the carrots, nuts, and raisins. Stir just until well incorporated. Spoon into pan.

Bake for 35–40 minutes or until a tester comes out clean and the cake has pulled from the sides of the baking pan. Cool before frosting. The usual frosting is a cream cheese one but you may choose another of your favorites.

For the Lighter Cream Cheese Frosting, see page 128. *Small cake makes 9–12 servings; large cake makes 16–24 servings.*

Nutrients per serving: Calories 190, Fat 6g, Cholesterol 35mg, Sodium 180mg, Carbohydrates 34g, Protein 3g.

Pumpkin-Pecan Bundt Cake

This moist, nutty cake is delicately flavored with pumpkin, orange, and pecans. It's easy to put together and a simple drizzle of confectioners' sugar mixed with orange juice finishes it to perfection.

2½ cups Four Flour Bean Mix
1 teaspoon xanthan gum
2 teaspoons baking powder
1 teaspoon baking soda
½ teaspoon salt
2 teaspoons dried orange peel
¾ cup white sugar
¾ cup brown sugar

½ cup (1 stick) margarine or butter
1 teaspoon Vanilla, Butter, & Nut
 flavoring or vanilla
1 cup canned pumpkin
3 eggs or ¾ cup liquid egg
 substitute
½ cup milk or nondairy substitute
¾ cup chopped pecans

Preheat oven to 350°. Grease a 10–12-cup bundt pan and dust lightly with rice flour.

In a medium bowl, whisk together the flour mix, xanthan gum, baking powder, baking soda, salt, and dried orange peel. Set aside.

In the bowl of your mixer, beat both sugars and margarine until light and fluffy. Add the flavoring and pumpkin, beating lightly. Add the eggs, one at a time, beating after each addition. Alternately beat in the dry ingredients with the milk. Stir in the nuts. Spoon into the prepared pan.

Bake for 40–45 minutes or until a tester comes out clean. Cool the cake for 5 minutes before reversing onto a cake plate.

For the glaze, combine ½ cup confectioners' sugar with enough orange juice to make a drizzling consistency. Drizzle it on immediately, letting it run down the sides in streaks. *Makes 16–20 servings.*

*Nutrients per serving: Calories 210, Fat 9g, Cholesterol 45mg,
Sodium 250mg, Carbohydrates 32g, Protein 3g.*

Lemon Ring Cake 350°

This lemony flavored bundt cake with nuts needs no mixer or special equipment to stir up. And since the frosting is the hot glaze brushed on after baking, it is extra easy to make.

CAKE:

1¾ cups Four Flour Bean Mix
  or GF Mix

1 scant teaspoon xanthan gum

2 teaspoons Egg Replacer

1 teaspoon unflavored gelatin

2 teaspoons baking powder

¼ teaspoon salt

1 cup sugar

½ cup (1 stick) margarine or butter

3 eggs, lightly beaten

½ cup citrus-flavored carbonated
  beverage

Grated zest of 1 lemon

½ cup chopped pecans
  or walnuts

GLAZE:

3 tablespoons lemon juice

¼ cup sugar

Preheat oven to 350°. Spray a bundt or tube pan with vegetable oil spray.

In the bowl of your mixer, whisk together the flour mix, xanthan gum, Egg Replacer, gelatin, baking powder, salt, and sugar. Add the margarine, working it into the flour as you would for pastry until the mix feels like crumbs.

In a small bowl, beat the eggs slightly and add the carbonated beverage. Pour this into the dry ingredients and beat about 20 strokes. Fold in the lemon zest and nuts. Spoon the batter into the prepared pan and bake for 35–40 minutes or until a tester comes out clean and the cake starts to pull away from the pan sides. Cool about 5 minutes before turning out onto a cake plate.

For the glaze, combine lemon juice and sugar. Heat to boiling. Using a pastry brush, brush the glaze over the hot cake, letting it soak in. If desired, sift confectioners' sugar over the top of the cake. *Makes 10–12 servings.*

*Nutrients per serving: Calories 330, Fat 5g, Cholesterol 65mg,
Sodium 260mg, Carbohydrates 47g, Protein 5g.*

Orange Coconut Pound Cake

This light, moist pound cake is so tender and tasty that no one will suspect it's gluten free. The orange-flavored syrup is frosting enough but you can top the slices with fresh fruit or whipped topping or, if you want a scrumptious dessert, use both.

Note: If you don't like coconut, you may substitute plain milk, NutQuik milk, or any other nondairy liquid.

For an 8½" × 4½" loaf pan

CAKE:
1½ cups GF Mix
¾ teaspoon xanthan gum
1½ teaspoons baking powder
1 teaspoon Egg Replacer
¾ cup (1½ sticks) butter or
   margarine
¾ cup sugar

3 eggs
2½ teaspoons orange zest
3 tablespoons coconut milk
   (see note)

SYRUP TOPPING:
½ cup sugar
⅓ cup orange juice

For a 10–12-cup bundt pan

CAKE:
3 cups GF Mix
1½ teaspoons xanthan gum
3 teaspoons baking powder
1 teaspoon Egg Replacer
1½ cups (3 sticks) butter or
   margarine
1½ cups sugar

6 eggs
5 teaspoons orange zest
⅓ cup coconut milk (see note)

SYRUP TOPPING:
½ cup sugar
⅓ cup orange juice

Preheat oven to 325°. Grease your chosen pan and dust with rice flour.

In a medium bowl, whisk together the flour mix, xanthan gum, baking powder, and Egg Replacer. Set aside.

In the bowl of your mixer, beat butter on medium for 30 seconds. Gradually add the sugar, beating on medium high. Continue beating until very light and fluffy. Add the eggs, one at a time, beating after each addition. Add the zest and dry ingredients, beating on medium until just combined. Beat in the coconut milk.

Spoon the batter evenly into the prepared pan. Bake for 55–60 minutes or until a tester comes out clean.

Meanwhile, make the syrup by combining the sugar and orange juice in a small pan and heating over medium heat to boiling. Remove from the heat.

To top, invert the cake onto a cake plate and prick the hot cake with a toothpick. Spoon on the hot syrup, using as much as the cake will absorb. Cool before serving plain, or top with fruit or whipped topping or both. *Makes 8 servings.*

Nutrients per serving: Calories 410, Fat 20g, Cholesterol 125mg,
Sodium 310mg, Carbohydrates 93g, Protein 4g.

Vanilla Pound Cake with Cinnamon Swirl 350°

This loaf cake is easy to stir up, needs no frosting, stays fresh for days, and can be made from either a rice or bean flour mix. For a change of flavor, try the chocolate swirl variation.

CAKE:

2 cups Four Flour Bean Mix or
   GF Mix
¾ teaspoon xanthan gum
   (optional)
2 teaspoons baking powder
1 teaspoon baking soda
1 teaspoon Egg Replacer
1 cup sugar
½ cup (1 stick) margarine or butter

1 cup sour cream or nondairy
   substitute
1 teaspoon vanilla
3 eggs

STREUSEL:

3 tablespoons brown sugar
1 teaspoon cinnamon
1 tablespoon chopped pecans
1 tablespoon butter or margarine

Preheat oven to 350°. Grease a 9" × 5" loaf pan and dust with rice flour.

In a medium bowl, whisk together the flour mix, xanthan gum (if used), baking powder, baking soda, and Egg Replacer. Set aside.

In the bowl of your mixer, beat the sugar and margarine until light and fluffy. Add the dry ingredients and beat just until blended. Beat in the sour cream and vanilla until smooth. Add the eggs and beat again.

Spoon half the batter into the prepared pan. Mix together the streusel ingredients and spread half over the batter. Spoon on the remaining batter and top with the remaining streusel. Use a knife to swirl the streusel into the batter.

Bake for about 55 minutes or until a tester comes out clean. Cool for 10 minutes in the pan before turning out to cool completely. *Makes 1 large loaf to serve 12–16.*

VARIATION:

VANILLA POUND CAKE WITH CHOCOLATE SWIRL: Grate 2 ounces semisweet chocolate and add 1 teaspoon cinnamon to the streusel. Follow the directions above for swirling this in.

Nutrients per serving: Calories 200, Fat 8g, Cholesterol 55mg,
Sodium 190mg, Carbohydrates 30g, Protein 3g.

---

*W*hen making a sponge cake, beat the egg yolks until thick and the color of lemons or your cake may form an eggy bottom layer.

Chocolate Pound Cake 325°

A new pound cake for chocolate lovers. This should be made at least one day before serving and can be made 3 days ahead. This will free up some time on the day of the party!

1½ cups Featherlight Mix
¾ teaspoon xanthan gum
1 teaspoon Egg Replacer (optional)
1½ teaspoons baking powder
½ teaspoon salt
⅓ cup Dutch processed cocoa
1 cup (2 sticks) butter or margarine

1⅔ cups sugar
4 eggs
1 cup sour cream (may use light)
1 tablespoon vanilla
¾ cup semisweet miniature
   chocolate chips

Preheat oven to 325°. Grease a 9" × 5" loaf pan.

In a medium bowl, whisk together the flour mix, xanthan gum, Egg Replacer (if used), baking powder, and salt. Set aside.

In the bowl of your mixer, beat the butter and sugar until well blended. Add the eggs one at a time, beating well after each addition. Add the sour cream and vanilla, beating in well. Beat in the dry ingredients in 3 additions, beating well after each addition. Fold in the chocolate chips. Spoon batter into prepared pan.

Bake for 1 hour 35 minutes. Cool for 15 minutes in pan. Cut between sides of cake and pan to turn out to cool. Wrap in foil and let stand at room temperature for at least 24 hours (can be made 3 days ahead of serving—keep at room temperature). Cut in ¾" slices. Serve with ice cream and berries or whipped nondairy topping. *Makes 12 servings.*

Nutrients per serving: Calories 430, Fat 24g, Cholesterol 120mg, Sodium 320mg, Carbohydrates 52g, Protein 4g.

Angel Food Loaf

Ever wish you could make just half a cake? Here it is. This small angel food cake can be made in a loaf pan or in a small, seven-inch tube pan. The flour can be rice or bean. Both turn out well. Frost this with Whipped Cream Frosting (page 130) or serve it topped with fresh fruit.

½ cup sifted flour (Four Flour Bean Mix or Featherlight Mix)
¾ cup sugar, divided
½ teaspoon vanilla powder
⅔ cup (4–5) egg whites, at room temperature

⅛ teaspoon salt
½ teaspoon cream of tartar
¼ teaspoon almond flavoring

Preheat oven to 375°.

Sift the flour before measuring. Add ¼ cup sugar and the vanilla powder to the flour. Sift 3 more times. Beat the egg whites and salt until foamy. Sprinkle in the cream of tartar and continue beating until the whites stand up in soft peaks. With the mixer on medium, sprinkle the remaining ½ cup sugar on very slowly. Add the almond flavoring and beat.

Sift about half the flour-sugar mix over the whites and fold in lightly. Add the last of the flour-sugar and fold in well. Turn into an ungreased 9" × 5" loaf pan or a 7" tube pan. Bake for 30–35 minutes until done.

Remove from oven and invert pan; let stand for 1 hour or until the cake is cool. *Makes 10–12 servings.*

Nutrients per serving: Calories 80, Fat 0g, Cholesterol 0mg, Sodium 45mg, Carbohydrates 18g, Protein 2g.

Apricot Cloud Cake

Not a sponge cake or angel food or chiffon, this springy, moist cake is one that melts on the tongue while the flavor of apricots and almonds lingers. This takes a little more fuss than some cakes but is well worth the trouble.

6 ounces (1 cup) dried apricots	1 cup almond meal
1½ cups orange or pineapple juice	1 teaspoon salt
1½ cups Four Flour Bean Mix	9 eggs, separated
¾ teaspoon xanthan gum	1¾ cups sugar, divided

Preheat oven to 350°. Have handy a 10" tube pan, ungreased.

In a small saucepan, cook the apricots in the orange juice by bringing it to a boil and simmering for 7–10 minutes or until the apricots are tender. Cool. Drain off ⅓ cup liquid and reserve. Puree the remaining sauce and set aside.

In a medium bowl, combine the flour mix, xanthan gum, almond meal, and salt. Set aside.

In a large mixing bowl, beat the egg yolks with 1¼ cups sugar until light. Add 1 cup of the apricot puree. Blend. Add the dry ingredients alternately with the reserved ⅓ cup liquid.

In a separate large mixing bowl, beat the egg whites until soft peaks form. Add the remaining sugar slowly and beat until stiff. Fold ¼ of this meringue into the batter. Add the remaining meringue, folding in gently. Spoon the batter into the tube pan.

Bake for 55–60 minutes or until a cake tester comes out dry. Invert the pan and let it cool. Cut from sides and center of pan with a knife and unmold onto a cake plate. Serve plain, with whipped topping, ice cream, or frozen yogurt. If desired, frost with any buttercream frosting. *Makes 12–16 servings.*

Nutrients per serving: Calories 260, Fat 8g, Cholesterol 120mg, Sodium 180mg, Carbohydrates 42g, Protein 7g.

Christmas Rum Cake

My original version of this rum cake was always a hit when I served it at a baking show for it tasted great even after several days. This new version with a change of flours became an instant success with my tasters for it rises higher, the texture is lighter, and the flavor more tasty. Remember to put the dried cranberries to soak overnight.

CAKE:

1 cup dried cranberries

⅓ cup dark rum

2½ cups Four Flour Bean Mix

4 teaspoons baking powder

1½ teaspoons baking soda

½ teaspoon salt

¼ teaspoon nutmeg

2 teaspoons xanthan gum

1 cup mayonnaise

1 cup sugar

3 eggs

1 cup buttermilk

2 teaspoons dried lemon peel

2 teaspoons dried orange peel

RUM SAUCE:

½ cup sugar

¼ cup water

2 tablespoons orange juice

2 tablespoons lemon juice

2 tablespoons dark rum

2 tablespoons confectioners' sugar
 (optional)

Preheat oven to 350°. Grease a bundt pan with 10–12-cup capacity and dust with rice flour.

Soak the dried cranberries in the rum overnight in a covered bowl until they are plump with rum and there is no moisture left in the bowl.

In a medium bowl, whisk together the flour mix, baking powder, baking soda, salt, nutmeg, and xanthan gum. Set aside.

In the bowl of your mixer, beat together the mayonnaise, sugar, and eggs on medium until they are well beaten. With the mixer on low, add the dry ingredients in 3 additions, alternating with the buttermilk. Then, by hand, stir in the lemon and orange peels and rum-soaked cranberries.

Pour the batter into the prepared pan and bake for approximately 50 minutes, or until a tester comes out clean. Let the cake stand in the pan for 10 minutes before turning out onto a cake plate.

For the rum sauce, boil the sugar and water together in small saucepan for 2 minutes. Remove from the heat and stir in the orange juice, lemon juice, and rum. Using a pastry brush, brush the warm rum sauce over the warm cake until it will absorb no more. Sprinkle the top with confectioners' sugar after cooling, if desired. *Makes 20 servings.*

Nutrients per serving: Calories 260, Fat 12g, Cholesterol 40mg, Sodium 340mg, Carbohydrates 34g, Protein 3g.

Peanut Butter and Jelly Cake

350°

A smooth-textured cake that will please anyone. Whether you're a peanut butter lover or not, you will enjoy the flavor of peanut butter and jelly in this adult form.

2 cups Featherlight Mix
1 teaspoon xanthan gum
1 teaspoon unflavored gelatin
2 teaspoons Egg Replacer
1 teaspoon baking soda
1 teaspoon baking powder
½ teaspoon salt
¾ cup (1½ sticks) butter
2 cups sugar

1 teaspoon vanilla
5 eggs
1 cup creamy peanut butter
1 cup buttermilk
One recipe Peanut Butter Icing
    (page 131)
¼ cup chopped peanuts (for
    decoration)

Preheat oven to 350°. Cut waxed or parchment paper to fit the bottoms of three 9" round cake pans. Grease paper and pan sides and lightly dust with rice flour.

In a medium bowl, whisk together the flour mix, xanthan gum, gelatin, Egg Replacer, baking soda, baking powder, and salt.

In the bowl of your mixer, cream the butter and sugar. Add the vanilla. Add the eggs, one at a time, beating well after each addition. Beat in the peanut butter. Add the dry ingredients alternately with the buttermilk, beating on low after each addition until just combined. Spoon into the prepared pans and bake for 25–30 minutes or until a tester comes out clean.

Cool slightly before removing from pans. Peel off the waxed paper and allow to cool completely before frosting.

To put the cake together, use your favorite jelly for the filling (I use raspberry), spread the icing on the sides and top, and scatter on the chopped peanuts for the final touch. *Makes 16 servings.*

*Nutrients per serving: Calories 570, Fat 24g, Cholesterol 92mg,
Sodium 399mg, Carbohydrates 82g, Protein 2g.*

Coconutty Layer Cake

Most coconut cakes get their name by just adding coconut flakes to the icing, but I wasn't satisfied with this. I looked and looked for a truly coconut-flavored cake until I found one and then reworked the recipe ingredients to make it gluten free. This has coconut flavor in the cake, in the filling, and in the icing. I hope you like this as much as my tasters did.

Note: *The cake calls for 1 cup of sweetened cream of coconut (such as Coco Lopez). Save the rest of the can for the icing.*

2¾ cups Featherlight Mix
1½ teaspoons xanthan gum
2½ teaspoons Egg Replacer
1 teaspoon unflavored gelatin
1 teaspoon baking powder
1 teaspoon baking soda
½ teaspoon salt
1½ cups sugar
1 cup butter or
   margarine

1 cup canned sweetened cream of
   coconut (such as Coco Lopez)
4 eggs, separated
1 teaspoon vanilla
1⅓ cups buttermilk
Pinch of salt
One recipe Microwave Custard
   Sauce (page 313)
One recipe Coconut Icing (page 131)
Sweetened shredded coconut

Preheat oven to 350°. Grease three 8" round pans. Line with waxed or parchment paper and grease paper.

In a medium bowl, whisk together the flour mix, xanthan gum, Egg Replacer, gelatin, baking powder, baking soda, and salt. Set aside.

In the bowl of your mixer, beat the sugar, butter, and sweetened cream of coconut until fluffy. Beat in egg yolks and vanilla. With the mixer on low, add the dry ingredients in 3 additions along with the buttermilk, beating until just blended.

In a large bowl and with clean beaters, beat the egg whites with the pinch of salt until stiff but not dry. Fold into the batter.

Divide between the 3 pans and bake for 25–30 minutes or until tester comes out clean. Let the cake cool in the pans for about 5 minutes before turning out onto racks to finish cooling. Remove the paper immediately.

To make the cake, layer with the Microwave Custard Sauce, sprinkling ¾ cup sweetened shredded coconut on top of the filling. Add the second layer, repeating the filling and coconut. Frost with the icing. Top this with shredded coconut. This is a rich cake so cut small pieces. *Makes 20 servings.*

Nutrients per serving: Calories 270, Fat 15g, Cholesterol 70mg, Sodium 270mg, Carbohydrates 33g, Protein 3g.

*T*o test a sponge or angel food cake for doneness, touch the top lightly. The cake is baked if the top springs back.

Coffee Bars

I wasn't sure whether these should be called cake or cookies. But they definitely can be called good. The adult flavor of these will please your palate while the ease of making them will please the cook. Top them with whipped cream or frozen yogurt for an easy dessert or finish them off with the Coffee Icing (page 125).

1 cup golden raisins

½ teaspoon cinnamon

⅔ cup strong hot coffee

1½ cups Four Flour Bean Mix or
    GF Mix

1 teaspoon xanthan gum

½ teaspoon baking soda

½ teaspoon baking powder

¼ teaspoon salt

½ cup (1 stick) margarine or butter

½ cup white sugar

½ cup brown sugar

2 eggs

Preheat oven to 350°. Grease a 9" × 13" oblong cake pan.

In a small bowl, combine the raisins, cinnamon, and hot coffee. Set aside.

In a medium bowl, whisk together the flour mix, xanthan gum, baking soda, baking powder, and salt. Set aside.

In the bowl of your mixer, cream the margarine and both sugars. Add the eggs, one at a time, beating after each addition. Stir in the dry ingredients. Add the raisin mix and beat with a spoon until well blended. Spoon the batter into the prepared pan and bake for 20–25 minutes or until the cake pulls away from the sides and a tester comes out clean. Cool and cut into squares to be topped as you desire. *Makes 12–15 servings.*

*Nutrients per serving: Calories 190, Fat 7g, Cholesterol 35mg,
Sodium 160mg, Carbohydrates 31g, Protein 2g.*

Banana Bars

This moist, tasty cake is made to be cut into bars to be served with fruit. It is low in fat because it uses fruit instead of fat for tenderness. And it stays moist for several days.

CAKE:
1¼ cups GF Mix
¼ teaspoon xanthan gum
2 teaspoons baking powder
¼ teaspoon salt
1 cup mashed ripe bananas
    (2 bananas)
¾ cup brown sugar
⅓ cup white sugar

¼ cup buttermilk
1 egg
1 tablespoon vegetable oil
2 teaspoons vanilla
½ cup chopped walnuts

DRIZZLE TOPPING:
¼ cup confectioners' sugar
2 teaspoons milk or juice

Preheat oven to 350°. Grease a 9" square cake pan with shortening or spray with vegetable oil spray.

In a small bowl, whisk together the flour mix, xanthan gum, baking powder, and salt. Set aside.

In the bowl of your mixer, beat together the mashed banana and both sugars until blended. Add the buttermilk, egg, oil, and vanilla. Beat well. Stir in the dry ingredients until just blended (do not beat). Fold in the nuts. Spoon the batter into the prepared pan. Bake for 25–30 minutes or until a tester comes out clean. Remove from the oven and keep the cake in the pan.

Stir together the confectioners' sugar and liquid until just thick enough to drizzle well. Drizzle in a zigzag pattern over the cooling cake. When cold, cut the cake into 12 bars.

Nutrients per serving: Calories 170, Fat 3g, Cholesterol 20mg,
Sodium 125mg, Carbohydrates 35g, Protein 2g.

Featherlight Sponge Roll

I have offered some versions of the old-fashioned jelly roll in the dessert section of every book, but using the new Featherlight Mix makes creating this now easier than ever. Make it plain with jelly or jam or serve it to company filled with Lemon Cream (page 316). If you have a special party coming up, make an Ice Cream Cake to freeze ahead. Any version of this dessert can be made ahead; it keeps well for two days in the refrigerator.

See below for the other variations.

⅔ cup Featherlight Mix
¼ teaspoon salt
1 teaspoon baking powder
⅔ cup sugar
1 teaspoon dried lemon peel
4 eggs, separated

½ teaspoon cream of tartar
Confectioners' sugar for dusting
Lemon curd (pages 314 and 315),
    berry jam, lemon cream, whipped
    cream, or nondairy topping for
    filling

Preheat oven to 375°. Grease the bottom and sides of a 10" × 15" jelly roll pan. Line the bottom with waxed paper and grease the paper.

In a medium bowl, sift together the Featherlight Mix, salt, baking powder, and all but 1 tablespoon of the sugar. Whisk in the dried lemon peel. Set aside.

Separate the eggs, placing the yolks in a small bowl and the whites in the bowl of your mixer. Beat the egg yolks until thick and lemon colored. Set aside.

Beat the whites until frothy. Add the reserved tablespoon of sugar and the cream of tartar. Continue beating until glossy and stiff. Remove the beaters.

Gently fold the egg yolks into the whites. Fold in the dry ingredients in 3 parts. Pour the batter into the prepared pan and bake for 15–18 minutes, or until the top springs back after being lightly pressed.

Invert immediately onto a smooth cotton tea towel dusted with confectioners' sugar. Remove the waxed paper and immediately roll the warm sponge cake and tea towel, making sure that the towel separates the sections of the cake. Let cool. Unroll and spread with desired filling. Roll up again (without the towel) and dust the top with confectioners' sugar (if desired). Rewrap with foil. To serve, cut into 1½" slices. *Makes 8 servings.*

VARIATIONS:

CHOCOLATE SPONGE ROLL: Replace the Featherlight Mix with Four Flour Bean Mix and add 3 tablespoons Dutch-style cocoa to the dry ingredients. Fill with cherry or raspberry jam and whipped nondairy topping.

MOCHA SPONGE ROLL: Replace the Featherlight Mix with Four Flour Bean Mix and add 3 tablespoons Dutch-style cocoa plus 1 tablespoon freeze-dried coffee crystals to the dry ingredients. A simple whipped-topping filling or apricot jam plus the whipped topping is excellent with mocha.

ICE CREAM CAKE: Instead of rolling, cool the cake flat on the towel, then cut into 3 sections (each 10" × 5"). Cut 1 quart of GF brick ice cream (vanilla is always good, but your favorite can be used) into ½" slices. Place a section of cake on a large piece of aluminum foil. Add a layer of ice cream, then another section of cake and another layer of ice cream. Top with cake. Frost top and sides with 1 cup whipped cream sweetened to taste (or nondairy topping) and colored, if desired, with food coloring. Tent in a large piece of foil and seal it around the cake without touching the frosting. Place in the freezer. Remove from the freezer 10 minutes before serving. Cut into 1" slices. *Makes 10 servings.*

Nutrients per serving (NA is based on a whipped cream filling): Calories 160, Fat 4g, Cholesterol 105mg, Sodium 150mg, Carbohydrates 29g, Protein 4g.

In my other books in the series, I gave forty-six recipes for cakes. I only repeated one in this book so I would have room for the wonderful new ones. To save you time, here is a list of the other cake recipes and their sources: *The Gluten-free Gourmet* (GFG), *The Gluten-free Gourmet*, revised edition (GFG rev), *More from the Gluten-free Gourmet* (More), *The Gluten-free Gourmet Cooks Fast and Healthy* (F&H). If cakes were listed in both the original GFG and the GFG rev, I only list them here as being in GFG, even though they're in GFG rev as well.

CAKES	BASE	BOOK	PAGE
A Lighter Chiffon Cake	GF Mix	F&H	118
Angel Food Cake	potato/corn	GFG	78
Apple Raisin Cake	rice/soy	GFG	75
Black Forest Cake	GF Mix	More	96
Carrot Cake Supreme	rice/soy	GFG	74
Chinese Five-Spice Cake	GF Mix	More	107
Chocolate-Applesauce Bundt Cake	GF Mix	More	99
Chocolate Mist Angel Food	potato/corn	More	102
Chocolate Rum Cake	corn/tapioca	F&H	126
Christmas Fruit Cake	rice/soy	GFG	215
Classic Sponge Cake	rice/tapioca	GFG	69
Country Jam Cake	rice/tapioca	GFG	77
Cranberry Cake	GF Mix	F&H	115
Curacao Orange Bundt Cake	GF Mix	More	103
Danish Spice Cake with Crumb Topping	GF Mix	More	108
Double Dutch Treat	GF Mix	More	111
Featherlight Yellow Cake	GF Mix	F&H	113
Fruit Cocktail Torte	GF Mix	GFG	73
Fruit Cocktail Torte with Bean Flour	bean	F&H	128
Gingerbread	GF Mix	More	105
Guilt-free Carrot and Plum Cake	brown rice	F&H	119
Hawaiian Isles Chiffon Cake	GF Mix	More	104
Katherine's Banana Cake	bean or rice	GFG rev	99
Lemon Pound Cake	bean or rice	GFG rev	100

Lemon Sheet Cake	GF Mix	GFG	68
Lemon Sheet Cake (Revised)	GF Mix/corn	GFG rev	92
Lemon Torte	GF Mix	More	98
Light Gingerbread	bean/corn	F&H	120
Mocha-Banana Bundt Cake	GF Mix	F&H	116
Mock Black Forest Cake	rice/potato/soy	GFG	72
No-Bake Fruitcake	crumbs	F&H	129
Orange Chiffon Cake	rice/potato	GFG	70
Pacific Rim Cake	GF Mix	More	100
Pineapple or Peach Upside-Down Cake	GF Mix	GFG	69
Pineapple Nut Cake	GF Mix	F&H	114
Raisin Rum Cake	rice/tapioca	GFG	76
Sacher Torte	GF Mix	More	110
Scandinavian Spice Cake	GF Mix	More	106
Simply Super Carrot Cake	bean/corn	F&H	127
Surprise Chocolate Cake	lentils	GFG	71
Tropical Fruitcake	fruit/nuts	GFG	214
Yellow Velvet Cake	GF Mix	More	97
Yogurt Chocolate Cake	GF Mix	F&H	117
Zucchini Bundt Cake	rice/tapioca	More	101
Zucchini Cake	bean or rice	GFG rev	101

Cakes from Mixes

With the variety of mixes now available from suppliers—or on the specialty store shelves—we can easily whip up white, chocolate, spice, or lemon cakes. This is a great improvement from past years, and I predict that in the future we are going to see more and more mixes to make life easier.

But for those of you who want to add your own twist to the basic cake, here are recipes that will fool your guests into thinking you started from scratch. Whether you want to add fruit or zucchini, there's a recipe for you here.

Although I've sometimes mentioned the name of the mix I used, you can replace these with any similar mix with approximately the same weight. An 11-ounce Authentic Foods mix can be replaced by a slightly larger mix package by increasing the additional ingredients by about one fourth. For example: if the recipe calls for ¼ cup of something, add an extra tablespoon; if ½ cup, add 2 tablespoons.

Lemon Spice Cake

With a few changes, that package of lemon cake mix can turn into a very special cake sure to win raves.

CAKE:

One 11-ounce package Authentic
  Foods lemon cake mix
½ cup tapioca flour
1 teaspoon baking powder
½ teaspoon baking soda
1½ teaspoons Chinese-style five
  spice mix
1 teaspoon Egg Replacer (optional)
2 eggs plus 1 egg white

4 tablespoons vegetable oil
½ cup citrus-flavored carbonated
  beverage
¼ cup lemon juice

GINGER-LEMON TOPPING:

1½ cups confectioners' sugar
3 tablespoons hot lemon juice
1½ tablespoons minced sugared
  ginger

Preheat oven to 350°. Grease an 8" square pan and dust with rice flour.

In a medium bowl, combine the cake mix, tapioca flour, baking powder, spice, and Egg Replacer (if used).

In a mixing bowl, beat the eggs, egg white, and oil until frothy and light. With a mixing spoon, beat in the dry ingredients alternately with the carbonated beverage and lemon juice in 3 additions, beating after each until just blended. Spoon into the prepared pan and bake for 25 minutes or until the cake tester comes out clean.

Cool before icing with the Lemon Frosting (page 131). Or try this Ginger-Lemon Topping: Let the cake set for 5 minutes and, with a large kitchen fork, poke holes into the top of the cake. In a bowl combine confectioners' sugar, hot lemon juice, and minced sugared ginger. Spread over the hot cake. *Makes 9 servings.*

Nutrients per serving: Calories 240, Fat 8g, Cholesterol 50mg,
Sodium 190mg, Carbohydrates 37g, Protein 3g.

Lemon Zucchini Cake 350°

Start with a mix and end up with a cake that tastes as if you started from scratch.

One 11-ounce pouch Dietary
   Specialties white cake mix
   (½ box)
½ cup tapioca flour
¼ teaspoon xanthan gum
½ teaspoon baking soda
1½ teaspoons Chinese-style five
   spice mix
1 teaspoon Egg Replacer

1 teaspoon dried lemon peel
⅔ cup grated zucchini, squeezed
   or patted dry
2 eggs
¼ cup lemon juice
½ cup plus 2 tablespoons citrus-
   flavored carbonated beverage
   (Sprite, etc.)

Preheat oven to 350°. Grease an 8" square pan.

Place the cake mix in the bowl of your mixer. Add the tapioca flour, xanthan gum, baking soda, spice mix, Egg Replacer, dried lemon peel, and grated zucchini.

In a separate bowl, beat the eggs lightly with a fork. Add the lemon juice and carbonated beverage. Pour this liquid mix into the cake mix and beat on medium until smooth, or about 1 minute. Do not overbeat. Spoon into your prepared pan and bake for 35–40 minutes or until a tester comes out clean. Cool before frosting with your favorite white or lemon icing. *Makes 9–12 servings.*

Nutrients per serving: Calories 140, Fat 3g, Cholesterol 125mg,
Sodium 150mg, Carbohydrates 23g, Protein 4g.

---

*W*hen using carbonated drinks as the liquid in cakes, do not use a diet soda.

Quick and Easy Blue Ribbon Chocolate Cake   350°

Using the secret ingredient from my Blue Ribbon Chocolate Cake on page 50, I created this one from a box mix. This recipe is for an 8" square pan. Double the recipe for a 9" × 13" oblong cake pan.

Note: If you don't have green tomatoes, the hard red ones in the grocery will work just as well.

One pouch Dietary Specialties
  chocolate cake mix (½ box)
¼ cup tapioca flour
¼ teaspoon xanthan gum
2 eggs

½ cup green tomatoes, peeled and
  pureed
⅓ cup cola drink
1 teaspoon almond flavoring

Preheat oven to 350°. Grease an 8" square cake pan.

In the bowl of your mixer, place the cake mix, tapioca flour, and xanthan gum. Blend on low.

In a small bowl, whisk together the eggs, tomato puree, cola, and flavoring. Pour into the dry ingredients and beat on medium just until smooth (less than 1 minute). Spoon the batter into the prepared pan and bake the 8" square pan for 35–40 minutes, the 9" × 13" pan for 40–45 minutes. This is delicious topped with whipping cream but may be frosted with any icing of your choice. *Small cake makes 9–12 servings; large cake makes 16–20 servings.*

Nutrients per serving: Calories 210, Fat 7g, Cholesterol 45mg,
Sodium 410mg, Carbohydrates 35g, Protein 4g.

Chocolate Bean Cake

This may start with a mix, but a few different ingredients will make that mix cake taste entirely different. This is a real winner, whether made into a cake or cupcakes.

2 eggs plus 1 egg white
3 tablespoons vegetable oil
One 11-ounce package Authentic
  Foods chocolate cake mix

¾ cup cherry cola
¼ cup chopped walnuts

Preheat oven to 350°. Grease an 8" square pan or 12 muffin cups.

In the bowl of your mixer, beat the eggs, extra egg white, and vegetable oil until fluffy. With a spoon, beat in the cake mix alternately with the cola in 3 additions, beating until just blended. Stir in the chopped nuts.

Spoon into the prepared pan and bake about 25 minutes for the cake and approximately 20 minutes for the muffins. Cool before frosting. *Makes 9–12 servings.*

Nutrients per serving: Calories 180, Fat 7g, Cholesterol 45mg,
Sodium 135mg, Carbohydrates 28g, Protein 4g.

Banana Nut Cake

This delicious moist cake can be stirred up in minutes using a boxed mix as a base.

Note: *If black walnut flavoring is unavailable, toast the walnuts for 5 minutes in a 350° oven before adding to the batter.*

2 eggs or ½ cup liquid egg
   substitute
¼ cup milk or nondairy substitute
¼ cup warm water
¼ cup (½ stick) butter or
   margarine, melted

2 mashed ripe bananas
1 teaspoon black walnut flavoring
  (see note)
One 11-ounce package Authentic
   Foods vanilla cake mix
½ cup chopped walnuts

Preheat oven to 375°. Grease a 9" square cake pan.

In the bowl of your mixer, beat the eggs, milk, and water until foamy. Add the melted butter. Blend in the bananas and flavoring. With the mixer on low, add the cake mix. Beat briefly but do not overbeat. Stir in the walnuts and spoon the batter into the prepared pan.

Bake for approximately 30 minutes. Cool before icing with your favorite butter cream frosting or serve unfrosted, topped with whipped cream or nondairy substitute. *Makes 9–12 servings.*

*Nutrients per serving: Calories 250, Fat 10g, Cholesterol 60mg,
Sodium 270mg, Carbohydrates 36g, Protein 4g.*

Peaches and Cream Cake

Moist, flavorful, and easy! Start with a cake mix, add canned sliced peaches and sour cream for topping. I used Dietary Specialties white cake mix for testing this, but other white, vanilla, or lemon cake mixes of approximately 13 ounces should work well, too.

½ cup (1 stick) margarine or butter
One 13-ounce pouch white cake mix
One 29-ounce can sliced peaches, drained

1⅓ cups sour cream or nondairy substitute
2 teaspoons brown sugar
2 eggs, slightly beaten
1 tablespoon lemon juice
Cinnamon for dusting

Preheat oven to 350°.

With a food processor or pastry blender, cut the margarine into the cake mix until it resembles coarse sand. Pack this into a 9" square pan and bake for 10 minutes.

Place the sliced, drained peaches on the hot crust. In a medium bowl, blend the sour cream, brown sugar, and beaten eggs until smooth. Pour over the peaches making sure the topping touches all sides. Dust with cinnamon and return to the oven for 30 minutes. Serve warm or at room temperature. *Makes 9 servings.*

Nutrients per serving: Calories 400, Fat 23g, Cholesterol 90mg, Sodium 410mg, Carbohydrates 45g, Protein 5g.

Peach Pandowdy

A great fruit cobbler–type dessert with very little work. Just stir up a cake mix and pour it on top of the fruit. For other fruits, see the variations below.

3 cups fresh peach slices or
  1 pound frozen (thawed) or one
  28-ounce can sliced peaches,
  drained
⅓ cup dark brown sugar

1 tablespoon lemon juice
1 teaspoon cinnamon
⅓ cup raisins or dried cranberries
One 13-ounce pouch or packet
  light cake mix

Preheat oven to 400°. Butter a shallow 2-quart casserole.

Combine the peaches, brown sugar, lemon juice, and cinnamon in a bowl. Tumble gently. Let stand for approximately 10 minutes before spooning into the casserole and sprinkling raisins over the top.

Prepare the cake mix as suggested on the box. Spoon this over the fruit. Bake for 30–40 minutes or until a tester comes out clean. To serve, spoon out and top with whipped topping or frozen yogurt. *Makes 8 servings.*

VARIATIONS:

APPLE PANDOWDY: Combine fresh apple slices as above, but microwave for 5 minutes on high before topping with the cake batter. Remember not to microwave in a metal pan. Bake as above.

CHERRY PANDOWDY: Replace peaches with an equal amount of fresh pitted cherries or thawed frozen fruit. Eliminate the raisins.

*Nutrients per serving: Calories 350, Fat 13g, Cholesterol 45mg,
Sodium 210mg, Carbohydrates 57g, Protein 4g.*

Raspberry Cake

350°

A magic medley of raspberry gelatin, raspberries, and white cake. Stir up this easy sheet cake and watch it go! This is best served on the day it's baked, so invite a crowd to share.

Note: I used Dietary Specialties cake mix for testing, but any mix of the same size should work as well.

4 cups miniature marshmallows
One pouch (½ box) Dietary
   Specialties white cake mix
One 3-ounce box raspberry gelatin

1 box fresh raspberries or one
   16-ounce carton frozen
   raspberries, partially thawed
⅔ cup cold water

Preheat oven to 350°. Grease an 9" × 13" pan. Sprinkle marshmallows evenly over the bottom.

Mix the cake according to the package directions and spread evenly over the marshmallows. Sprinkle on the dry gelatin. Spoon the raspberries over the gelatin. Drizzle the water over the top. Do not mix!

Bake for 45–50 minutes or until a tester inserted in the center comes out clean. Cool in the pan for at least 30 minutes before cutting. If desired, top with a dab of whipped cream or nondairy topping and add a raspberry for color. *Makes 12 servings.*

*Nutrients per serving: Calories 230, Fat ½g, Cholesterol 0mg,
Sodium 180mg, Carbohydrates 49g, Protein 8g.*

CAKES FROM MIXES RECIPES FROM OTHER BOOKS IN THE
GLUTEN-FREE GOURMET SERIES

See page 92 for book title abbreviations.

Individual Cakes and Filled Favorites

*A*lmost any cake recipe can be converted to cupcakes by dividing the dough into greased or paper-lined muffin tins. Then why do I have a special chapter on cupcakes? This chapter contains cupcakes grand enough for a party dessert or something special for that luncheon or bridge club. Many of these would not bake as well in round or square cake pans. All of them are so good, you wouldn't be embarrassed to feed them to any guest.

For celiacs, this is a good way to keep treats for yourself; you can hide some in the freezer. Pull them out when there is no other dessert you can eat.

As for children's parties or school treats, these special cupcakes are so tasty that you won't have to send just your child's special cake but can serve the whole class. Many of these are not only good, they are good for them. But don't tell any child that!

And finally, there are two of the special cakes that children love: twinkies and whoopie pies, created gluten free especially for them.

At the end of the chapter you will find a list of the sources for individual cakes from other books in this series.

Jam-Filled Cupcakes 350°

Absolutely delicious with a surprise in the middle. These may sound a bit complicated because they have a filling, but once the filling is made and put aside, there is nothing more left but to stir up the recipe.

Note: I give directions for a cherry-cheesecake center in the recipe, but this can be changed to apricot or pineapple by using apricot or pineapple jam, changing the liquid flavoring to fresh lemon zest, and replacing the cola with a citrus-flavored carbonated beverage.

FILLING AND TOPPING:

⅓ cup cream cheese, softened

3 tablespoons confectioners' sugar

⅓ cup whole cherry jam (see note)

2 tablespoons finely chopped nuts
  (walnuts, pecans, macadamia)

DOUGH:

2 cups GF Mix

1 teaspoon xanthan gum

3 teaspoons baking powder

1 teaspoon Egg Replacer

½ teaspoon salt

⅔ cup butter or margarine

¾ cup sugar

2 eggs plus 1 egg white

1 teaspoon cherry or vanilla
  flavoring

1 cup cherry cola

Preheat oven to 350°. Grease twelve 2½" or eighteen 2" muffin tins or line with paper liners and spray with vegetable oil spray.

In a small bowl, blend the cream cheese with the confectioners' sugar.

In a medium bowl, whisk together the flour mix, xanthan gum, baking powder, Egg Replacer, and salt.

In the bowl of your mixer, cream the butter and sugar. Beat in the eggs, one at a time. Add the flavoring. Add the dry ingredients and liquid alternately in 3 sections, beating after each addition.

Spoon half the mix into the prepared muffin tins. Then spoon in the cream cheese topped with a spoonful of the cherry jam, being careful that neither the cream cheese nor the jam touches the sides of the tins. Top with the remaining batter and sprinkle on the nuts, pressing them in gently. Bake for 25–30 minutes or until the top springs back when pressed. *Makes 12–18 cupcakes.*

Nutrients per cupcake: Calories 230, Fat 10g, Cholesterol 50mg,
Sodium 240mg, Carbohydrates 33g, Protein 2g.

Cooking oils cannot replace solid fats in a recipe that depends on air being beaten in for lightness, as oils do not hold air as solid fats do.

Carrot Cupcakes

These are a winner! The combination of GF Mix and soy gives them a springy texture studded with the fruit and nuts. It's hard to stop with just one. And why should you since they are full of fiber and protein as well as lactose free.

2 cups GF Mix
¼ cup soy flour
1 rounded teaspoon xanthan gum
3 teaspoons baking powder
1 teaspoon baking soda
1 teaspoon Egg Replacer
1 teaspoon cinnamon
1 teaspoon nutmeg
½ teaspoon salt

1⅓ cups sugar
½ cup mayonnaise
½ cup sour cream substitute
3 eggs
1 large apple, peeled, cored, and chopped fine
1 cup grated carrot
1 cup chopped walnuts
½ cup chopped dates

Preheat oven to 375°. Grease 18 muffin tins or line with a paper liner and spray with vegetable oil spray.

In a medium bowl, whisk together the flour mix, soy flour, xanthan gum, baking powder, baking soda, Egg Replacer, cinnamon, nutmeg, and salt.

In the bowl of your mixer, beat together the sugar, mayonnaise, and sour cream substitute until smooth. Beat in the eggs, one at a time. Add the dry ingredients and beat until smooth. Remove the bowl from the stand and stir in the prepared apple, carrots, walnuts, and dates.

Spoon into prepared muffin tins and bake for 25 minutes or until a tester comes out clean. Cool before frosting with a simple cream cheese frosting (see pages 126–28). *Makes 18 cupcakes.*

Nutrients per cupcake: Calories 240, Fat 11g, Cholesterol 40mg, Sodium 250mg, Carbohydrates 35g, Protein 4g.

Double Fruit Carrot Cupcakes
(Lactose Free, Rice Free)

Pineapple and prunes or apricot join the carrots to bring high fiber and great taste to these moist cupcakes. The recipe doubles easily.

1¼ cups Four Flour Bean Mix
¾ teaspoon xanthan gum
1 teaspoon apple pie spice (if using prunes) or dried lemon peel (if using apricots)
1 teaspoon baking powder
1 teaspoon baking soda
½ teaspoon salt

2 eggs or ½ cup liquid egg substitute
⅔ cup sugar
¼ cup vegetable oil
One 6-ounce jar junior baby fruit (plum or apricot)
1 cup grated carrots
One 8-ounce can crushed pineapple, well drained

Preheat oven to 350°. Line 12 to 15 muffin cups with paper liners or lightly grease them with vegetable oil or shortening.

In a medium bowl, combine the flour mix, xanthan gum, apple pie spice, baking powder, baking soda, and salt.

In the bowl of your mixer, beat together the eggs, sugar, and oil until light and creamy (about 5 minutes). With the mixer on low, add the dry ingredients. Beat only until blended. Stir in the carrots and drained pineapple. Spoon into the muffin cups and bake for 25–30 minutes or until a tester comes out clean. *Makes 12–15 cupcakes.*

Nutrients per cupcake: Calories 150, Fat 5g, Cholesterol 30mg, Sodium 210mg, Carbohydrates 25g, Protein 2g.

Black Forest Cupcakes

*The combination of chocolate and cherries has always been a winner, but here the rich-
ness of bean flour is added. These are not low calorie but they are worth saving calorie
points for.*

½ cup chopped dried cherries

2¼ cups Four Flour Bean Mix

1 rounded teaspoon xanthan gum

1 teaspoon Egg Replacer (optional)

1 teaspoon baking soda

2½ teaspoons baking powder

⅓ cup cocoa powder

½ teaspoon salt

½ cup mayonnaise

½ cup sour cream substitute

¾ cup brown sugar

½ cup white sugar

2 teaspoons molasses

2 eggs plus 1 egg white

½ cup cherry-flavored cola

Reconstitute the cherries by placing them in a bowl and covering them with boiling
water. Soak for 1 to 4 hours. Drain before adding to batter.

Preheat oven to 350°. Grease 18 muffin tins and dust them with rice flour or line
them with paper liners.

In a medium bowl, whisk together the flour mix, xanthan gum, Egg Replacer (if
used), baking soda, baking powder, cocoa, and salt.

In the bowl of your mixer, cream the mayonnaise, sour cream substitute, and both
sugars. Add the molasses and the eggs, one at a time, beating after each addition. Add
the dry ingredients and the cola, alternately, in 3 additions, beating slightly to blend
after each addition. Add the cherries and beat with a mixing spoon.

Spoon into the prepared muffin tins and bake for 22–25 minutes or until the top
springs back when gently pressed. Frost as desired. *Makes 18 cupcakes.*

*Nutrients per cupcake: Calories 210, Fat 8g, Cholesterol 25mg,
Sodium 240mg, Carbohydrates 34g, Protein 3g.*

Chocolate Peanutty Cupcakes 350°

For chocolate and peanut butter lovers. This is a rich-tasting, high-fiber treat for children and the child in all of us. I top this with a confectioners' sugar frosting with a dash of peanut butter and then sprinkle on a few toasted, chopped peanuts.

2¼ cups Four Flour Bean Mix
1 rounded teaspoon xanthan gum
1 teaspoon Egg Replacer (optional)
1 teaspoon baking soda
2½ teaspoons baking powder
⅓ cup cocoa powder
½ teaspoon salt
⅔ cup margarine or butter

½ cup chunky-style peanut butter
1 teaspoon vanilla
½ cup brown sugar
¾ cup white sugar
2 teaspoons molasses
2 eggs plus 1 egg white
1 cup plus 2 tablespoons
 cherry-flavored cola

Preheat oven to 350°. Grease 18 muffin tins and dust them with rice flour or line them with paper liners.

In a medium bowl, whisk together the flour mix, xanthan gum, Egg Replacer (if used), baking soda, baking powder, cocoa, and salt.

In the bowl of your mixer, blend the margarine and peanut butter. Add the vanilla and both sugars. Beat until creamy. Add the molasses and the eggs, one at a time, beating after each addition. Add the dry ingredients and cola, alternately in 3 additions, beating just until blended after each.

Spoon into the muffin tins, filling ⅔ full. Bake for 22–25 minutes or until tester comes out clean. When cool, frost as desired. *Makes 18 cupcakes.*

Nutrients per cupcake: Calories 240, Fat 11g, Cholesterol 40mg,
Sodium 300mg, Carbohydrates 33g, Protein 4g.

Easy

Mocha Madness Cupcakes
(Lactose and Rice Free, Low Fat)

350°

A wonderful new chocolate-coffee taste with little fat! Make them with 1 jar of baby prunes or plums, apricots, or applesauce. Vary the flavor by adding fruit or nuts and different flavorings. This just may become your basic cupcake because it's moist, flavorful, and easy!

2 cups Four Flour Bean Mix
1 teaspoon xanthan gum
1½ cups sugar
⅓ cup cocoa powder
2 teaspoons baking soda
½ teaspoon salt
1 teaspoon baking powder

One 6-ounce jar baby prunes or
    plums
¼ cup vegetable oil
2 eggs
3 tablespoons espresso powder
½ cup warm water
2 teaspoons vanilla

Preheat oven to 350°. Grease, or line with paper cups, 18 standard-size muffin cups or 15 large muffin cups (2½").

In a medium bowl, whisk together the flour mix, xanthan gum, sugar, cocoa powder, baking soda, salt, and baking powder.

In another mixing bowl, stir together the prune puree, oil, and eggs. Dissolve the espresso powder in the water. Add to prune mixture, along with the vanilla.

Stir the dry ingredients into the liquids until blended. Do not beat. Spoon the batter evenly into the prepared muffin cups, filling each about ⅔ full.

Bake for 18–20 minutes or until tops spring back when lightly touched. Cool for about 3 minutes and then remove from pan. Cool and frost with your favorite frosting or serve with a dab of whipped topping. *Makes 15–18 cupcakes.*

VARIATIONS:

Try baby apricots or applesauce in place of the prune or plum puree. Add chopped dried apricots to the apricot-flavored cupcakes, dried cherries or dried cranberries to the plum- or prune-flavored ones, or almond flavoring and chopped almonds to the ones flavored with applesauce.

Nutrients per cupcake: Calories 180, Fat 4g, Cholesterol 25mg, Sodium 250mg, Carbohydrates 34g, Protein 3g.

Mini Fruitcakes

325°

These are not your typical heavy fruitcakes but light and filled with dates, nuts, and cherries. If made in the mini muffin tins, they fit in well on the Christmas cookie tray. In the small muffin tins, they become a complete dessert. If desired, candied pineapple can replace some of the cherries.

1 cup Four Flour Bean Mix
½ teaspoon xanthan gum
1½ teaspoons baking powder
2 cups pitted dates, chopped and
  tumbled in sugar
2 cups walnuts, chopped

2 cups red and green candied
  cherries, chopped
1 cup (2 sticks) butter or margarine, melted and cooled
4 eggs, separated
1 cup sugar
2 tablespoons fruit brandy

Preheat oven to 325°. Prepare the muffin tins by inserting paper liners and spraying with vegetable oil (4 dozen mini muffin cups or 1½ to 2 dozen small muffin cups).

In a mixing bowl, whisk together the flour, xanthan gum, and baking powder. Stir in the dates, nuts, and cherries. Blend butter into the mixture. Beat the egg yolks, sugar, and brandy; blend into the batter. Beat the egg whites to soft peaks and fold into the mixture.

Spoon the batter into the prepared pans. Bake for 22 minutes for mini pans, 30 minutes for the small muffin pans. *Makes approximately 48 mini cakes, 18–24 small cakes.*

*Nutrients per mini cake: Calories 240, Fat 14g, Cholesterol 60mg,
Sodium 125mg, Carbohydrates 28g, Protein 4g.*

Whoopie Pies

350°

A taste of childhood! We can still have these icing-filled, chocolate cookie cakes in a lunch box or for a special treat. Both cakes and icing are easy to make so let children enjoy them while the adult celiacs have a taste of yesterday.

CAKE COOKIES:
2 cups Four Flour Bean Mix
1 rounded teaspoon xanthan gum
1 teaspoon baking powder
1 teaspoon baking soda
2 teaspoons Egg Replacer
1 teaspoon salt
½ cup cocoa
½ cup shortening
1 cup brown sugar
1 egg

1 cup buttermilk
1 teaspoon vanilla

FILLING:
1 cup shortening
1 cup confectioners' sugar
One 7-ounce jar marshmallow
  creme
¼ teaspoon salt
1 tablespoon water
1½ teaspoons vanilla

Preheat oven to 350°. Lightly grease 2 cookie sheets.

For the cakes, in a medium pan, whisk together the flour mix, xanthan gum, baking powder, soda, Egg Replacer, salt, and cocoa.

In the bowl of your mixer, cream the shortening, brown sugar, and egg. Add the dry ingredients, alternately with the buttermilk, to which the vanilla has been added, beating each time until smooth. Drop the dough in goose egg size spoonfuls onto prepared cookie sheets and spread slightly to about 3½" size. Bake for 15 minutes or until firm to the touch. Cool completely before filling.

For the filling, in the bowl of your mixer, beat together the shortening, confectioners' sugar, and marshmallow creme. Dissolve the salt in the water and add to shortening mixture, with the vanilla. Spread approximately ¼" thick over bottom of half the cakes. Top with the remaining half. *Makes 9 cakes.*

Nutrients per serving (½ pie): Calories 410, Fat 22g, Cholesterol 15mg, Sodium 300mg, Carbohydrates 50g, Protein 5g.

Twinkies

These old-fashioned filled sweets were created by request of the celiac children at a summer camp so they could have the same treat the wheat-eaters enjoyed. Thanks to Cynthia Kupper, R.D., and her staff: these were a complete success!

Note: *English muffin rings may be squeezed into an elongated oval or you can create the shape by using 20 pieces of aluminum foil cut into 12 " × 14 " pieces and folded and refolded to 1 " × 14 ". Seal ends together with masking tape and bend into the long oval shape. These may be washed and used several times. If you prefer testing the recipe without investing in either of the above, bake the dough in muffin tins and fill the centers as explained below in the filling section.*

1 cup Featherlight Mix	1 teaspoon orange extract
1 teaspoon baking powder	¾ cup sugar
¼ teaspoon salt	1 teaspoon cream of tartar
7 eggs, separated	One recipe Whoopie Pies filling
1 teaspoon dried orange peel	(page 118)

Preheat oven to 300°. Grease one or two baking sheets and place the rings on them.

In a medium bowl, whisk together the flour mix, baking powder, and salt.

Separate the eggs, placing the yolks in a 1½ quart bowl and the whites in a large mixing bowl. With electric mixer, whip the yolks on high speed for 3–5 minutes. Add the orange peel and continue to whip until thick and pale yellow.

With clean beaters in the bowl of your mixer, whip the whites for 1 minute. Add 1 tablespoon sugar and the cream of tartar. Continue whipping until the whites are glossy and stiff. Remove mixer. Pour the yolks onto the whites and gently fold in. Sprinkle ⅓ of the remaining sugar over surface and fold to incorporate. Add the rest in 2 more foldings. Add the dry ingredients in the same way, folding each time until just incorporated.

Divide the dough into the prepared rings. Bake for 40–45 minutes or until the top springs back when gently pressed. Remove from the rings while still warm and cool before filling.

Prepare the filling on page 118 for Whoopie Pies. To make holes in the twinkies, either use a skewer or a chopstick pushed lengthwise through the cake. Make 1 to 3 holes in the bottom. Squeeze in the filling with an icing bag with a very small hole or use a strong Baggie with a small corner nipped off at an angle. It is easier to fill halfway from each end until the icing starts to ooze out of the bottom holes. *Makes 20 filled cakes.*

Nutrients per twinkie: Calories 80, Fat 2g, Cholesterol 75mg,
Sodium 70mg, Carbohydrates 13g, Protein 2g.

Doughnut Drops

A very easy-to-make doughnut with a lot of flavor!

1½ cups Four Flour Bean Mix or
  GF Mix

1 scant teaspoon xanthan gum

1 tablespoon baking powder

½ teaspoon salt

⅓ cup sugar

1 teaspoon pumpkin pie spice

1 teaspoon gelatin (optional)

1 egg, slightly beaten

½ cup mashed cooked pumpkin
  (canned or fresh)

¼ cup milk or nondairy substitute

2 tablespoons vegetable oil

½ teaspoon vanilla

Oil for deep frying

In a mixing bowl, whisk together the flour mix, xanthan gum, baking powder, salt, sugar, pumpkin pie spice, and gelatin (if used).

In a small bowl, beat the egg and add the pumpkin, milk, oil, and vanilla. Add this to the dry ingredients, stirring just until moistened.

Pour oil to the depth of 2 inches in your deep fryer and heat to 375°. Fill a level teaspoon and, with a rubber scraper, roll the batter into the hot oil, cook until brown, turning once. Drain in a bowl with crushed paper towels. *Makes 24 drops.*

*Nutrients per drop: Calories 60, Fat 1½g, Cholesterol 10mg,
Sodium 100mg, Carbohydrates 10g, Protein 1g.*

INDIVIDUAL CAKES AND FILLED FAVORITES FROM OTHER BOOKS IN THE
GLUTEN-FREE GOURMET SERIES

See page 92 for book title abbreviations.

INDIVIDUAL CAKES	BASE	BOOK	PAGE
Almond-Lace Dessert Cups	rice	More	173
Chocolate Eclairs	potato/rice	GFG	83
		GFG rev	112
Cream Puffs	potato/rice	GFG	82
		GFG rev	111
Eskimo Pie (Ice Cream Bars)	cereal	More	151
Fruit Crepes with Wine Sauce	rice	GFG	200
	rice or bean	GFG rev	175
Pecan Brownie Cupcakes	rice	GFG	84
		GFG rev	113
Pineapple Upside-Down Cupcakes	cake mix	F&H	125
Raised Doughnuts	rice	More	89
Surprise Doughnut Holes	potato	GFG	113
		GFG rev	221

Frostings, Fillings, and Sauces

*M*any of our cakes can be eaten with just a dab of whipped cream or GF ice cream. Others, like gingerbread, may call for a lemon sauce. But a three-layer party cake needs the decorative touch of a rich and fluffy icing.

There are many frostings or icings in any market that are gluten free. But if you don't want to read ingredient labels for half a day, or pay the price, any of the following recipes will make your GF cake a winner.

See the back of the chapter for many more icings and frostings from other books in the series.

Light White Icing

For a creamy appearance and ease of handling, nothing beats the confectioners' sugar icing. This one has some shortening for extra body and keeping quality. For a creamy color use Butter Flavor Crisco; for a pure white, use white shortening.

Note: This basic recipe is a bland, sweet-tasting frosting. See below for several adaptations of this one icing, making it tastier.

1½ pounds confectioners' sugar	⅓ cup boiling water
⅓ cup shortening	Pinch of salt (to taste)
2 teaspoons vanilla	

In a chilled bowl, whip the confectioners' sugar, shortening, and vanilla. Add enough boiling water to make the icing fluffy and smooth. Beat well. *Makes about 1½ cups icing.*

VARIATIONS:

COFFEE ICING: Replace the boiling water with extra strong coffee.

CHOCOLATE AND COFFEE ICING: Add ⅓ cup cocoa powder to the confectioners' sugar and replace the boiling water with extra strong coffee.

LEMON-LEMON ICING: Replace the vanilla with fresh lemon zest and the water with hot lemon juice. (For a lighter lemon taste, use lemonade in place of lemon juice.)

MAPLE ICING: Replace the vanilla with maple flavoring, and replace 2 tablespoons of the water, before boiling, with 2 tablespoons maple syrup.

Nutrients per serving (2 tablespoons): Calories 116, Fat 2g, Cholesterol 0mg, Sodium 8mg, Carbohydrates 18g, Protein 0g.

Fluffy Cream Cheese Frosting

A wonderful topping for that occasion when you want your cake to be special. Is it someone's birthday or anniversary? Then treat them to this and use the Raisin/Brandy Filling suggested below to make it even more special. A full recipe makes enough to fill and frost a 3-layer cake. The recipe can easily be halved for the top of a 9" × 13" cake.

Three 8-ounce packages cream cheese at room temperature	2 tablespoons maple syrup
	1 teaspoon orange zest
1 cup confectioners' sugar	1½ cups nondairy whipped topping

Place cream cheese in the bowl of your mixer and beat on high until smooth. Reduce speed to low and beat in the rest of the ingredients. *Makes 3 cups filling.*

VARIATION:

RAISIN-BRANDY FILLING: If desired, half of the above may be changed to a filling by adding ½ cup chopped raisins or dates soaked in 2 tablespoons brandy or rum. Use this to spread between the layers. Use the rest of the frosting for the top and sides.

Nutrients per serving (2 tablespoons): Calories 140, Fat 11g, Cholesterol 30mg, Sodium 105mg, Carbohydrates 9g, Protein 1g.

Special Cream Cheese Frosting

Although I've given a recipe for a frosting much like this in another book, this is lighter and large enough to fill and frost a 3-layer cake, so I've included it here.

¼ cup heavy cream
12 ounces cream cheese
½ teaspoon flavoring (vanilla, maple, etc.)

6 tablespoons (¾ stick) butter or margarine
1 pound (3 cups) confectioners' sugar

In the bowl of your mixer, beat the cream, cream cheese, flavoring, and butter until smooth. Add the confectioners' sugar and beat until consistency is good for spreading. If necessary, refrigerate to thicken. *Makes enough to fill and frost a 3-layer cake.*

Nutrients per serving (2 tablespoons): Calories 110, Fat 8g, Cholesterol 35mg, Sodium 70mg, Carbohydrates 10g, Protein 1g.

---

*W*hen cutting a cake with fluffy frosting, dip the knife in hot water between cuts and shake to remove the water without drying completely.

Lighter Cream Cheese Frosting

Although lighter, this frosting still has the flavor and texture of your old cream cheese frosting.

One 8-ounce package reduced-fat
    cream cheese
2 tablespoons butter
1 teaspoon lemon juice

1 teaspoon orange or lemon zest
½ teaspoon lemon flavoring or
    vanilla
3 cups confectioners' sugar

In the bowl of your mixer, beat the cream cheese, butter, lemon juice, zest, and flavoring until smooth. Beat in the confectioners' sugar, 1 cup at a time, until the frosting is a good spreading consistency. Add additional sugar if needed. *Makes approximately 2 cups frosting.*

Nutrients per serving (2 tablespoons): Calories 100, Fat 3g, Cholesterol 10mg, Sodium 100mg, Carbohydrates 17g, Protein 1g.

Sour Cream Frosting

This variation of the old Cream Cheese Frosting can be made with nondairy sour cream, thus allowing the lactose intolerant to enjoy a popular and easy to make frosting again.

⅓ cup sour cream or nondairy
   sour cream
¼ cup butter or margarine,
  softened

1 teaspoon vanilla
3 cups sifted confectioners' sugar

In a medium bowl, beat together the sour cream, butter, and vanilla until smooth. With a mixer on low, gradually beat in the confectioners' sugar till smooth and spreadable. *Makes 1½ cups frosting.*

Nutrients per serving (2 tablespoons): Calories 160, Fat 5g, Cholesterol 10mg, Sodium 45mg, Carbohydrates 30g, Protein 0g.

Whipped Cream Frosting

Does your whipped cream frosting start to weep or run just when you serve your cake? With this trick you can have whipped cream that stands up for a couple of days. This formula is for 1 pint of whipping cream but it will work with 3 cups also.

1 packet unflavored gelatin	2 or 3 cups whipping cream
¼ cup cold water	Sugar to taste

Dissolve the packet of gelatin in cold water in a small glass or metal bowl. When dissolved, place the bowl in warm water to soften the gelatin until it will pour into the cream. Place all ingredients in a mixer and whip to firm peaks. Add sugar to taste. Frost your cake and keep refrigerated until serving. If any is left, return to refrigerator. This will keep well up to two days. *Makes approximately 1 quart frosting. Enough for top and sides of a large cake.*

Nutrients per serving (2 tablespoons): Calories 110, Fat 10g, Cholesterol 35mg, Sodium 15mg, Carbohydrates 1g, Protein 6g.

Bakers' Secret Icing
(with Variations)

This is an egg-free, easy-to-make, never-fail, fluffy icing that can be varied with different flavored liquids. This keeps a long time in the refrigerator.

Note: *Use white shortening for a white frosting; use Butter Flavor Crisco for a creamy off-white frosting that makes a fine topping for spice and ginger cakes.*

2 tablespoons sweet rice flour
2 tablespoons cornstarch
1 cup milk or nondairy liquid
  (see below for other liquids)
1 cup sugar

1 cup vegetable shortening
  (see note)
1 teaspoon salt
1 teaspoon vanilla

In a small saucepan, blend the flour and cornstarch. Add a bit of the milk to form a paste; stir in the remaining milk. Cook over medium heat, stirring constantly, until the paste is thick. Set aside to cool completely, or place in the refrigerator.

In a medium bowl, whip together the sugar and shortening; add the salt and vanilla. Blend in the milk paste. Beat hard until the icing is fluffy. *Makes about 2½ cups.*

VARIATIONS:

MOCHA FROSTING: Replace the milk with 1 cup strong coffee and add 2 tablespoons cocoa with the sugar.

LEMON FROSTING: Replace the milk with 1 cup lemonade and add 1 tablespoon lemon zest to the finished frosting. Use Butter Flavor Crisco for the shortening.

COCONUT ICING: Replace ½ cup milk with ½ cup sweetened cream of coconut (such as Coco Lopez). Use white shortening in the icing.

PEANUT BUTTER ICING: Replace ¼ cup shortening with ¼ cup peanut butter.

MAPLE FROSTING: Place 2 tablespoons maple syrup in a 1-cup measuring cup and fill to the top with milk. Use maple flavoring instead of vanilla.

Nutrients per serving (2 tablespoons): Calories 150, Fat 11g, Cholesterol 0mg, Sodium 115mg, Carbohydrates 12g, Protein 0g.

Lemon or Orange Filling

Fillings like this help keep our cakes moist and flavorful to the last bite. Although the bean flour–based cakes do not dry out as fast as the rice-based ones, if you plan to keep the cake more than one day, a moist filling will make it stay tastier.

½ cup water
¼ cup sugar
1 tablespoon lemon or orange zest
¼ cup lemon or orange juice

4 teaspoons cornstarch
¼ teaspoon salt
1 tablespoon margarine or butter

In a small saucepan, blend the water, sugar, zest, juice, cornstarch, and salt. Cook over medium heat, stirring constantly, until thick and boiling briskly. Reduce heat and cook 1 minute, stirring constantly. Remove from heat and stir in the margarine. *Makes about 1 cup.*

Nutrients per serving (1 tablespoon): Calories 45, Fat 1½g, Cholesterol 5mg, Sodium 85mg, Carbohydrates 8g, Protein 0g.

Coconut-Pecan Frosting

This frosting, usually used on German chocolate cakes, dresses up any other chocolate cake. It may be found on grocery shelves but often contains gluten, so it's safer to make your own. Cut the recipe by one third if frosting only the top of a 9" × 13" oblong cake.

1 cup evaporated milk
1 cup sugar
3 egg yolks, lightly beaten
½ cup (1 stick) butter or margarine

1 teaspoon vanilla
1⅓ cups flaked coconut
1 cup chopped pecans

In a medium saucepan, combine milk, sugar, egg yolks, butter, and vanilla. Stir while cooking over medium heat until thickened. Remove from heat and stir in coconut and pecans. Beat until frosting is cool and reaches desired spreading consistency. *Makes approximately 3 cups, which fills and frosts a 2-layer cake.*

Nutrients per serving (2 tablespoons): Calories 110, Fat 8g, Cholesterol 35mg, Sodium 70mg, Fiber 0g, Carbohydrates 10g, Protein 1g.

FROSTINGS, FILLINGS, AND SAUCES FROM OTHER BOOKS IN THE
GLUTEN-FREE GOURMET SERIES

See page 92 for book title abbreviations.

FROSTING	BOOK	PAGE
Butterscotch Icing	F&H	133
Coffee Icing	F&H	133
Cream Cheese Frosting	GFG	85
	GFG rev	114
Easy Chocolate Icing	GFG	85
	GFG rev	114
Fluffy White Frosting	F&H	134
Lemon Sauce	More	121
Mocha Cream Frosting	More	120
Mock Raspberry Filling	F&H	135
Orange Cream Frosting	F&H	134
Penuche Frosting	GFG	86
	GFG rev	115
Raspberry Sauce	F&H	136

Cookies

Shaped Cookies

Mock Oreo Cookies (page 165)
Mary Lou's Fig Newtons (page 166)
Black and White Biscotti (page 168)
Chocolate-Cherry Biscotti (page 169)
Lemon-Tipped Pistachio Biscotti
   (page 170)
Peanut Butter–Chocolate Cookies
   (page 172)
Double Ginger Cookies (page 173)

Christmas Cookies

Spritz Cookies (page 174)
Dutch Sugar Cookies (page 175)
Nut Butter Thumbprints (page 176)
Scandinavian Almond Bars (page 177)
Cranberry Swirls (page 178)

Florentines (page 180)
Walnut-Caramel Bars (page 181)
Zucchini Bars (page 182)
Fruit-Filled Biscotti (page 183)

See Also

Nut Butter Drops (page 288)
Orange Shortbread (page 289)
Lemon Melts (page 290)
Marshmallow Krisp Bars (page 291)
Mocha Puffs (page 292)
Date-Nut Kisses (page 293)
Caramel-Pecan Kisses (page 294)
Coconut Macaroons (page 295)
Raspberry Whispers (page 296)
Haystacks (page 297)
Fruit and Nut Dessert Bars (page 298)
Rice Balls with Fruit and Nuts (page 299)

*Y*ou don't have to be an expert baker to make great cookies. You don't even need to know much about baking because cookies are so easy to make—even using gluten-free flours. And these taste so good that everyone (even those wheat-eaters in the family) will want to eat them by the handful.

Whether you're looking for cookies for the lunch box, biscotti for traveling, or something special as a finish for that fancy luncheon, you'll find them in the following pages. You'll also discover gluten-free versions of some of your favorite holiday cookies, along with some exciting new ones.

With a choice of rice, sorghum, or bean flour as a base, you can have a variety of tastes and textures. You'll even find you can rekindle some of your childhood taste memories with those old favorites made with the new flours: Fig Newtons, Oreos, oatmeal or peanut butter cookies, and gingersnaps.

At the end of this chapter you'll find a list of cookies featured in my other books.

If you really don't want to start from scratch, you'll find that many of the companies listed at the back of this book sell either mixes or ready-baked cookies. These will be much more expensive than homemade ones, especially if you have to pay shipping charges. But there are a growing number of mixes to be found on the shelves of specialty markets and even a few at your regular grocer.

The Ultimate Brownie

So rich and fudgy, it's absolutely decadent! This brownie, with its baked-on frosting, tastes so much like fudge that a little piece packs as much flavor as the candy.

Note: By lining the baking pan with foil with extra long edges as "handles," it's easy to remove the whole cake. It makes cutting the cake into the tiny pieces without damaging the pan bottom much easier.

BATTER:
1 cup Featherlight Mix
½ rounded teaspoon
   xanthan gum
¼ teaspoon baking powder
½ cup toasted chopped nuts
   (walnuts or pecans)
3 ounces unsweetened chocolate,
   chopped
½ cup (1 stick) butter or
   margarine
1½ cups sugar

3 eggs
1 teaspoon vanilla

TOPPING:
3 ounces semisweet chocolate,
   chopped
6 ounces cream cheese
1 egg
¼ cup sugar
1 tablespoon milk or nondairy
   liquid
½ teaspoon vanilla

Preheat oven to 350°. Prepare a 9" × 13" pan by spraying with cooking spray. Then line with foil, leaving 4" extra hanging out both 13" sides. Spray again.

In a medium bowl, whisk together the flour mix, xanthan gum, and baking powder. Stir in the toasted nuts. Set aside.

In a double boiler, over water, melt the chocolate and the butter. Remove from over the water and pour into a mixing bowl. Beat in the sugar. Whip the eggs with a fork, add the vanilla, and blend with a mixing spoon, beating lightly. Do not overbeat or the brownies will rise during baking and then fall and crack. Stir in the flour mixture and spoon into the prepared pan. Bake for 35 minutes. Remove from the oven to spread on the topping.

For the topping, melt the chocolate as above and remove from heat. Let cool while beating the cream cheese slightly. Add the chocolate, egg, sugar, milk, and vanilla. Beat until well combined and smooth.

Spread the topping evenly over the hot base. Return to oven for 10–12 minutes or until the topping is set. Cool slightly before removing the whole cake from pan by the "handles" of foil. Let cool for 2–3 hours before cutting into very small pieces about ¾" × 1". *Makes 75 to 90 pieces.*

Nutrients per brownie: Calories 60, Fat 4g, Cholesterol 15mg,
Sodium 25mg, Carbohydrates 7g, Protein 1g.

Apple-Walnut Brownie Squares

350°

This is a brownie for those who prefer fruit to chocolate. Frosted with a nonchocolate topping, it can be as tasty as the caffeine-saturated chocolate counterpart.

BATTER:
1¼ cups Four Flour Bean Mix
¾ teaspoon xanthan gum
1 teaspoon Egg Replacer (optional)
1 teaspoon baking powder
½ teaspoon baking soda
1 teaspoon cinnamon
½ cup (1 stick) margarine or butter
1 cup brown sugar
2 eggs

¼ cup apple juice
1 large apple, peeled, cored, and
 chopped
1 cup walnuts, chopped

FROSTING:
¼ cup cream cheese, softened
1 tablespoon apple juice
1 cup confectioners' sugar

Preheat oven to 350°. Grease a 9" square pan.

In a medium bowl, whisk together the flour mix, xanthan gum, Egg Replacer (if used), baking powder, baking soda, and cinnamon. Set aside.

In the bowl of your mixer, cream the margarine and brown sugar. Add the eggs and apple juice and beat until fluffy. Add the dry ingredients and continue beating until smooth. By hand, stir in the apple and nuts. Spoon batter into the prepared pan and bake for 35 minutes or until a tester comes out clean.

Cool. Meanwhile, beat the frosting ingredients to a smooth, spreadable consistency. Spread over the cooled brownies. Cut after the frosting is set. *Makes 18 brownies.*

*Nutrients per brownie: Calories 200, Fat 9g, Cholesterol 40mg,
Sodium 130mg, Carbohydrates 28g, Protein 3g.*

Peanut Butter Brownies

Chunky peanut butter and white chocolate chips plus pecans make these brownies irresistible.

1 cup Four Flour Bean Mix	¾ cup brown sugar
½ teaspoon xanthan gum	3 eggs
1 teaspoon baking powder	1 teaspoon vanilla
½ cup (1 stick) margarine or butter	One 6-ounce package white
½ cup crunchy peanut butter	chocolate chips
¾ cup white sugar	1 cup chopped pecans

Preheat oven to 350°. Grease a 9" × 13" oblong baking pan.

In a medium bowl, blend the flour mix, xanthan gum, and baking powder. Set aside.

In the bowl of your mixer, cream the margarine and peanut butter. Gradually add both sugars, beating on medium until light and fluffy. Add the eggs, one at a time, beating after each addition.

Stir in the flour and mix until well blended. Add the vanilla, chocolate chips, and pecans. Spoon into the prepared pan and bake for 30 minutes or until lightly browned. Cool before cutting into bars. *Makes 3 dozen bars.*

Nutrients per brownie: Calories 140, Fat 8g, Cholesterol 25mg, Sodium 50mg, Carbohydrates 16g, Protein 2g.

Lemon Bars

350°

This easy-to-make dessert cookie has a creamy lemon topping over a rich, buttery crust. If made ahead it can be stored in a closed container in the refrigerator for up to a week. For a different base, use only ½ cup (1 stick) butter and substitute 3 tablespoons cream cheese for the rest.

CRUST:

2 cups GF Mix

½ teaspoon xanthan gum

½ cup confectioners' sugar

½ teaspoon salt

¾ cup (1½ sticks) butter or margarine, chilled

2 tablespoons NutQuik or finely ground almonds (optional)

FILLING:

1⅓ cups sugar

3 tablespoons GF Mix

½ teaspoon baking powder

⅓ cup lemon juice

3 eggs

2 teaspoons fresh lemon zest

Confectioners' sugar for dusting

Preheat oven to 350°. Lightly grease a 9" × 13" pan.

In the bowl of your food processor, combine the flour mix, xanthan gum, confectioners' sugar, salt, butter (cut in small chunks), and NutQuik (if used). Pulse on and off until the mixture resembles coarse meal. (If you don't have a food processor, cut in the butter as you would for a pie crust.) Spread into the prepared pan and pat down. Bake for 20 minutes or until lightly colored.

Meanwhile, prepare the filling: In the bowl of your food processor, or the same bowl you used before, combine the sugar, flour mix, baking powder, lemon juice, and eggs. Whirl or beat until well blended. Pour this over the hot crust. Bake for another 20 minutes. Remove and cool slightly before dusting with the confectioners' sugar. Cut into 2" × 1¼" bars. *Makes 36 bars.*

VARIATION:

LEMON COCONUT BARS: Add 1 cup flaked coconut to the lemon filling.

Nutrients per bar: Calories 110, Fat 5g, Cholesterol 30mg,
Sodium 80mg, Carbohydrates 17g, Protein 1g.

Easy Pecan Bars

350°

A cookie for pecan pie lovers. The recipe calls for maple syrup, but dark corn syrup may be substituted.

CRUST:
1 cup Featherlight Mix
1 teaspoon xanthan gum
¼ cup confectioners' sugar
½ cup (1 stick) margarine or
  butter

TOPPING:
2 tablespoons GF Mix
2 tablespoons brown sugar
1 egg or ¼ cup liquid egg substitute
⅓ cup maple syrup
½ cup chopped pecans

Preheat oven to 350°. Grease an 8" square pan.

In a medium bowl, combine the flour mix, xanthan gum, and confectioners' sugar. Cut in the margarine, working until crumbly. Pat into the bottom of the prepared pan. Bake for about 15 minutes.

Meanwhile in the same bowl, beat together the flour mix, brown sugar, egg, and syrup. Add the nuts.

Pour the thin batter over the baked crust and spread evenly. Bake for about 20 minutes or until set in the center. Cool and cut into 1½" squares. *Makes 25 bars.*

Nutrients per bar: Calories 100, Fat 6g, Cholesterol 20mg,
Sodium 40mg, Carbohydrates 11g, Protein 1g.

Frosted Macadamia Bars

350°

This deliciously different bar is an adaptation of a recipe put out by Jowar Flour Company using their sorghum flour. It's absolutely delicious and my wheat-eating friends declare it "one of the very best."

Note: *Toasting the chopped nuts for about 8 minutes in a 350° oven will give more flavor.*

BASE:
¾ cup plus 2 tablespoons sorghum
   flour
2 tablespoons tapioca flour
¼ rounded teaspoon xanthan gum
½ teaspoon baking soda
½ cup sugar
½ teaspoon vanilla
2 tablespoons honey

1 large egg or ¼ cup liquid egg
   substitute
½ cup finely chopped macadamia
   nuts

FROSTING:
1 cup confectioners' sugar
2 tablespoons mayonnaise
1 tablespoon water
1 teaspoon vanilla

Preheat oven to 350°. Grease a 9" × 13" pan.

Place all ingredients for the base in a mixing bowl and (with mixer on low) blend until they appear as large crumbs. Press into the prepared pan and bake for 8 to 10 minutes. While the base is baking, mix the frosting.

Frost while still warm, so the frosting becomes firm as a glaze. Cut in 1½" × 2" bars. *Makes 3 dozen bars.*

Nutrients per bar: Calories 60, Fat 2½g, Cholesterol 5mg,
Sodium 25mg, Carbohydrates 10g, Protein 1g.

Lemon Cheesecake Bars 350°

Make these creamy-tasting, rich dessert bars with little fuss. Serve them beside a dish of fruit to top off any dinner. Or pass them as dessert at the next luncheon.

CRUST:
¾ cup GF Mix
¼ cup sweet rice flour
½ teaspoon xanthan gum
⅓ cup brown sugar
⅓ cup (5½ tablespoons) margarine or butter, melted
¼ cup finely chopped walnuts or pecans

TOPPING:
One 8-ounce package cream cheese
¼ cup sugar
1 egg
1 teaspoon vanilla
1 teaspoon lemon zest
1½ tablespoons fresh lemon juice
2 tablespoons cream or nondairy creamer

Preheat oven to 350°. Grease an 8" square pan.

In a small bowl, combine the flour mix, sweet rice flour, xanthan gum, brown sugar, melted margarine, and nuts. Pat all but ½ cup of the crumb mix into the prepared pan. Bake for 12–15 minutes or until lightly brown at the edges.

In the bowl of your mixer, cream the cream cheese and sugar. Add the egg, vanilla, lemon zest, lemon juice, and cream. Beat until blended. Pour over the baked crust and top with the remaining crumb mix. Bake for 30 minutes. Cool and cut into 1½" squares. *Makes 25 bars.*

Nutrients per bar: Calories 100, Fat 6g, Cholesterol 25mg, Sodium 55mg, Carbohydrates 10g, Protein 1g.

Cheesecake Honey Bars

An easy but tasty cookie bar that can serve as a whole dessert when topped with fresh fruit, a dab of whipped topping, or a bit of ice cream. This should be stored in the refrigerator to keep.

CRUST:

1 cup GF Mix

¼ teaspoon xanthan gum

⅓ cup brown sugar

⅓ cup (5½ tablespoons) margarine or butter

¾ cup chopped walnuts or pecans

FILLING:

¼ cup honey

1 egg

1 tablespoon lemon juice

One 8-ounce package cream cheese

2 tablespoons milk or nondairy liquid

½ teaspoon almond flavoring (pineapple or lemon may be substituted)

Preheat oven to 350°. Grease a 9" × 13" pan.

In a medium bowl, combine the flour mix, xanthan gum, and brown sugar. Cut in the butter with a pastry blender or work it in with your fingers. Stir in the nuts. Press the mix into the prepared pan. Bake for 12–15 minutes or until very slightly browned.

For the filling, in the same mixing bowl, beat together the honey, egg, lemon juice, cream cheese, milk, and flavoring. Spoon the filling over the baked crust. Bake for 25 minutes or until set. Cool in the pan before cutting. Refrigerate after cooling. *Makes 20 bars.*

Nutrients per bar: Calories 150, Fat 10g, Cholesterol 30mg, Sodium 70mg, Carbohydrates 14g, Protein 3g.

Raspberry Bars

These bars with their sorghum shortbread base will have everyone reaching for more. They are easy to make, even though the list of ingredients may look a bit long. See below for the changes to make Pineapple Bars.

BASE:

1¼ cups sorghum flour

3 tablespoons tapioca flour

1 teaspoon xanthan gum

2 tablespoons almond meal or
    NutQuik

2 egg yolks

1 teaspoon dried lemon peel

½ cup (1 stick) butter or margarine

½ cup confectioners' sugar

TOPPING:

1 cup raspberry preserves

¾ cup chopped walnuts

GLAZE (OPTIONAL):

⅓ cup confectioners' sugar

1¼ teaspoons lemon juice

Preheat oven to 350°. Prepare a 9" × 13" pan by lining it with aluminum foil and extending the foil enough up the ends of the pan to be able to lift out the whole cookie base before cutting it. Grease well or spray with liquid vegetable oil.

In a medium bowl, whisk together the sorghum flour, tapioca flour, xanthan gum, and almond meal. Set aside. In the bowl of a mixer, beat the egg yolks, lemon peel, butter, and confectioners' sugar on medium until blended. Turn mixer to low and add the dry ingredients, beating until moist crumbs form. Spoon this mixture over the bottom of the prepared pan and press into an even layer. Bake for 18 minutes or until set.

For the topping, spread the preserves over the crust; sprinkle with the walnuts. Bake for 15 minutes or until the walnuts are toasted.

For the glaze, combine the sugar and lemon juice and squeeze out the corners of a small plastic bag in a zigzag pattern over the hot topping.

Remove from the pan by the foil handles and transfer to a cutting board. Cool slightly and cut into bars. *Makes 48 bars.*

VARIATION:

PINEAPPLE BARS: Use pineapple in place of raspberry preserves. Substitute macadamia nuts for the walnuts.

Nutrients per bar: Calories 70, Fat 3g, Cholesterol 15mg,
Sodium 20mg, Carbohydrates 10g, Protein 1g.

Caramel-Pecan Bars

350°

Pecan pie flavor in a cookie! These easy-to-make bars keep well and are good travelers.

BASE:
1¼ cups sorghum flour
¼ cup tapioca flour
1 teaspoon xanthan gum
½ cup (1 stick) butter or margarine
½ cup brown sugar
1 egg yolk
½ teaspoon vanilla

TOPPING:
1 cup brown sugar
½ cup (1 stick) butter or margarine
 (cut up)
¼ cup dark corn syrup
½ cup cream or nondairy creamer
2 cups chopped pecans

Preheat oven to 350°. Line a 9" × 13" pan with foil, letting the foil extend over the short edges of the pan. Spray with vegetable oil.

In a medium bowl, whisk together the sorghum flour, tapioca flour, and xanthan gum. Set aside.

In the bowl of your mixer, beat the butter, brown sugar, egg yolk, and vanilla until fluffy. Turn the mixer to low and blend in the flour mix. With your hands, press into the bottom of the prepared pan. Bake for 15 minutes.

For the topping, combine the brown sugar, butter, and corn syrup in a medium saucepan. Bring to a boil and boil for 2 minutes. Remove from the heat; add the cream and nuts. Pour over the baked crust and return to the oven. Bake for 22 minutes. Cool and lift from the pan with the foil ends. Cut into bars 6 across and 6 lengthwise. *Makes 36 bars.*

*Nutrients per bar: Calories 150, Fat 10g, Cholesterol 20mg,
Sodium 60mg, Carbohydrates 16g, Protein 1g.*

Macadamia and White Chocolate Bars

With a rich filling over a flavorful shortbread crust, this cookie is sure to make a hit with everyone. Testers report that on a scale of 1 to 10, this is a 15.

CRUST:
1¼ cups sorghum flour
¼ cup tapioca flour
1 teaspoon xanthan gum
½ cup confectioners' sugar
½ cup (1 stick) butter or
   margarine
1 egg yolk
½ teaspoon vanilla

TOPPING:
1 cup sugar
½ cup Four Flour Bean Mix
2 large eggs
¼ cup (½ stick) butter or
   margarine, melted
1 teaspoon vanilla
1 cup white baking chips
1 cup chopped macadamia nuts

Preheat oven to 350°. Grease a 9" × 13" pan.

Blend the sorghum flour, tapioca flour, xanthan gum, and sugar in a food processor or bowl. Add the margarine, egg yolk, and vanilla and process using on/off pulses until mixture resembles coarse meal. Or cut in the butter with a pastry cutter until you get the same texture. Transfer the mixture to the prepared baking pan and press onto the bottom. Bake for about 15 minutes.

(For a firmer crust: In a medium bowl, whisk together the sorghum flour, tapioca flour, and xanthan gum. Set aside. In the bowl of your mixer, cream the sugar, butter, egg yolk, and vanilla. Add the flour mix and blend on low until a soft ball forms. Press into pan, making sure it is even. Bake for 15 minutes.)

For the topping, whisk the sugar, flour mix, eggs, melted butter, and vanilla in a large bowl until well blended. Stir in the baking chips and nuts. Pour the filling over the warm crust, making sure all is covered. Bake for about 30 minutes or until the filling is slightly browned. If using a tester, it should come out with moist crumbs attached. Cool in the pan and cut into 1½" × 2" bars. *Makes 40 bars.*

VARIATIONS:

RASPBERRY CHOCOLATE PECAN BARS: Increase the sugar in the filling to ¾ cup and use raspberry chocolate bits in place of the white chocolate bits. Use pecans in place of macadamia nuts.

CHOCOLATE-MACADAMIA BARS: Increase the sugar to 1 cup in the filling and use semisweet chocolate bits instead of the white baking bits.

Nutrients per bar: Calories 190, Fat 14g, Cholesterol 25mg, Sodium 45mg, Carbohydrates 17g, Protein 2g.

Lime Bars with a Coconut Crust

Savor the tang of lime combined with the sweetness of coconut.

BASE:
1 cup sorghum flour
¼ cup tapioca flour
1 teaspoon xanthan gum
½ cup (1 stick) margarine or
   butter
1 egg yolk
½ cup brown sugar
½ teaspoon vanilla

1 cup dried sweetened coconut,
   chopped fine, divided

TOPPING:
¾ cup sugar
Zest from 1 lime
½ cup lime juice (2–3 limes)
¼ cup (½ stick) margarine or butter
2 eggs, slightly beaten

Preheat oven to 350°. Line a 9" × 13" oblong cake pan with foil, allowing it to come up over the sides and fold back to use for a handle. Spray with vegetable oil cooking spray.

Place the first 7 ingredients for the base in the bowl of your mixer and beat slowly until they form crumbs. Add ¾ cup of the coconut and continue blending until the dough forms a ball. Flatten with your hand and press the mixture into the prepared pan. Bake for 10 minutes.

Meanwhile, in a medium saucepan, blend the topping ingredients and cook over medium-low heat, stirring until thickened (about 10 minutes). Do not boil. Remove from the heat and pour over the baked base. Sprinkle the top with the reserved coconut and bake for 10 minutes. Cool before cutting into 1¼" × 2" bars. *Makes 36 bars.*

Nutrients per bar: Calories 100, Fat 5g, Cholesterol 30mg,
Sodium 50mg, Carbohydrates 13g, Protein 1g.

*M*ake fine-cut macaroon coconut from flake or shredded coconut by processing in a food processor until the desired texture is reached.

Butterscotch Bars with Peanuts   350°

A very different chewy-topped bar with its combination of caramel and peanuts that is sure to please.

2 cups Four Flour Bean Mix or
   Featherlight Mix
¾ teaspoon xanthan gum
½ cup brown sugar
⅔ cup margarine or butter
2 cups roasted peanuts

1 cup butterscotch bits
1 cup butterscotch or caramel ice
   cream topping
3 tablespoons Featherlight Mix
   or GF Mix

Preheat oven to 350°. Line a 10" × 15" baking pan with foil.

In a mixing bowl, whisk together the flour mix, xanthan gum, and brown sugar. Cut in the margarine with a pastry blender until the mixture is crumbly. Press into the bottom of the prepared pan and bake for 12 minutes.

While still hot from oven, sprinkle the peanuts and butterscotch bits over the top. In a small bowl, blend the topping and the 3 tablespoons of the flour mix. Drizzle evenly over the top. Bake for 12–15 minutes or until caramel is bubbly. Cool and cut into bars. *Makes 36 bars.*

*Nutrients per bar: Calories 180, Fat 9g, Cholesterol 5mg,
Sodium 95mg, Carbohydrates 24g, Protein 3g.*

Pecan Sandies

This shortbread is delightfully different as it's flavored with the crunch of toasted pecans.

Note: *To toast the pecans, spread on a baking sheet and bake at 300° for 5–6 minutes. Watch to be sure they don't get too brown.*

1 cup toasted pecans	1 cup (2 sticks) butter or margarine
2 cups Featherlight Mix	¾ cup brown sugar
¾ teaspoon xanthan gum	1 teaspoon vanilla

Preheat oven to 300°. Line a 9" × 13" oblong baking pan with aluminum foil, leaving the ends to hang over as handles. Grease lightly.

In a food processor, finely grind the pecans with the flour mix and xanthan gum. Set aside.

In the bowl of your mixer, beat the butter, brown sugar, and vanilla on medium until creamy. Gradually add the flour-nut mixture on low until a soft dough forms. Spoon this into the prepared pan and smooth evenly to about ¼" thickness overall.

Bake for 30–35 minutes or until the edges brown lightly. Cool slightly before removing from the pan, using the foil as handles. Cut while still warm into 1½" squares. *Makes about 4 dozen bars.*

Nutrients per bar: Calories 120, Fat 8g, Cholesterol 15mg, Sodium 60mg, Carbohydrates 13g, Protein 1g.

Apricot-Pineapple Bars

This great-tasting fruit-filled bar cookie is so easy to make it's sure to become a favorite in your family, as it is in ours. The filling is purchased jam and there's no rolling out. What could be easier?

1¼ cups Four Flour Bean Mix	¾ teaspoon cinnamon
1 cup almond meal	⅓ teaspoon cloves
1 teaspoon xanthan gum	⅛ teaspoon salt
¾ cup (1½ sticks) butter or margarine	1 egg plus 1 egg yolk
	1 teaspoon almond flavoring
1 cup sugar	¾ cup apricot-pineapple preserves

Preheat oven to 350°. Line a 9" × 13" oblong baking pan with aluminum foil, allowing extra to hang out on both ends as a handle. Grease the foil and pan sides.

In a medium bowl, whisk together the flour mix, almond meal, and xanthan gum. Set aside.

In the bowl of your mixer, beat the butter on medium for about 30 seconds. Add the sugar, cinnamon, cloves, and salt. Beat until well combined, scraping down the sides of the bowl as needed. Beat in the egg and egg yolk until well blended. Beat in as much of the dry ingredients as you can. Mix in the rest with a spoon, if necessary.

Spread 2 cups of the batter evenly in the prepared pan. Spoon the preserves over batter to within ½" of the edges. (Drop the remaining batter by small spoonfuls evenly over the batter and gently spread over the preserves with the tip of a knife.)

Bake for 35–40 minutes or until tester comes out clean. Let cool for about 5 minutes and then remove the whole from the pan using the foil handles. Let cool completely before cutting into bars. *Makes 30 bars.*

Nutrients per bar: Calories 140, Fat 7g, Cholesterol 25mg,
Sodium 60mg, Carbohydrates 18g, Protein 1g.

Mock Toll House Cookies

Donna Jo, hungering for the original Toll House cookies, created these, and once you've tasted them you won't believe they're gluten free. These are not good long-distance travelers but just right for taking to that school party or on the family picnic.

1¾ cups Featherlight Mix
½ cup sorghum flour
½ teaspoon xanthan gum
½ cup (1 stick) margarine
½ cup Butter Flavor Crisco
¾ cup white sugar
¾ cup brown sugar

1 teaspoon baking soda
1 scant teaspoon salt
1 teaspoon vanilla
2 eggs
One 12-ounce package semisweet
   chocolate chips
1 cup chopped walnuts or pecans

Preheat oven to 375°. Have ready, but do not grease, 2 cookie sheets.

In a medium bowl, blend the flour mix, sorghum flour, and xanthan gum. Set aside.

In the bowl of your mixer, cream the margarine, Crisco, and both sugars. Add the baking soda, salt, and vanilla. Beat in the eggs, one at a time. Add the dry ingredients and beat well. Stir in the chocolate chips and nuts.

Spoon the dough onto the cookie sheets, using approximately 1½ teaspoons at a time, spacing the cookies 3 inches apart. Bake for 7–9 minutes for soft cookies, 9–11 minutes for firm ones. Cool slightly before removing from the sheets. *Makes 5½ dozen 2" cookies.*

Nutrients per cookie: Calories 100, Fat 5g, Cholesterol 5mg,
Sodium 70mg, Carbohydrates 12g, Protein 1g.

Gingersnaps

I introduced these as a midnight snack at a celiac convention and got raves. The sorghum and bean flours combine magically to give these cookies all the taste and texture of the wheat ones some of us still remember.

1 cup Garfava bean flour

1 cup cornstarch

1 cup tapioca flour

1 cup sorghum flour

1 scant teaspoon xanthan gum

½ teaspoon salt

3 teaspoons baking soda

2½ teaspoons ground ginger

1½ teaspoons ground cinnamon

1½ teaspoons ground cloves

½ cup (1 stick) margarine or butter

½ cup Butter Flavor Crisco

1⅓ cups sugar

½ cup molasses

2 eggs, beaten slightly

Preheat oven to 350°. Grease 2 cookie sheets.

In a medium bowl, whisk together the bean flour, cornstarch, tapioca flour, sorghum flour, xanthan gum, salt, baking soda, ginger, cinnamon, and cloves. Set aside.

In the bowl of your mixer, cream the margarine, Crisco, and sugar until fluffy and light colored. Beat in the molasses and eggs until well blended. Set the mixer to low and add the dry ingredients, a spoonful at a time until it is all used. Turn the mixer to medium and beat until the dough is smooth and well blended.

To form cookies, roll the dough from the tip of a tablespoon in balls about 1½" in size onto the prepared cookie sheets, leaving 2½" between the balls. Bake for 11 minutes (do not overbake). *Makes 6½ dozen cookies.*

Nutrients per cookie: Calories 45, Fat 1½g, Cholesterol 5mg,
Sodium 45mg, Carbohydrates 8g, Protein 0g.

158   *The Gluten-free Gourmet Makes Dessert*

Chocolate Chip Cookies

This crispy chocolate and nut cookie, a favorite with children and adults alike, is rich and buttery. A lower-fat version can be made by substituting one stick of margarine and half a cup of fat-free ricotta cheese for the butter. Eliminate the nuts.

1¼ cups GF Mix
1 cup soy flour
2 teaspoons baking soda
1 teaspoon salt
1 cup (2 sticks) butter or margarine
1½ cups packed brown sugar

2 eggs
1 teaspoon vanilla
1 cup semisweet chocolate chips
½ cup coarsely chopped walnuts
  or pecans

Preheat oven to 375°.

In a small bowl, whisk together the flour mix, soy flour, baking soda, and salt. Set aside.

In the bowl of your mixer, cream the butter and brown sugar. Add the eggs and beat until smooth. Beat in the vanilla. Add the dry ingredients, beating only until mixed. By hand, stir in the chocolate chips and nuts.

Drop by spoonfuls on ungreased cookie sheets, leaving 2 inches between mounds. Bake for 12–15 minutes. Cool slightly and remove to finish cooling. *Makes about 4½ dozen cookies.*

Nutrients per cookie: Calories 100, Fat 5g, Cholesterol 15mg, Sodium 130mg, Carbohydrates 13g, Protein 1g.

---

*I*f stored cookies get dry, add a slice of apple to the closed container to soften them.

Old-Fashioned Peanut Butter Cookies 375°

I'd forgotten how wonderfully satisfying this cookie tasted until I made these to take on a trip. The high protein will keep you going when you're traveling and the kids will love them—even those who can have wheat. Make these a must for trips away from home.

1¾ cups GF Mix
½ teaspoon xanthan gum
¾ teaspoon salt
¾ teaspoon baking soda
¾ cup peanut butter
½ cup Butter Flavor Crisco

1½ cups brown sugar
3 tablespoons milk or nondairy liquid
1 tablespoon vanilla
1 egg

Preheat oven to 375°.

In a small bowl, whisk together the flour mix, xanthan gum, salt, and baking soda. Set aside.

In the bowl of your mixer, combine the peanut butter, Crisco, brown sugar, milk, and vanilla. Beat on medium until well blended. Add the egg and beat just until blended. Add the dry ingredients and beat on low until blended.

Drop by teaspoonfuls onto ungreased cookie sheets, about 2 inches apart. Flatten with a fork, making crisscross marks on the dough. Bake for 7–8 minutes or until set. Cool for a few minutes on the cookie sheet before removing to cool on a rack. *Makes about 4 dozen cookies.*

Nutrients per cookie: Calories 90, Fat 4g, Cholesterol 15mg, Sodium 60mg, Carbohydrates 12g, Protein 1g.

Choc-O-Nut Jumbles

Chocolate and nuts fill this rich cookie while bean and sorghum add to the flavor. A true chocoholic's treat.

1¼ cups Four Flour Bean Mix
¼ teaspoon salt
1 teaspoon baking powder
6 squares semisweet baking chocolate
4 squares unsweetened baking chocolate
½ cup (1 stick) margarine or butter

¾ cup brown sugar
½ cup white sugar
3 eggs, lightly beaten with fork
2 teaspoons Vanilla, Nut, & Rum flavoring or vanilla
1 cup chopped walnuts or pecans
1 cup vanilla baking chips

Preheat oven to 325°.

In a small bowl, mix the flour mix, salt, and baking powder. Set aside.

In a microwave proof bowl, heat the semisweet chocolate, baking chocolate, and margarine on high for 1½–2 minutes, stirring once during the heating time. Pour into your mixing bowl.

Stir in both sugars until blended. Beat in the eggs and flavoring. Add the dry ingredients and stir until well blended; add the nuts and baking chips. Drop by rounded teaspoonfuls onto ungreased cookie sheets, leaving 1½ inches between rounds. Bake for 10–12 minutes or until set. Do not overbake or they will be dry. Let cool for a minute or two on the cookie sheet before removing them to cool. *Makes 4½ dozen cookies.*

Nutrients per cookie: Calories 90, Fat 5g, Cholesterol 70mg,
Sodium 45mg, Carbohydrates 11g, Protein 1g.

New "Oatmeal" Cookies

350°

"Wonderful!" report my testers. "These taste like real old-fashioned oatmeal cookies!" The secret is the addition of the new rolled soy flakes now available.

Note: To crush the almonds, place them in a plastic bag and roll with a rolling pin to achieve a texture resembling oats.

1 cup sweet rice flour
½ cup white rice flour
½ teaspoon salt
1 teaspoon baking soda
1 cup Butter Flavor Crisco
1 cup white sugar
1 cup brown sugar

2 eggs
1 teaspoon vanilla
2 cups thin-shaved almonds
    crushed to oatmeal size (see note)
1 cup soy flakes
¾ cup raisins

Preheat oven to 350°. Lightly grease 2 cookie sheets.

In a medium bowl, whisk together the sweet rice flour, white rice flour, salt, and baking soda. Set aside.

In the bowl of your mixer, cream the Crisco and both sugars. Beat in the eggs, one at a time. Add the vanilla. Stir in the dry ingredients. Add the almonds, soy flakes, and raisins. Drop by rounded teaspoonfuls onto the prepared cookie sheets and bake for 10 minutes, or until lightly browned.

Remove from pan immediately and cool flat on waxed paper. *Makes 6½ dozen cookies.*

Nutrients per cookie: Calories 80, Fat 4g, Cholesterol 5mg, Sodium 35mg, Carbohydrates 10g, Protein 2g.

Apricot-Almond Chews

Think of these as adult oatmeal cookies flavored with apricot and almonds. This is a wonderful way to use the new textured soy protein found in many health food stores and available by order from several suppliers. If you don't have the textured soy protein, these can be made by substituting sliced almonds, crushed with a rolling pin, for the soy. Cut the chopped almonds to ½ cup.

1¼ cups Featherlight Mix or Four
   Flour Bean Mix
½ teaspoon xanthan gum
1 cup (2 sticks) margarine or butter
¾ cup brown sugar
½ cup white sugar
½ teaspoon baking soda

1 egg
1 teaspoon almond flavoring
2 tablespoons apricot or orange
   juice
1½ cups textured soy protein
1 cup chopped dried apricots
1 cup chopped almonds

Preheat oven to 375°.

In a medium bowl, measure flour mix and whisk in the xanthan gum. Set aside.

In the bowl of your mixer, cream the margarine and both sugars. Add the baking soda and beat until combined and smooth. Add the egg. Then add the almond flavoring plus the juice. Beat again.

With the mixer on low, spoon in the flour slowly and beat until all is incorporated. Stir in the soy protein, dried apricots, and chopped almonds. Drop by rounded teaspoonfuls onto an ungreased cookie sheet. Bake for 8–10 minutes or till done. Cool for 1 minute before removing to cool completely. *Makes approximately 65 chews.*

*Nutrients per cookie: Calories 70, Fat 4g, Cholesterol 10mg,
Sodium 40mg, Carbohydrates 9g, Protein 2g.*

Potato Chip Cookies

350°

A drop cookie with the texture of shortbread with a crunch. These are tender cookies and do not travel well.

1 cup (2 sticks) butter	1½ cups GF Mix
½ cup sugar	½ teaspoon xanthan gum
1 teaspoon vanilla	2 cups crushed potato chips
1 egg	½ cup chopped pecans

Preheat oven to 350°.

In the bowl of your mixer, cream the butter and sugar until light and fluffy. Add the vanilla and egg. Beat well. Beat in the flour mix blended with the xanthan gum. Stir in the potato chips and pecans. Drop by teaspoonfuls onto ungreased baking sheets. Bake for 10–12 minutes. Cool slightly before removing from sheets. *Makes 4½ dozen cookies.*

*Nutrients per cookie: Calories 70, Fat 5g, Cholesterol 15mg,
Sodium 45mg, Carbohydrates 6g, Protein 1g.*

---

*I*nsulated cookie sheets are not suitable for cookies high in fat or shaped cookies. They are best for pale drop cookies with soft centers.

Mock Oreo Cookies

350°

Remember when we split these cookies apart and licked the frosting from each side before eating the cookies? Do that with these and you'll think they are the "real" thing.

Note: *If you have a cookie stamp, press onto sliced cookies before baking to give a more authentic look to the cookies.*

DOUGH:
2¼ cups Featherlight Mix
1 scant teaspoon xanthan gum
2 teaspoons Egg Replacer
⅔ cup cocoa
1 teaspoon baking powder
1 teaspoon baking soda
½ teaspoon salt
¾ cup (1½ sticks) margarine
  or butter
1 cup sugar

1 egg
1 teaspoon vanilla
1–2 tablespoons milk or nondairy
  substitute

FILLING:
2 cups confectioners' sugar
3 tablespoons shortening
¼ teaspoon vanilla
2 tablespoons hot water

Preheat oven to 350°.

In a medium bowl, whisk together the flour mix, xanthan gum, Egg Replacer, cocoa, baking powder, baking soda, and salt. Set aside.

In the bowl of your mixer, cream the margarine and sugar until light. Add the egg and vanilla and beat well. Add the dry ingredients in 3 additions. If the dough becomes too stiff, add the milk as needed. Shape the dough into two 10" × 1½" rolls. Wrap in foil and chill. Cut into ⅛" slices (see note) and bake on an ungreased cookie sheet for 10 minutes. Let cool for only a few minutes before removing from the cookie sheet. Cool thoroughly on a rack.

For the filling, combine the confectioners' sugar, shortening, vanilla, and hot water (use enough to create a good spreading texture). *Makes about 45 filled cookies.*

Nutrients per cookie: Calories 70, Fat 3g, Cholesterol 15mg,
Sodium 95mg, Carbohydrates 10g, Protein 1g.

Mary Lou's Fig Newtons

"They taste just like 'real' Fig Newtons," the testers agreed. These may seem a lot of trouble, but if you miss your Fig Newtons, they are well worth it.

Note: *If you use the GF Mix, you may eliminate the extra ⅓ cup sweet rice flour, but to firm up the dough to correct consistency, refrigerate for 2–3 hours before rolling out.*

FILLING:
One 10-ounce bag dried figlets
½ cup water
½ cup orange juice
⅓ cup sugar

COOKIE DOUGH:
2½ cups Four Flour Bean Mix or
   GF Mix (see note)
2 teaspoons xanthan gum

3 teaspoons baking powder
½ teaspoon baking soda
½ teaspoon salt
⅓ cup (5½ tablespoons) margarine
   or butter
⅔ cup brown sugar
2 eggs or ¼ cup liquid egg
   substitute
1 teaspoon vanilla
⅓ cup sweet rice flour (see note)

Grease a 10" × 15" cookie sheet.

Chop or grind the figlets and place in a medium saucepan. Add the water, orange juice, and sugar. Bring to a boil; reduce heat and simmer, uncovered, for 15–20 minutes or until thickened. Remove to a refrigerator dish and chill.

In a medium bowl, whisk together the flour mix, xanthan gum, baking powder, baking soda, and salt. Set aside.

In the bowl of your mixer, cream the margarine and brown sugar. Add the eggs, one at a time, beating well after each addition. Stir in the vanilla. Add the dry ingredients, mixing well, stirring in the sweet rice flour last.

Divide the dough into 3 sections and roll out the first section between sheets of plastic wrap into a rectangle 4" wide and about 15" long. Remove the top plastic wrap and spread ⅓ of the fig mixture in a 1" strip down the length of the dough. Brush water on the edges of the dough and fold over the filling, using the bottom plastic wrap to help mold the dough. Seal the edges and again using the plastic wrap, lift the roll onto your prepared cookie sheet and turn it with the seamed side down. Repeat with the remaining dough and filling.

Bake in a 350° preheated oven for about 20 minutes or until lightly browned. Remove from oven and cool. Slice crosswise into ¾" slices.

If you plan to freeze these cookies, do not cut into slices first. Just cut the bars in half and wrap well in plastic wrap or foil and place in a freezer bag. To serve, slice after thawing. *Makes about 4½ dozen cookies.*

Nutrients per cookie: Calories 60, Fat 1½g, Cholesterol 10mg,
Sodium 70mg, Carbohydrates 12g, Protein 1g.

Black and White Biscotti

350°–325°

If you've dreamed of a chocolate biscotti, here's the answer to that dream with the addition of vanilla chips thrown in for extra pizazz. Bake these up and watch your wheat-eating friends grab them.

2 cups Featherlight Mix
¼ cup sweet rice flour
1 teaspoon xanthan gum
¼ teaspoon salt
⅓ cup cocoa powder
3 teaspoons baking powder

⅔ cup white sugar
⅓ cup brown sugar
¼ cup (½ stick) margarine or butter
3 eggs
3 tablespoons cherry or regular cola
1 cup white vanilla chips

Preheat oven to 350°. Grease 2 cookie sheets.

In a medium bowl, whisk together the flour mix, sweet rice flour, xanthan gum, salt, cocoa powder, and baking powder. Set aside.

In the bowl of your mixer, cream both sugars with the margarine until light. Add the eggs, one at a time, beating after each addition. Spoon in the cola liquid and blend. With a spoon or the mixer on low, blend in the dry ingredients. Add the vanilla chips. The dough will be stiff.

Divide the dough into 3 sections. With each, spoon out a log on the sheets about ½" high, 2½" wide, and almost the length of the sheet. Bake for about 25 minutes, reversing the position of the pans in the oven halfway through baking.

Remove and cool for about 5 minutes. Turn the oven to 325°. Slice diagonally across the logs in ½" slices. Lay, cut side up, on the baking sheets and return to the oven for 12–14 minutes, again reversing the position of the sheets halfway through baking but turning the slices over at this point.

Cool and store airtight for up to a month. Or freeze for later use. *Makes about 4 dozen cookies.*

Nutrients per cookie: Calories 80, Fat 2½g, Cholesterol 15mg, Sodium 55mg, Carbohydrates 13g, Protein 1g.

Chocolate-Cherry Biscotti

The addition of cherries and walnuts makes this my favorite chocolate biscotti.
Note: If you like your chocolate dark, increase the cocoa powder to ½ cup.

⅔ cup chopped dried cherries
2½ cups Four Flour Bean Mix
⅓ cup sweet rice flour
1 teaspoon xanthan gum
1 teaspoon Egg Replacer
¼ teaspoon salt
3 teaspoons baking powder
⅓ cup cocoa powder (see note)

⅔ cup white sugar
⅓ cup brown sugar
¼ cup (½ stick) margarine or butter
3 eggs
1 teaspoon cherry flavoring
3 tablespoons cherry cola or cherry
 juice
½ cup chopped walnuts

Place the dried cherries in a small bowl and cover with boiling water. Let soak for about 25 minutes.

Preheat oven to 350°. Grease 2 cookie sheets or spray with vegetable oil spray. In a medium bowl, whisk together the flour mix, sweet rice flour, xanthan gum, Egg Replacer, salt, baking powder, and cocoa. Set aside.

In the bowl of your mixer, cream both sugars with the margarine until fluffy. Add the eggs, one at a time, beating after each addition. Add the flavoring and spoon in the cola. With a spoon or the mixer on low, blend in the dry ingredients. Stir in the walnuts. The dough will be stiff.

Divide the dough into 3 sections. Spoon each one out into a log on the sheets about ½" high, 2½" wide, and almost the length of the baking sheet. Bake for about 25 minutes, reversing the position of the pans in the oven halfway through baking.

Remove and cool for about 5 minutes. Turn the oven down to 325°. Slice diagonally across the logs in ½" slices. Lay, cut side up, on the baking sheets and return to the oven for 12–14 minutes, again reversing the position of the sheets halfway through baking. Turn the slices over at the halfway point in baking. Cool and store airtight for up to a month. Or freeze for later use. *Makes about 4 dozen cookies.*

Nutrients per cookie: Calories 70, Fat 2g, Cholesterol 15mg, Sodium 50mg, Carbohydrates 13g, Protein 1g.

Lemon-Tipped Pistachio Biscotti 350°–375°–350°

My absolute favorite biscotti. These are crisp, crunchy, and tangy with the lemon icing. The twice baking required for biscotti and the lemon tipping may seem like a lot of work, but these are well worth the time and effort.

COOKIE:
1½ cups GF Mix
½ cup sweet rice flour
¼ teaspoon salt
1 teaspoon xanthan gum
1 tablespoon baking powder
1 teaspoon Egg Replacer
1 teaspoon unflavored gelatin
6 tablespoons (¾ stick) butter or
  margarine
½ cup sugar
1 tablespoon grated lemon peel

2 eggs
1 teaspoon vanilla
1 cup shelled pistachios
¾ cup chopped white chocolate
  or vanilla chips, chopped
1–3 tablespoons milk, if needed

LEMON ICING:
2 cups confectioners' sugar, sifted
3–4 tablespoons lemon juice
1 teaspoon grated lemon peel

Preheat oven to 350°. Toast pistachios for 4–5 minutes.

Turn oven up to 375°. Lightly grease 1 cookie sheet.

In a medium bowl, combine the flour mix, sweet rice flour, salt, xanthan gum, baking powder, Egg Replacer, and gelatin. Set aside.

In the bowl of your mixer, beat the butter, sugar, and lemon peel on medium until well blended. Add eggs, one at a time, beating well after each addition. Beat in the vanilla. Gradually add the dry ingredients, beating only until smooth. If the dough is too thick and dry, add the milk, 1 tablespoon at a time, until the dough forms a ball in the hand. Stir in the pistachios and white chocolate.

Divide the dough in half. Shape each piece into a 9" × 1½" log and flatten to ¾" thick and 3" wide. (An easy way is to form the dough into a log with your hand and place on a tray to flatten.) Bake for 18–20 minutes until edges are lightly browned. Cool for 10 minutes.

Reduce oven to 350°. Cut each log (on an angle across the width) into ½" slices. Lay slices, cut side down, on the cookie sheet and bake for 8–10 minutes. Turn over and bake for an additional 8 minutes. Cool before dipping in the icing.

For the icing, combine the confectioners' sugar, lemon juice, and lemon peel in a small bowl. Stir until smooth. Dip one end (to the halfway point) in the icing and let stand upright between rows in a wire rack until the icing sets. Store, with layers separated by waxed paper, in an airtight container for up to 2 months. *Makes 3 dozen biscotti.*

Nutrients per cookie: Calories 70, Fat 2g, Cholesterol 15mg,
Sodium 50mg, Carbohydrates 11g, Protein 1g.

Peanut Butter–Chocolate Cookies

375°

Add chocolate to the already popular peanut butter cookie and you have a double treat. I thought the chocolate would drown out the peanut butter, but they are a perfect combination.

2½ cups Four Flour Bean Mix or GF Mix

1 teaspoon xanthan gum

3 tablespoons cocoa powder

1 teaspoon baking powder

2 teaspoons Egg Replacer

1 cup (2 sticks) butter or margarine

1¼ cups creamy peanut butter

1 cup white sugar

1 cup brown sugar

2 eggs

1½ cups vanilla drops or chopped white baking bar

Preheat oven to 375°. Grease 2 baking sheets.

In a medium bowl, whisk together the flour mix, xanthan gum, cocoa powder, baking powder, Egg Replacer, and salt. Set aside.

In the bowl of your mixer, beat the butter, peanut butter, and both sugars until well blended. Add the eggs, one at a time, beating after each addition. With the mixer on low, add the dry ingredients and mix until just combined. Stir in the vanilla chips.

Form dough into 1" balls and place on baking sheet, 2 inches apart. Using a fork, flatten the cookies by making a crisscross pattern on top of each. Bake for about 11 minutes or until dry on top and slightly brown on the bottom. Cool on a rack. *Makes about 6 dozen cookies.*

Nutrients per cookie: Calories 110, Fat 6g, Cholesterol 25mg, Sodium 40mg, Carbohydrates 13g, Fiber 0g, Protein 2g.

Double Ginger Cookies   350°

An extra spicy cookie for those who love the taste of ginger. These are shaped like gingersnaps but the flavor is doubled with the added chopped crystallized ginger.

2¼ cups Four Flour Bean Mix
¾ teaspoon xanthan gum
2 teaspoons baking soda
1 teaspoon cinnamon
1 teaspoon cloves
¾ teaspoon salt
¾ cup crystallized ginger, chopped

1 cup dark brown sugar
½ cup shortening
¼ cup (½ stick) butter or margarine
1 egg
¼ cup molasses
White sugar for rolling

Preheat oven to 350°. Grease 2 baking sheets.

In a medium bowl, whisk together the flour mix, xanthan gum, ginger, baking soda, cinnamon, cloves, and salt. Stir in the crystallized ginger. Set aside.

In the bowl of your mixer, cream the brown sugar, shortening, and butter until fluffy. Add the egg and molasses and beat until blended. Add the dry ingredients and mix well. Cover and refrigerate for 1 hour.

Spoon about ½ cup white sugar into a flat bowl. With wet hands, form the dough into balls the size of a walnut, roll in the sugar, and place on the baking sheets 2 inches apart. Bake for about 12 minutes. They should be cracked on top but still soft to the touch. Let cool slightly before transferring to a cooling rack. *Makes about 4 dozen cookies.*

*Nutrients per cookie: Calories 80, Fat 3g, Cholesterol 5mg,
Sodium 65mg, Carbohydrates 12g, Protein 1g.*

Spritz Cookies

I was never happy with the taste or texture of any Spritz cookies I attempted with rice flour but, with this new bean/sorghum mix, the cookies taste as I remember. They are so easy that they should be a must at the holidays.

2 cups Four Flour Bean Mix
½ cup sweet rice flour
¾ teaspoon xanthan gum
1 teaspoon dried lemon peel
1 teaspoon baking powder
¼ teaspoon salt

1 cup (2 sticks) butter or margarine
¾ cup sugar
1 large egg
1 teaspoon vanilla
Colored sugar or candies for
    decorating

Preheat oven to 350°.

In a medium bowl, blend together the Four Flour Bean Mix, sweet rice flour, xanthan gum, dried lemon peel, baking powder, and salt. Set aside.

In the bowl of your mixer, cream the butter and sugar. Beat in the egg and vanilla until smooth. With the mixer on low, gradually beat the dry ingredients into the butter mixture. The dough will be very thick. If too thick, thin with 1–3 teaspoons of orange juice.

Fill a cookie press with dough and press onto ungreased cookie sheets. Decorate with colored sugars or candies. Bake for 11–13 minutes or until cookies are beginning to brown at the edges. Remove to cool on racks. *Makes 6 dozen cookies.*

Nutrients per cookie: Calories 50, Fat 2½g, Cholesterol 10mg,
Sodium 40mg, Carbohydrates 6g, Protein 0g.

Dutch Sugar Cookies

350°

My first sugar cookies were difficult to handle and had to be refrigerated before rolling out. These cookies are far easier to handle (you even knead in some of the flour!), require no chilling, and have a melt-in-your-mouth texture.

2½ cups Featherlight Mix
1 teaspoon baking powder
2½ teaspoons xanthan gum
1 teaspoon salt
1 cup sugar

1 cup Butter Flavor Crisco
1 egg or ¼ cup liquid egg substitute
2 teaspoons vanilla
¼ cup (or more) potato starch for
   kneading

Preheat oven to 350°. Have on hand 2 ungreased cookie sheets.

In a small bowl, whisk together the flour mix, baking powder, xanthan gum, and salt. Set aside.

In the bowl of your mixer, cream the sugar and Crisco. Beat in the egg and vanilla. Add the dry ingredients, mixing enough to combine. The dough will be a soft ball. With your hands, knead in enough of the potato starch to make the dough easy to handle and roll out.

Using about half at a time, place a piece of plastic wrap over the ball and roll out to about ⅛" thickness. Cut into desired shapes and place on pan. Decorate with colored sugars before baking or use frosting to decorate after baking. (With this dough, you can use all the scraps. Just scrape them together and roll out again. They will not get tough.)

Bake for about 13 minutes. Cool very slightly before removing from pan. *Makes 3 dozen 2½" cookies.*

*Nutrients per cookie: Calories 140, Fat 7g, Cholesterol 5mg,
Sodium 75mg, Carbohydrates 18g, Protein 1g.*

Nut Butter Thumbprints 375°

Use any of the nut butters (cashew, peanut, almond, or hazelnut) to make these melt-in-your-mouth cookies baked with a dab of jam in the center. Use a red jam for the festive Christmas touch and pineapple or other light-colored jam for any other season.

Note: *See page 267 for making your own nut butters.*

1½ cups Featherlight Mix	½ cup shortening
¼ teaspoon xanthan gum	½ cup white sugar
1 teaspoon baking soda	½ cup brown sugar
½ teaspoon salt	2 eggs
¾ cup nut butter	Jam or preserves of your choice

Preheat oven to 375°.

In a medium bowl, whisk together the flour mix, xanthan gum, baking soda, and salt. Set aside.

In the bowl of your mixer, beat the nut butter, shortening, and both sugars until well blended. Beat in the eggs. Add the dry ingredients and beat only until smooth.

Shape the dough into 1" balls and place on ungreased cookie sheet with 2 inches between cookies. Press thumb in center to make depression to fill with jam. Bake for 8–10 minutes or until set. Cool slightly before removing from cookie sheets. *Makes 4 dozen cookies.*

*Nutrients per cookie: Calories 90, Fat 4g, Cholesterol 10mg,
Sodium 75mg, Carbohydrates 13g, Protein 1g.*

---

*T*o make your own nut butter, place nuts in a food processor and process until the desired texture is reached.

Scandinavian Almond Bars

325°

These delicately light, decorative cookies are comparatively easy to make but will make a great show on that holiday tray. Just press the dough out on the cookie sheets and then slice the cookies at an angle to make the shape.

DOUGH:
1¾ cups Featherlight Mix
1 scant teaspoon xanthan gum
2 tablespoons almond meal
½ cup (1 stick) margarine or butter
1 cup sugar
2 teaspoons baking powder
¼ teaspoon salt
1 egg
½ teaspoon almond flavoring

Milk for brushing
½ cup coarsely chopped sliced
   almonds

ICING:
1 cup confectioners' sugar
¼ teaspoon almond flavoring
1 tablespoon of milk or enough to
   make consistency to drizzle

Preheat oven to 325°.

In a medium bowl, whisk together the flour mix, xanthan gum, and almond meal. Set aside.

In the bowl of your mixer, beat the margarine and sugar until blended. Add the baking powder and salt and beat again. Add the egg and almond flavoring, beating until well combined. Beat in the dry ingredients. Divide the dough into 4 parts, forming rolls about 10 inches long with each, placing them on 2 ungreased cookie sheets and flattening to about 2½" inches wide.

Brush the dough with milk and sprinkle with the chopped almonds. Bake for 12–14 minutes or until the edges are lightly browned. While the cookies are still warm, cut diagonally into 1" strips. Cool and drizzle the almond icing in thin threads across the cookies. *Makes 40 cookies.*

Nutrients per bar: Calories 90, Fat 4g, Cholesterol 10mg,
Sodium 60mg, Carbohydrates 13g, Protein 1g.

Cranberry Swirls

These are a bit fussy to make but the taste and looks add so much to the Christmas cookie plate that they are well worth the trouble.

DOUGH:

2½ cups Four Flour Bean Mix

½ cup sweet rice flour

1¼ teaspoons xanthan gum

1 cup ground walnuts

1 teaspoon baking powder

1 teaspoon unflavored gelatin

½ teaspoon salt

1 tablespoon brown sugar

⅔ cup butter or margarine

½ cup sugar

½ cup honey

1 egg

2 teaspoons vanilla

FILLING:

One 6-ounce package dried
   cranberries

1 cup cranberry juice cocktail

1½ teaspoons grated ginger

In a medium bowl, whisk together the flour mix, sweet rice flour, xanthan gum, walnuts, baking powder, gelatin, salt, and brown sugar. Set aside.

In the bowl of your mixer, beat the butter, sugar, and honey until fluffy. Beat in the egg and vanilla. Turn mixer to low and beat in the dry ingredients. Halve the dough and flatten each section into a rectangle and wrap in plastic wrap. Chill for 1 hour.

For the filling, gently boil the cranberries, juice, and ginger in a small saucepan for 7 minutes, stirring often. Puree in a food processor.

To assemble cookies, dust 2 sheets of waxed paper with rice flour and roll ½ the dough between these sheets into an 8½" × 12" rectangle. Remove the top sheet of paper and spread with ½ the filling. Roll up from the long side. (You may have to use the paper on the bottom to help roll, as the dough is sticky.) Place the roll in foil and rechill for several hours. Repeat with the other ½ of dough and filling.

Heat the oven to 350°. Grease the baking sheets with shortening. Slice the dough ¼" thick and place 1" apart on sheets. Bake for 12 minutes or until golden. Cool slightly before transferring to racks. Store airtight for up to 10 days. *Makes 6 dozen cookies.*

Nutrients per cookie: Calories 60, Fat 2½g, Cholesterol 10mg,
Sodium 40mg, Carbohydrates 9g, Protein 1g.

---

*T*oo much flour can cause baked goods to be dry. To measure, stir or whisk flour in the container, then spoon it into a measuring cup and level with a knife.

Florentines

These crisp cookies filled with nuts and candied fruit are a European favorite. Most of the recipes I saw called for a frosting of white or dark chocolate spread on the smooth (bottom) side of the cookie, but I like them plain or with a lighter-flavored frosting of melted white Almond Bark so the full flavor of the cookie can be savored.

⅓ cup butter or margarine
⅓ cup milk or nondairy liquid
¼ cup sugar
1 cup chopped almonds, toasted
¾ cup fruit glace, chopped fine

1 teaspoon orange zest
¼ cup Featherlight Mix
2 ounces Almond Bark for frosting
  (optional)

Preheat oven to 350°. Grease and dust cookie sheets with rice flour.

Place the butter, milk, and sugar in a heavy saucepan and bring to a rolling boil, stirring occasionally. Remove from heat.

Combine the chopped almonds, fruit glace, and orange zest with the flour mix. Tumble well and stir into the liquids in the saucepan. Drop 1 tablespoonful for each cookie at least 2" apart. Spread the dough out into thin circles and bake for 8–10 minutes or until the edges are lightly browned. Remove while still warm and repeat the greasing and flouring of the cookie sheet before making the next batch of cookies.

If desired, when the cookies are cool, frost the bottoms with either chocolate or Almond Bark melted in a saucepan over very low heat (or over hot water). Each cookie should take a scant teaspoon of frosting. Store the frosted cookies in the refrigerator, covered. Plain cookies may be stored in a closed container without refrigerating. *Makes 2 dozen cookies.*

*Nutrients per cookie: Calories 90, Fat 5g, Cholesterol 5mg,
Sodium 35mg, Carbohydrates 11g, Protein 1g.*

Walnut-Caramel Bars

With a thick topping of walnuts in a base of caramel, these cookies just beg to be eaten.

CRUST:
½ cup (1 stick) margarine or butter
½ cup brown sugar
1 egg yolk
1 cup rice flour
½ cup soy flour

TOPPING:
1 cup brown sugar
½ cup (1 stick) margarine or butter
¼ cup honey
½ cup cream or nondairy creamer
4 cups chopped walnuts

Preheat oven to 350°. Line the bottom of an oblong 9" × 13" pan with foil, extending up the short sides to make a handle for removing. Grease this foil lightly and extend greasing up the edges of the pan.

In the bowl of your mixer, beat the margarine, brown sugar, and egg yolk until fluffy. Turn mixer to low and beat in the flour. Press this onto the pan bottom. Bake for 15 minutes or until golden.

For the topping, in a medium saucepan heat the brown sugar, margarine, and honey until the margarine melts. Bring to a boil and boil for 3 minutes. Remove from the heat and add the cream and nuts. Pour over the crust and bake for 24 minutes.

Cool slightly before cutting around the edges and lifting the foil to a cutting board. Let cool completely before cutting into 1¼" × 2" bars. *Makes 3 dozen bars.*

*Nutrients per bar: Calories 200, Fat 14g, Cholesterol 25mg,
Sodium 55mg, Carbohydrates 17g, Protein 4g.*

Zucchini Bars

This cakelike bar with drizzled icing is a good keeper and fancy enough for any party.

DOUGH:

1¾ cups Four Flour Bean Mix

1 (scant) teaspoon xanthan gum

¾ cup (1½ sticks) margarine or butter

½ cup white sugar

½ cup brown sugar

1 teaspoon baking soda

2 eggs

1 teaspoon vanilla

2 cups grated zucchini

1 cup flaked coconut

¾ cup chopped pecans

ICING:

1 tablespoon margarine or butter

1 cup confectioners' sugar

2–3 tablespoons orange juice

Preheat oven to 350°. Grease a 15" × 10" jelly roll pan.

In a medium bowl, whisk together the flour mix and xanthan gum. Set aside.

In the bowl of your mixer, beat the margarine for about 30 seconds. Add the two sugars and baking soda. Beat until fluffy. Add the eggs one at a time, beating after each addition. Beat in the vanilla until combined. Add the dry ingredients to blend. With a spoon, stir in the zucchini, coconut, and pecans.

Spoon the mixture into the prepared pan and spread to smooth. Bake for 25–30 minutes or until the top springs back when touched lightly and the dough starts to shrink from the pan edges. Cool in the pan and cut into thirty 2" × 1½" bars.

For the icing, blend the margarine into the confectioners' sugar and add enough of the orange juice to make an icing soft enough to drizzle on the bars. Place in a plastic bag with ⅛" diagonal cut across 1 bottom corner. Squeeze the icing in a zigzag pattern across the bars while still in the pan. Remove the bars from pan and store in a closed plastic container for up to several days, or freeze for later use. *Makes 30 bars.*

*Nutrients per bar: Calories 150, Fat 8g, Cholesterol 15mg,
Sodium 85mg, Carbohydrates 18g, Protein 2g.*

Fruit-Filled Biscotti

These twice-baked cookies are full of candied fruit and nuts. Make them for your Christmas tray and wait for the raves. If desired, add ½ teaspoon finely chopped anise seeds for a true Italian flavor.

1½ cups GF Mix

½ cup sweet rice flour

1 scant teaspoon xanthan gum

½ teaspoon salt

1 teaspoon baking powder

½ cup (1 stick) butter or
  margarine

1½ cups sugar

2 teaspoons grated lemon peel

2 teaspoons vanilla

½ teaspoon anise seed, chopped
  (optional)

4 eggs

1 cup sliced almonds

½ cup red candied cherries,
  chopped

½ cup candied pineapple, chopped

½ cup dried cranberries, chopped

½ cup shelled pistachios, chopped

⅓ cup candied orange peel, chopped

Preheat oven to 350°. Grease 2 baking sheets.

In a medium bowl, whisk together the flour mix, sweet rice flour, xanthan gum, salt, and baking powder. Set aside.

In the bowl of your mixer, beat the butter until creamy. Add the sugar, lemon peel, vanilla, and anise seed (if used). Beat until light and fluffy. Beat in the eggs, one at a time, until well blended. Beat in the dry ingredients and stir in the candied fruit and nuts. Divide the batter into 3 parts, spooning each part in a strip about 2" wide down the length of the baking sheets, using one sheet for 2 strips and putting 1 on the other. Bake for 25–30 minutes or until slightly brown and a tester comes out clean.

Reduce temperature to 325°. Let cookie strips cool for 10 minutes before slicing at an angle into strips ½"–¾" wide. Arrange on sheets with cut side down. Bake for 20 minutes, turning the cookies after 10 minutes. *Makes 6½ dozen cookies.*

*Nutrients per cookie: Calories 65, Fat 2½g, Cholesterol 14mg,
Sodium 32mg, Carbohydrates 9g, Protein 1g.*

I did not repeat any of the cookie recipes from former books, although I have revised and perfected a few for this book, usually using one of the new flour mixes. But if you had a favorite from another book in this series, you can check this list to find it. See page 92 for book title abbreviations.

COOKIES	BASE	BOOK	PAGE
Almond Dollars	no flour	More	131
Almond-Orange Biscotti	rice	More	137
Almond-Rice Cookies	rice	More	136
Apricot Bars	rice	F&H	144
Butterscotch Bites	rice/soy	GFG	50
Butterscotch Brownies	rice/soy	GFG	54
Butterscotch Chip Dreams	soy	GFG	50
Carrot Raisin Drop Cookies	rice	GFG	53
Chewy Fruit Bars	rice/soy	GFG	58
Chinese Gingers	rice	More	136
Chocolate Cherry Chews	bean or soy	F&H	151
Chocolate Surprise Rounds	rice	More	140
Christmas Fruit Mounds	rice	More	128
Chunky Chocolate Squares	rice/soy	GFG	55
Coconut Macaroons	no flour	GFG	52
Crunchy Chocolate Drops	rice	F&H	149
Date Roll-ups	rice	GFG	63
Crescent Crisps	rice/soy	More	141
Fig Bars	rice/soy	GFG	57
Forgotten Dreams	no flour	GFG	51
Frosted Fudge Squares	rice/soy	F&H	142
Fruitcake Bars	cookie crumbs	F&H	146
Ginger Almond Sticks	rice	GFG	62
Gingersnaps	rice	GFG	58
Granola Cookies	rice/soy	More	130
Hawaiian Fruit Drops	rice	F&H	150

Hello Dollys	cookie crumbs	GFG	56
Jam-Filled Crunchies	rice/soy	GFG	61
Lebkuchen	rice	More	139
Mediterranean Fruit Bars	rice	More	134
Mocha-Rum Biscotti	rice	F&H	154
Mock Oatmeal Cookies with Fruit and Spice	rice	F&H	147
No-Bake Peanut Butter Bars	rice	GFG	54
Nutty Pumpkin Treats	rice/soy	More	129
Oatmeal Cookies (Mock)	rice	More	127
Old-Fashioned Sugar Cookies	potato	GFG	59
Orange Slice Bars	rice/soy	GFG	56
Paradise Drops	rice/soy	More	126
Peanut Butter Drops	no flour	GFG	51
Peanut Toffee Bars	cookie crumbs	F&H	141
Pecan Bites	no flour	GFG	52
Pecan Pie Squares	rice	F&H	143
Pralines	rice/soy	GFG	60
Refrigerator Roll	rice/soy	GFG	60
Regency Bars	rice	More	132
Rum Balls	cookie crumbs	More	135
Sesame Dollars	no flour	More	131
Shortbread	cornstarch	More	133
Sugar Cookies II	potato, corn, tapioca	F&H	155
Tasters' Choice Peanut Butter Cookies	bean	F&H	148
Vanilla Wafers	rice/soy	F&H	152
Velvet Brownies	rice	F&H	140
White Chocolate and Macadamia Nut Biscotti	rice	F&H	153

Cheesecakes

Cheesecakes

Tiramisu

See Also

While cheesecakes may seem one of the most glamorous of desserts, they can be one of the easiest to make. Since they can be made a day ahead, they also save time for the cook on party day. So why do you hesitate?

If it's calories that bother you, look at some of the low-calorie ones in this chapter. If it's worry over the crust, check out the many crusts. Some of them can be as simple as crushed cookie crumbs patted into the pan. If it's dairy that stops you, I created one that is dairy free, egg free, and cholesterol free for you.

These cover a wide range from a simple crustless cheesecake to tiramisu, that cake-and-cheesecake combination now appearing on almost every dessert board or cart.

You may be imagining that heavy and very rich New York cheesecake, but cheese-cakes have taken on new appearances and tastes. Try one of the following for your next special dinner or party.

If you remember a favorite from another book, I've listed those at the end of the chapter to save you from having to thumb through the other volumes.

Key Lime Cheesecake

A rich-tasting cheesecake with a flavor between lemon pie and New York cheesecake. This takes any kind of crust but I've suggested here a cookie crumb crust. I've given a family-sized recipe and a 16-serving recipe suitable for a party.

Note: Key lime juice is available in most grocery stores. If unavailable, use regular lime juice.

9" pie tin

CRUST:
2 cups GF cookie crumbs
¼ cup (½ stick) butter or margarine, melted
¼ cup finely chopped pecans

FILLING:
½ cup Key lime juice (see note)
2 tablespoons cold water

1 envelope unflavored gelatin
¾ cup sugar
3 small eggs, slightly beaten
1 teaspoon fresh lime zest
¼ cup (½ stick) butter or margarine
One 8-ounce package cream cheese
¼ cup whipping cream, whipped, or ½ cup nondairy whipped topping

10" springform pan

CRUST:
3 cups GF cookie crumbs
⅓ cup butter or margarine, melted
⅓ cup finely chopped pecans

FILLING:
1 cup Key lime juice
¼ cup cold water
2 envelopes unflavored gelatin

1½ cups sugar
5 large eggs, slightly beaten
2 teaspoons fresh lime zest
½ cup (1 stick) butter or margarine
Two 8-ounce packages cream cheese
½ cup whipping cream, whipped, or 1 cup nondairy whipped topping

In a small bowl (or plastic bag) mix together the cookie crumbs, melted butter, and pecans. Pat into the bottom and up the sides of the chosen pan.

For the filling, place the lime juice and water in a saucepan and sprinkle on the gelatin. Let stand for about 5 minutes to soften. Add the sugar, beaten eggs, and zest, and cook over medium-high heat for about 7 minutes or until the liquid reaches a temperature of 160° and is thickened (do not boil). Remove from heat.

Beat the butter and cream cheese in a large bowl. Slowly beat in the cooked lime mixture. Refrigerate until the mixture forms a slight mounding when dropped from a spoon. Fold in the whipped cream or topping and pour into the prepared shell. Refrigerate until firm or at least 3 hours. Keep refrigerated until serving. Garnish with whipped cream and thin slices of lime, if desired. *Small recipe serves 6–8. Large recipe serves 14–16.*

Nutrients per serving: Calories 450, Fat 32g, Cholesterol 150mg, Sodium 400mg, Carbohydrates 37g, Protein 6g.

*T*o avoid lumps always allow cream cheese to come to room temperature before processing into cheesecake batter.

Party Cheesecake

This very special cheesecake, with its dramatic swirl of lemon curd and sour cream topping, had my guests begging for the recipe. See pages 314 and 315 for making your own lemon curd if you can't find a gluten-free jar at the market.

CRUST:

1 cup GF cookie or graham cracker crumbs

¾ cup pecans or walnuts, toasted

3 tablespoons margarine or butter, melted

2 teaspoons fresh grated lemon zest

FILLING:

Two 8-ounce packages light cream cheese, softened

½ cup sugar

½ tablespoon frozen lemonade concentrate

1 tablespoon fresh lemon zest

¾ cup sour cream or nondairy substitute

2 eggs

TOPPING:

1 cup sour cream or nondairy substitute

One 10-ounce jar GF lemon curd

½ cup nondairy whipped topping (optional)

Preheat oven to 350°.

In the bowl of a food processor, grind the crumbs until fine; add the toasted nuts and process slightly until coarsely chopped. Add the margarine and lemon zest and process just until the crumbs are moist. Press these onto the bottom of a 9" springform pan. Bake for 10 minutes.

For the filling, with a handheld mixer, beat the cream cheese, sugar, lemonade concentrate, and lemon zest until smooth. Beat in the ¾ cup sour cream. Add the eggs, one at a time, beating only until blended. Pour the filling over the crust and bake for 50 minutes. Cool for 5 minutes before topping.

For the topping, beat the 1 cup sour cream in one bowl until smooth; beat the lemon curd in another bowl until smooth. Spoon onto the cheesecake in alternating dollops. When the cake is covered, use a knife tip to swirl these for a marbled look.

Using a sharp knife, cut around the sides and remove the outer ring of the springform pan. Frost the sides of the cake with the whipped topping if desired. Chill for 6 hours or overnight. *Makes 12 servings.*

Nutrients per serving: Calories 580, Fat 34g, Cholesterol 120mg, Sodium 620mg, Carbohydrates 57g, Protein 12g.

Macadamia-Pineapple Cheesecake 350°

If cheesecakes top the dessert chart, this one tops the cheesecake list. It's still full of calories but I've lowered the cholesterol by using tofu and low-fat cream cheese.

Note: *To toast the macadamia nuts, spread them in a shallow pan and place in 350° oven for 8–10 minutes. Watch carefully to be sure they don't burn.*

CRUST:
1½ cups crushed GF cookie
   crumbs
½ cup flake coconut
½ cup finely chopped macadamia
   nuts, toasted (see note)
⅓ cup (5½ tablespoons) margarine
   or butter, melted

FILLING:
16 ounces silken tofu, drained
1 tablespoon cornstarch

One 8-ounce package light cream
   cheese
1 cup sugar
2 teaspoons pineapple or vanilla
   flavoring
1 teaspoon lemon juice
3 eggs, slightly beaten
One 8-ounce can crushed pineapple, drained
⅓ cup finely chopped macadamia
   nuts, toasted (see note)

Preheat oven to 350°.

Combine the cookie crumbs, coconut, nuts, and margarine, and press into the bottom and slightly up the sides of a 9" springform pan. Set aside.

For the filling, in a large mixing bowl, beat together the tofu, cornstarch, and cream cheese until smooth. Add the sugar, beating on medium until well combined. Beat in the flavoring, lemon juice, and eggs on low, just until combined. Stir in the pineapple and nuts.

Pour the filling into the prepared crust and bake for 45–50 minutes or until the center appears nearly set when shaken. Remove from the oven and cool for 15 minutes before loosening around the crust and removing the ring of the pan. Cool for another hour and then place in the refrigerator and chill for approximately 4 hours. This can be served plain or topped with slices of star fruit or kiwi. *Makes 12 servings.*

Nutrients per serving: Calories 340, Fat 22g, Cholesterol 65mg,
Sodium 310mg, Carbohydrates 31g, Protein 8g.

*N*ever substitute the "tub" or soft cream cheese for that sold in blocks for a cheesecake recipe unless the recipe suggests this exchange.

Ginger-Ricotta Cheesecake

My tasters said, "Keep this." The unusual flavor adds a nip to the usual bland but rich taste. Using low-fat ricotta cheese cuts the calories.

CRUST AND TOPPING:
¾ cup GF Mix
½ teaspoon xanthan gum
⅓ cup brown sugar
3 tablespoons melted margarine
¼ teaspoon salt
2 tablespoons almond meal
½ cup minced candied ginger, divided

FILLING:
One 15-ounce carton ricotta cheese
4 egg whites
2 tablespoons lemon juice
One 8-ounce package low-fat cream cheese
1 cup sugar
1 teaspoon grated lemon peel
2 kiwis, peeled and thinly sliced for decorating

Preheat oven to 350°. Grease an 8" springform pan.

Combine the flour mix, xanthan gum, brown sugar, margarine, salt, almond meal, and ¼ cup of the minced ginger. Press into the prepared pan and bake for 10 minutes.

Meanwhile, in the bowl of your food processor, whirl the ricotta cheese, egg whites, lemon juice, and cream cheese until smooth. Add the sugar and lemon peel and mix until blended. Pour into the baked shell and return to the oven for 50–55 minutes or until the center barely jiggles when shaken. Remove from the oven and sprinkle the reserved ginger on the hot top.

Refrigerate for at least 2 hours before serving (may be refrigerated for up to 2 days if wrapped in plastic wrap). If desired, place the sliced kiwis in an overlapping ring around the top edge just before serving. *Makes 10 servings.*

Nutrients per serving: Calories 320, Fat 14g, Cholesterol 35mg, Sodium 330mg, Carbohydrates 40g, Protein 10g.

No-Bake Chiffon Cheesecake
(Cholesterol Free, Egg Free, Lactose Free)

350°

Delicate and light, this cheesecake, topped with fresh berries or a canned pie filling, will please those watching their cholesterol count.

CRUST:
1 cup GF cookie crumbs
2½ tablespoons margarine, melted
2 tablespoons finely chopped
  pecans or walnuts

FILLING:
1 cup nondairy milk substitute

4 teaspoons (2 packets) unflavored
  gelatin
⅞ cup sugar
1 tablespoon vanilla
2 cups nondairy sour cream
  substitute
1 cup tofu (silken or soft), drained
1 tablespoon lemon zest

Preheat oven to 350°.

Place the cookie crumbs in a plastic bag. Add the melted margarine and nuts. Knead a bit until all the crumbs are moist. Pour into an 8" springform pan and pat even. Bake for 10–12 minutes.

For the filling, place the milk substitute in a small saucepan and sprinkle the gelatin on top. Heat over low heat until the gelatin is dissolved.

In the bowl of your mixer, place the sugar, vanilla, sour cream substitute, tofu, and lemon zest. Beat until well blended and smooth. Add the milk and gelatin and beat until incorporated. Pour gently into the prepared crust and refrigerate until set (about 3 hours). Serve topped with fresh crushed berries or one of the gluten-free berry pie fillings. *Makes 6 servings.*

*Nutrients per serving: Calories 440, Fat 26g, Cholesterol 0mg,
Sodium 260mg, Carbohydrates 47g, Protein 7g.*

Coffee and Cream Cheesecake

350°–325°

Cheesecake without a zillion calories? Yes, it's possible, by using nonfat or low-fat yogurt and cream cheese and by cutting the egg yolks. You still retain the flavor. Cut fat even more by using the Low-Fat Crumb Crust.

1½ cups nonfat plain yogurt
1 cup recipe of Low-Fat Crumb
    Crust (page 246)
1 tablespoon instant espresso
    powder
¼ cup hot water
One 8-ounce package nonfat
    cream cheese

One 8-ounce package ⅓-reduced-
    fat cream cheese
¾ cup sugar
2 eggs plus 3 egg whites
¼ cup GF Mix
1 teaspoon vanilla

Drain the yogurt in a yogurt filter (or strainer lined with a coffee filter) over a bowl deep enough to keep the filter at least ½" from the bottom. Let stand for 30 minutes.

Heat oven to 350°. Spray a 9" springform pan with vegetable cooking spray. Wrap the bottom and 1½" up the sides with foil. Pat the crumb mix over the bottom of pan. Bake for 8 minutes. After removing, reduce oven to 325°.

Dissolve the espresso powder in the hot water. Beat the cream cheeses on medium until smooth. Beat in the sugar. Add the eggs and whites, one at a time, beating until just blended. Add the yogurt, espresso, flour mix, and vanilla and beat again until smooth. Pour into prepared pan.

Place the pan in a large shallow dish and fill around it with hot water to 1" depth. Bake for 55–60 minutes or until the center is just set. Cool in the water bath and remove to refrigerator for 4 hours or overnight. Remove the sides of the pan. Garnish with chocolate curls if desired. *Makes 12 servings.*

*Nutrients per serving: Calories 200, Fat 9g, Cholesterol 65mg,
Sodium 340mg, Carbohydrates 21g, Protein 8g.*

Almost Fat-free Cheesecake

300°

Unbelievable! A wonderfully tasty cheesecake using fat-free cream cheese and fat-free sweetened condensed milk. If you want a bit more flavor (and don't mind the fat and calories), add 1 tablespoon ground almond meal or finely chopped pecans or macadamia nuts to the crumb crust.

¼ cup GF cookie crumbs or dry
   bread crumbs sweetened with
   1 tablespoon sugar
Two 8-ounce packages fat-free
   cream cheese
One 10-ounce can fat-free
   sweetened condensed skimmed
   milk

4 egg whites
1 egg
⅓ cup lemon juice
1 teaspoon vanilla
¼ cup GF Mix
Assorted fruit for topping if desired
   (strawberries, blueberries, kiwis,
   etc.)

Preheat oven to 300°. Spray an 8" springform pan with cooking spray and sprinkle the crumbs on the bottom of the prepared pan.

In the bowl of your mixer, beat the cream cheese until fluffy. Gradually beat in the sweetened condensed milk. Add the egg whites and the egg, beating until well incorporated. Add the lemon juice and vanilla and sprinkle the flour mix into the bowl. Beat on low until well blended. Pour into the crumb-lined pan and bake for 45–50 minutes or until the center is set.

Cool and chill to serve with fruit topping. *Makes 10–12 servings.*

Nutrients per serving: Calories 180, Fat 3g, Cholesterol 35mg,
Sodium 390mg, Carbohydrates 25g, Protein 13g.

> *W*hen making cheesecakes, remember that springform pans can leak, so it's wise to wrap the bottom in foil before placing in oven.

Peanut Butter Cheesecake 325°

A rich-tasting cheesecake that can be made with only the crust baked. This can be topped easily with a scattering of nuts or finished off with a rich chocolate topping that makes it look like a dessert from the finest bakery.

CRUST:

6 tablespoons (¾ stick) margarine
  or butter
2 cups GF chocolate cookie crumbs
⅓ cup sugar
1 teaspoon cinnamon

FILLING:

1½ cups creamy peanut butter
Two 8-ounce packages ⅓-fat-
  reduced cream cheese
2 cups confectioners' sugar
2 tablespoons vanilla

2 cups whipping cream, whipped,
  or 16 ounces nondairy whipped
  topping

TOPPING:

½ cup whipping cream
¼ cup sugar
1 tablespoon instant espresso
  powder
6 ounces semisweet chocolate,
  chopped
1 teaspoon vanilla
¼ cup chopped walnuts

Preheat oven to 325°. Lightly butter a 10" springform pan.

Melt the margarine and combine with the cookie crumbs, sugar, and cinnamon in a plastic bag. Pour into the prepared pan and press onto the bottom and up the sides. Bake for about 15 minutes or until the crust darkens slightly. Cool.

For the filling, blend the peanut butter and cream cheese in the bowl of your mixer. Add the confectioners' sugar and vanilla and beat until smooth. In another bowl, beat the 2 cups whipping cream until stiff peaks form (or use the nondairy topping straight from the carton). Fold this into the peanut butter mixture in 4 additions. Spoon the filling into the prepared crust.

For the topping, combine the ½ cup whipping cream, sugar, and espresso powder in a medium saucepan. Stir over medium heat until the powder and sugar dissolve and the mixture comes to a simmer. Remove from the heat and add the chopped chocolate. Whisk until melted and smooth. Cool for about 5 minutes before spreading evenly over the filling. Top with the chopped walnuts. Chill before serving. *Makes 12 servings.*

Nutrients per serving: Calories 610, Fat 40g, Cholesterol 145mg, Sodium 350mg, Carbohydrates 52g, Protein 14g.

---

*I*f your cheesecake is not going to be spread with a meringue or other baked top, place the foil-wrapped springform pan in a large pan with hot water 1" deep. This prevents cracking on top.

Rhubarb-Topped Cheesecake Squares

Simple but spectacular! This is an easy, make-ahead dessert sure to bring raves. The rhubarb topping can be changed to a can of GF pie filling such as cherry, blackberry, or blueberry when rhubarb is not available.

For 8" square cake pan

CRUST:
¾ cup GF Mix
¼ teaspoon xanthan gum
⅓ cup brown sugar
¼ teaspoon salt
3 tablespoons butter or margarine
⅓ cup chopped walnuts
1 scant teaspoon vanilla

FILLING:
One 8-ounce package cream cheese
⅓ cup sugar

6 tablespoons liquid egg substitute
½ teaspoon vanilla

TOPPING:
1½ cups rhubarb (fresh or frozen)
½ cup sugar
2 tablespoons water
1½ teaspoons cornstarch
⅛ teaspoon cinnamon
1 teaspoon raspberry or cherry-
   flavored gelatin

For 9" × 13" oblong pan

CRUST:
1 cup GF Mix
½ teaspoon xanthan gum
½ cup brown sugar
¼ teaspoon salt
4 tablespoons butter or margarine
1 teaspoon vanilla
½ cup chopped walnuts

FILLING:
Two 8-ounce packages cream
   cheese

¾ cup sugar
¾ cup liquid egg substitute
1 teaspoon vanilla

TOPPING:
3 cups rhubarb (fresh or frozen)
1 cup sugar
½ cup water
1 tablespoon cornstarch
¼ teaspoon cinnamon
2 teaspoons raspberry or cherry
   flavored gelatin

Preheat oven to 375°. Grease your chosen pan. Set aside.

In a mixing bowl, whisk together the flour mix, xanthan gum, brown sugar, and salt. Cut in butter until mixture resembles coarse crumbs. Stir in vanilla and walnuts. Press into your pan. Bake for 10 minutes.

While the crust is baking, beat cream cheese and sugar in the same bowl until light and fluffy. Add the egg substitute and vanilla. Pour over the baked crust and return to the oven to bake for 20–25 minutes or until the center is set. Cool.

While the filling is baking, prepare the topping by combining the rhubarb, sugar, water, cornstarch, and cinnamon in a saucepan. Bring to a boil over medium heat and cook, stirring constantly, until the mixture thickens (about 5 minutes). Stir in the gelatin. Cool and pour over the filling. Cover and refrigerate for at least 1 hour. *Small recipe makes 6 servings; large recipe makes 12.*

Nutrients per serving: Calories 230, Fat 11g, Cholesterol 30mg, Sodium 135mg, Carbohydrates 30g, Protein 3g.

Cut cheesecakes with a straight-edged (not serrated) knife dipped in hot water and dried for each cut. Plain dental floss also works as a tool for slicing cheesecake layers horizontally.

Raspberry Cheesecake Squares

A cheesecake with lower calories and the added flavor of fresh fruit, this should appeal to all cheesecake lovers, even those who are watching their cholesterol. Use the canned raspberry pie filling to save time or when raspberries are not in season.

FRUIT FILLING:
2 cups fresh or frozen raspberries
½ cup sugar
2 tablespoons quick tapioca

CRUST:
1½ cups GF Mix
¾ teaspoon xanthan gum
2 tablespoons almond meal or
  finely chopped pecans

3 tablespoons confectioners' sugar
¾ cup (1½ sticks) margarine or
  butter

CHEESECAKE FILLING:
One 8-ounce package reduced-fat
  cream cheese, softened
½ cup sugar
1 egg
1 teaspoon vanilla

Preheat oven to 350°. Lightly spray an 8" × 10" oblong or 9" square baking pan with cooking spray.

In a small saucepan, bring the slightly crushed raspberries, sugar, and tapioca to a boil. Reduce the heat and boil for about 2 minutes. Cool.

For the crust, whisk together the flour mix, xanthan gum, almond meal, and confectioners' sugar in a medium bowl. Cut the margarine into the mix until it resembles coarse crumbs. Press half the mixture into the prepared pan. Bake for 8 minutes.

For the cheesecake filling, beat together the cream cheese and sugar. Add the egg and vanilla. Spread this over the cooked crust. Pour the raspberry filling over the top. Sprinkle remaining crust mixture on top. Bake for 25–30 minutes. Cool and store in the refrigerator. Serve cold. *Makes 12–16 servings.*

Nutrients per serving: Calories 250, Fat 13g, Cholesterol 25mg,
Sodium 220mg, Carbohydrates 30g, Protein 3g.

Tiramisu

This Italian cake and cheesecake combination will make a hit at any party with its combination of coffee-soaked cake and rum in the topping.

CAKE:
¾ cup Four Flour Bean Mix
½ teaspoon xanthan gum
1 teaspoon Egg Replacer
1 rounded teaspoon baking
  powder
¼ teaspoon salt
¼ cup (½ stick) margarine or
  butter
¼ cup milk (not fat-free)
2 eggs
¾ cup sugar
¼ teaspoon vanilla

¾ cup hot strong coffee
1 tablespoon sugar

TOPPING:
12 ounces ⅓-reduced-fat cream
  cheese
⅓ cup confectioners' sugar
2 tablespoons dark rum
1½ cups whipping cream or one
  12-ounce carton nondairy
  whipped topping
½ cup chopped pecans, toasted

Preheat oven to 375°. Grease an 8" × 12" oblong or 10" square cake pan.

In a medium bowl, whisk together the flour mix, xanthan gum, Egg Replacer, baking powder, and salt. Set aside.

In a 2-cup microwaveable bowl, heat the margarine and milk until steaming (about 1 minute on high).

In the bowl of your mixer, beat the eggs on high until light and lemon colored. Gradually beat in the sugar. Beat for an additional 2 minutes. Add the dry ingredients with the hot milk mixture and beat on low until smooth. Pour into the prepared pan and bake for 14–16 minutes or until the cake springs back when touched lightly.

Combine the coffee with the tablespoon of sugar and drizzle over the hot cake. Cool before adding the topping.

For the topping, place the cream cheese in the bowl of your mixer and beat until smooth. Beat in the confectioners' sugar and rum. In another bowl, beat the whipping cream until stiff peaks form. Sugar slightly to taste. Fold this (or the nondairy whipped topping) into the cream cheese mixture. Spread evenly on the cake. Sprinkle with the pecans. *Makes 12–15 servings.*

Nutrients per serving: Calories 280, Fat 19g, Cholesterol 85mg,
Sodium 290mg, Carbohydrates 23g, Protein 5g.

Bette's Favorite Tiramisu

This no-bake dessert may seem to be a bit of trouble to make, but most of it can be done ahead of time and then put together 10–12 hours before serving, as it is best refrigerated overnight. The sponge cake "fingers" can be made 1–5 days ahead, as they should be slightly stale. The microwave custard sauce can be stirred up a day early.

Note: *If mascarpone cheese is unavailable, turn to page 269 for making a substitute.*

SPONGE CAKE:
⅔ cup Featherlight Mix
¼ teaspoon salt
1 teaspoon baking powder
⅔ cup sugar
1 teaspoon dried lemon peel
4 eggs, separated
½ teaspoon cream of tartar

MICROWAVE CUSTARD SAUCE:
¼ cup sugar
3 tablespoons cornstarch
1½ cups milk or nondairy
   substitute

2 egg yolks
1 tablespoon butter
1½ teaspoons vanilla

TO ASSEMBLE:
2 tablespoons rum
½ cup strong black coffee
One 8-ounce container mascarpone
   cheese
1 cup nondairy whipped topping or
   ½ cup heavy cream, whipped
1 square semisweet chocolate,
   grated

Preheat oven to 375°. Grease the bottom and sides of a 10" × 15" jelly roll pan and dust with rice flour.

In a medium bowl, sift together the flour mix, salt, baking powder, and all but 1 tablespoon of the sugar. Whisk in the dried lemon peel.

Separate the eggs, placing the yolks in a small bowl and the whites in the bowl of your mixer. Beat the egg yolks until thick and lemon colored.

Beat the whites until frothy. Add the reserved tablespoon of sugar and the cream of tartar. Continue beating until glossy and stiff. Remove the beaters and gently fold the egg yolks into the whites. Fold in the dry ingredients in 3 parts. Pour the batter into the prepared pan and bake for 15–18 minutes or until the top springs back after being lightly pressed. Cool and cut into 1" × 4" "fingers." Store in a plastic bag in the refrigerator until used.

For the microwave custard sauce, combine the sugar and cornstarch in a 4-cup microwave-safe bowl. Add about ¼ cup milk and stir until the cornstarch is dissolved and smooth. Whisk in the remaining milk. Cover with waxed paper and cook on high for 5–7 minutes, stirring twice, until the mixture comes to a boil and thickens. Whisk smooth.

In a small bowl, beat the egg yolks lightly. Gradually whisk in about ½ cup of the hot mixture. Whisk into the remaining milk mixture and return the custard to microwave and cook, uncovered on high, for 1 minute more. While still hot, blend in the butter and vanilla. Refrigerate until chilled (2 hours) or ready to assemble.

To assemble, line a 9" square cake pan with foil, leaving enough hanging over 2 sides to use as handles to lift the finished cake from the pan. Line the bottom of the pan with enough of the sponge "fingers" to cover completely.

Add the rum to the cold, strong black coffee and sprinkle half over the cake. Stir the marscapone cheese and the whipped topping into the custard and spread half over the cakes. Top with 1 tablespoon of the sweetened chocolate. Repeat by layering on more cake, sprinkling with the rum/coffee liquid, and spreading on the other half of the custard. Top with the remaining chocolate. Cover with plastic and refrigerate for at least 4 hours or overnight. To serve, lift from the pan by the foil "handles" and cut into squares. *Makes 9 servings.*

Nutrients per serving: Calories 390, Fat 21g, Cholesterol 160mg,
Sodium 170mg, Carbohydrates 40g, Protein 6g.

Easy No-Bake Tiramisu

With all the restaurants featuring this cheesecake and cake dessert, I finally figured out the easy way to make one that can be varied in many ways. This uses leftover cake or cookies or purchased GF cookies as the cake base layered with a brandy custard.

Note: I use cherry brandy with chocolate chip or chocolate cookies, and apricot brandy with orange cake, orange shortbread, or vanilla wafers, but they can be vanilla wafers, chocolate chip or any flavored shortbread or even leftover cake.

3 eggs

3 tablespoons sugar

2½ tablespoons fruit-flavored brandy (see note)

12 ounces cream cheese (light is okay)

¾ cup water

½ cup sugar

1 tablespoon espresso powder or orange zest

⅓ cup plus 1 tablespoon whipping cream or nondairy creamer

About eighteen 2½" crisp cookies or enough leftover cake to slice thin, to cover bottom of an 8½" square pan twice

In the top of a double boiler over simmering water, whisk the eggs with the sugar until the thermometer registers 160° (about 10 minutes). Set the double-boiler top in a pan of ice water and continue whisking until cool. Whisk in the brandy.

In a medium bowl, whisk the cream cheese until fluffy; fold in the cooled custard.

In a medium saucepan, bring the water to a simmer. Add the sugar and whisk until it dissolves. Add the espresso powder (chocolate for mocha-flavored tiramisu; the orange zest for citrus flavor) and the cream. Cool.

Dip the cookies or cake in the liquid until saturated and place on bottom of an 8½" square pan to cover. Spread half the cream cheese custard mixture over cookies. Repeat the soaking process with the remaining cookies, in a single layer. Top with the remaining custard mixture. Refrigerate for 2 hours or overnight.

If desired, you may top the mocha-chocolate mix with chocolate curls or a dusting of cocoa powder. For the citrus, place twisted half slices of orange on each piece just before serving. *Makes 9–12 servings.*

Nutrients per serving: Calories 330, Fat 17g, Cholesterol 110mg, Sodium 480mg, Carbohydrates 35g, Protein 7g.

*A*lways use large (not extra large or jumbo) eggs in recipes and allow them to come to room temperature before using.

Chocolate Tiramisu Squares

A chocoholic's dream with three kinds of chocolate! Start with a chocolate cake mix and add the topping of chocolate cheesecake filled with chocolate chips. I used Dietary Specialties' single pouch (13 ounces), but you can use any comparable cake mix. This can be made with reduced-fat cream cheese (not nonfat) and nonfat ricotta cheese to reduce calories.

Note: *This is a good way to use up leftover chocolate cake. Save leftovers and freeze them until you have enough to line the bottom of a 9" × 13" pan ½" deep.*

One GF chocolate cake prepared as directed except for using cherry cola for the liquid (or make a chocolate cake from scratch) (see note)

3 tablespoons kirschwasser (cherry brandy)

One envelope unflavored gelatin

¼ cup cold water

One 15-ounce container ricotta cheese

Two 8-ounce packages cream cheese (light okay)

1½ cups confectioners' sugar

3 tablespoons cocoa powder

¾ cup minichocolate bits

Slice the cake into ½" thick slices and cover the bottom of a 9" × 13" baking pan in a single layer. Sprinkle on the kirschwasser.

Soften the gelatin in cold water in a heatproof dish; place the dish in a pan of simmering water to dissolve the gelatin.

In the bowl of your food processor, place ricotta cheese, cream cheese, confectioners' sugar, and cocoa. Process until smooth. Add the gelatin mixture and process to blend. Pour in the chocolate bits and process just to combine. Spoon onto the cake and spread in an even layer. Cover with plastic wrap and chill for 3 hours or until set. *Makes 15 squares.*

*Nutrients per square: Calories 280, Fat 9g, Cholesterol 25mg,
Sodium 390mg, Carbohydrates 25g, Protein 13g.*

CHEESECAKE RECIPES FROM OTHER BOOKS IN THE
GLUTEN-FREE GOURMET SERIES

Although I did include a few cheesecake recipes at the end of each cake chapter, I never dedicated a whole chapter to this dessert, ever growing in popularity with its redesigned appearance as tiramisu. The following are a few from other books. If you have the revised edition of the *Gluten-Free Gourmet*, the ones listed here will be included in your version, but the page numbers may be different. See page 92 for book title abbreviations.

CHEESECAKES	BASE	BOOK	PAGE
Black Forest Cheesecake	rice	More	116
Cranberry Cheesecake with Pecan Crust	rice or bean	GFG rev	200
Easy Mini-Cheesecakes	rice or bean	GFG rev	110
Fruit Cheesecake Pie	rice or bean	More	154
Light Lemon Cheesecake	rice or bean	F&H	131
Linda's Lighter Cheesecake	rice or bean	GFG	80
Mocha Cheesecake	cereal	F&H	130
No-Bake Pineapple Cheesecake	rice or bean	F&H	132
Orange Cheesecake	rice or bean	GFG	80
Ricotta-Pineapple Cheesecake	rice/corn	More	117
Simply Scrumptious Cheesecake	rice or bean	GFG	79
White Chocolate Cheesecake	rice or bean	More	115

> *T*he true root of the cheesecake goes back to ancient Greece when honey and flour were added to a strained soft cheese and baked.

Coffee Cakes and Tea Breads

Although these may not seem to be true desserts, they are the "sweet" served at the "coffee" hour of morning social or business gatherings. While we may not often have time for afternoon "teas" as such, these make wonderful breads for luncheons or afternoon breaks.

You should find one for any of the above special occasions or, if you prefer, try one for that special Sunday brunch.

Other coffee cakes and breakfast sweets you may remember from other books are listed at the end of this chapter so you won't have to search them out in the books.

Apricot-Filled Coffee Cake

325°

This moist fruit-filled cake is so elegant tasting that you could serve it anytime from a morning coffee dessert to a luncheon or for a midnight snack. Serve it plain or topped with whipped cream or nondairy topping.

FILLING:
One 17-ounce can apricot halves
½ cup chopped walnuts
¼ cup brown sugar

BATTER:
1 cup Four Flour Bean Mix
½ rounded teaspoon xanthan gum
1 teaspoon Egg Replacer (optional)

1 teaspoon baking powder
½ teaspoon baking soda
¼ teaspoon salt
2 eggs
6 tablespoons (¾ stick) butter
  or margarine
⅔ cup sugar
1 teaspoon almond or Vanilla,
  Butter, & Nut flavoring or vanilla

Preheat oven to 325°. Grease a 9" springform pan or cake pan. Set aside.

To prepare the filling, drain the apricots and place cut side down on several layers of paper towels. In a small bowl, combine the walnuts and brown sugar until well blended. Set aside.

For the batter, whisk together the flour mix, xanthan gum, Egg Replacer, baking powder, baking soda, and salt in a mixing bowl. In a smaller bowl, whisk the eggs until foamy and light. Melt the butter and add that plus the sugar and flavoring. Whisk to blend.

Add the liquids to the dry ingredients and stir together until evenly blended. Spoon half the batter into the prepared pan and spread evenly. Place the drained apricots, cut side up, over the batter and sprinkle the walnut-brown sugar mix over the top with the remaining batter. (Don't worry if it doesn't completely cover the filling. It is interesting to have some of it show through the top.)

Bake for 45 minutes or until just beginning to pull away from the sides of the pan. Wait for about 15 minutes before removing the springform ring. If using a cake pan, do not turn out, but serve from the pan. Serve either hot or at room temperature. *Makes 6–8 servings.*

Nutrients per serving: Calories 290, Fat 13g, Cholesterol 75mg, Sodium 310mg, Carbohydrates 41g, Protein 5g.

Streusel-Filled Banana Coffee Cake 350°

Make this tasty, not-too-sweet snacking cake in either a loaf or bundt shape. Either way, your guests (or family) will love it.

For an 8½" × 4½" loaf pan

STREUSEL:

2 tablespoons margarine or butter

½ cup brown sugar

1½ teaspoons cinnamon

¼ teaspoon nutmeg

½ cup chopped walnuts or pecans

CAKE BATTER:

1½ cups Four Flour Bean Mix

¾ teaspoon xanthan gum

1 teaspoon baking powder

½ teaspoon baking soda

½ teaspoon salt

2 tablespoons margarine or butter

½ cup sugar

1 egg plus 1 egg white or ⅓ cup plus 1 tablespoon liquid egg substitute

1 teaspoon orange zest

⅔ cup mashed bananas (2 bananas)

⅓ cup buttermilk

For an 8-cup bundt pan

STREUSEL:

¼ cup (½ stick) margarine or butter

½ cup brown sugar

1½ teaspoons cinnamon

¼ teaspoon nutmeg

½ cup chopped walnuts or pecans

CAKE BATTER:

3 cups Four Flour Bean Mix

1½ teaspoons xanthan gum

2 teaspoons baking powder

1 teaspoon baking soda

½ teaspoon salt

¼ cup (½ stick) margarine or butter

1 cup sugar

3 large eggs or ¾ cup liquid egg substitute

2 teaspoons orange zest

1¼ cups mashed bananas (3–4 bananas)

⅔ cup buttermilk

Preheat oven to 350°. Grease your preferred pan.

For the streusel, melt the margarine. Add the brown sugar, cinnamon, nutmeg, and nuts. Sprinkle bottom of the pan with half the mixture. Save the rest.

For the cake batter, in a medium bowl, whisk together the flour mix, xanthan gum, baking powder, baking soda, and salt. Set aside.

In the bowl of your mixer, cream the margarine and sugar. Add the eggs, one at a time, beating after each addition. Beat in the orange zest and bananas. Add the dry ingredients and buttermilk and stir until well blended. Don't overbeat.

Pour half the batter into the prepared pan; spoon the remaining streusel over the dough evenly. Top with the remaining batter. Bake for about 50 minutes or until a tester comes out clean. Cool slightly and then invert the loaf or bundt pan onto a cake plate. Serve the cake warm or cool. *Loaf pan makes 8 servings; bundt pan makes 14–16 servings.*

Nutrients per serving: Calories 260, Fat 8g, Cholesterol 20g, Sodium 30mg, Carbohydrates 44g, Protein 4g.

Apple-Topped Coffee Cake 350°

With apples on top and in the cake, this moist and not-too-sweet cake should make the coffee hour a wonderful treat to the gluten-free or wheat-eater alike.

2 cups Featherlight Mix or Four Flour Bean Mix

1 teaspoon xanthan gum

2 teaspoons Egg Replacer

½ teaspoon salt

¼ teaspoon cinnamon

¾ cup (1½ sticks) margarine or butter

1 teaspoon lemon zest

1¾ cups plus 1 tablespoon sugar

4 eggs

3 tablespoons sweet white dessert wine

1 cooking apple, peeled, cored, and cut into small bits

2 cooking apples, peeled, cored, and thinly sliced to top batter

Preheat oven to 350°. Grease a 10" springform pan and dust with rice flour.

In a medium bowl, whisk together the flour mix, xanthan gum, Egg Replacer, salt, and cinnamon. Set aside.

In the bowl of your mixer, beat the margarine and lemon zest until fluffy. Gradually add the 1¾ cups sugar, beating until well blended. Add the eggs, one at a time, beating well after each addition. Mix in all but 1 tablespoon of the dry ingredients. Add the wine. Tumble the small bits of apple with remaining flour mix and stir into the batter.

Spoon the batter into the pan and place the sliced apples in concentric circles on top of the cake. Sprinkle with the 1 tablespoon sugar. Bake for about 1 hour 30 minutes or until tester inserted in the center comes out with just a few moist crumbs. To prevent browning too much, cover loosely with foil midway in the baking. Let cool for about 10 minutes before loosening sides of the springform pan after running a knife around the edges. *Makes 8–10 servings.*

Nutrients per serving: Calories 420, Fat 16g, Cholesterol 85g, Sodium 190mg, Carbohydrates 65mg, Protein 5g.

Green Tomato Tea Bread

Absolutely wonderful with a light springy texture and terrific flavor! If you don't have green tomatoes in your garden, just purchase the hardest and greenest you can find at the store. You will need about 2 large ones to chop and puree in a food processor.

⅔ cup raisins

⅔ cup boiling water

3⅓ cups Four Flour Bean Mix

2 teaspoons xanthan gum

2 teaspoons baking soda

1 teaspoon baking powder

2 teaspoons Egg Replacer

1½ teaspoons salt

1 teaspoon cinnamon

½ teaspoon nutmeg

⅔ cup shortening

⅔ cup white sugar

⅓ cup brown sugar

4 eggs

2 cups green tomato puree

⅔ cup walnuts or pecans, chopped

Preheat oven to 350°. Grease two 8½" × 4½" loaf pans and dust lightly with rice flour.

Place the raisins in a small bowl and add boiling water. Let sit until cool.

In a medium bowl, combine the flour mix, xanthan gum, baking soda, baking powder, Egg Replacer, salt, cinnamon, and nutmeg. Set aside.

In a mixing bowl, cream the shortening and the two sugars until light and fluffy. Beat in the eggs; stir in the tomato puree and raisins with their water. Beat well. Add the dry ingredients, 1 cup at a time, beating until smooth after each addition. Stir in the chopped nuts. Spoon the dough into the prepared pans and bake for 65–70 minutes, or until a tester inserted in the center comes out clean. Cool slightly before tipping from pans. Slice when completely cold. *Makes 2 loaves, 10 servings per loaf.*

*Nutrients per serving: Calories 140, Fat 6g, Cholesterol 25mg,
Sodium 200mg, Carbohydrates 21g, Protein 3g.*

Baba au Rhum

For a special brunch try this very exciting tea bread made with yeast, filled with raisins and citron, and soaked with a rum sauce. Babas are often baked in small molds but I tried mine in a bundt pan and had wonderful luck. (It's also much easier to cut and serve.)

BATTER:

3 cups Four Flour Bean Mix or Featherlight Mix, divided

1½ teaspoons xanthan gum

¼ cup sugar

¼ teaspoon salt

1½ tablespoons yeast

2 tablespoons almond meal or NutQuik

½ cup water

½ cup (1 stick) butter or margarine

6 eggs

1 cup (scant) glacé cake mix or candied citron

2 tablespoons raisins

RUM SAUCE:

½ cup sugar

¼ cup water

2 tablespoons lemon juice

2 tablespoons orange juice

2 tablespoons rum

Grease a 10–12-cup bundt pan by spraying with vegetable oil cooking spray.

In a medium bowl, whisk together the flour mix and xanthan gum.

In the bowl of your mixer, combine the sugar, salt, yeast, and ¾ cup of the flour.

In a small saucepan heat the water and butter until very warm (120°–130°); butter does not need to be completely melted. With the mixer on low, beat the liquid into the dry ingredients until just mixed. Beat at medium for 2 minutes. Add the eggs and 1 cup more flour and continue beating for 2 more minutes. Stir in the glacé cake mix and raisins and remaining flour. (Dough should be the texture of cake batter.)

Spoon into prepared pan, cover and let rise in a warm place for 35–40 minutes if using rapid rising yeast, 50–60 minutes for regular yeast or until the dough has doubled in bulk. Bake in a preheated 350° oven for 45 to 50 minutes, covering with foil after 10 minutes. Allow to cool for a few minutes and then turn out onto foil-covered cake plate. Immediately brush with rum sauce.

For the rum sauce, boil the sugar and water in a small saucepan for 2 minutes. Remove from the heat and stir in the lemon juice, orange juice, and rum. Using a pastry brush, brush the hot rum sauce over the hot bread until it will absorb no more. Let cool before cutting. *Makes 16 servings.*

Nutrients per serving: Calories 270, Fat 8g, Cholesterol 95g, Sodium 150mg, Carbohydrates 45mg, Fiber 5g.

*F*or greasing pans, use shortening rather than butter or margarine. If you are avoiding fat, spray with vegetable oil only if the pan is glass or a metal that is not finished with stick-resistant material.

COFFEE CAKE, BREAKFAST SWEETS, AND TEA BREAD RECIPES FROM OTHER
BOOKS IN THE *GLUTEN-FREE GOURMET* SERIES

To save you time searching the index of my other books, I've listed those sweet baked items here. I also refer to *The Gluten-Free Gourmet Bakes Bread* (Bread). See page 92 for other book title abbreviations.

COFFEE CAKES AND TEA BREADS	BASE	BOOK	PAGE
Apple Bundt Coffee Cake	rice	GFG	112
Apple Bundt Coffee Cake	bean	GFG rev	220
Basic Featherlight Sweet Bread	rice	Bread	122
Bear Claws with Fig and Raisin Filling	rice	More	164
Cranberry-Plus Coffee Cake	rice/soy	GFG	111
Cranberry-Plus Coffee Cake	rice or bean	GFG rev	219
Cranberry Swirl Bread	bean	Bread	116
Danish Kringle	rice	More	162
Fruit Danish	rice	More	163

Pies and Pastries

As most canned fruit fillings and many of the packaged ones are already gluten free (always read the ingredient labels), I've only included some extra special pie fillings in this book. I've also added a few tarts and one amazing upside-down cobbler that my testers love.

For your fresh fruit pies just follow your own recipe, but exchange the wheat-based flour used for thickening with tapioca, my GF Mix, or sweet rice flour.

The real problem with pies and our diet will come with the crust, and you'll be happily surprised to find that, if you're a dedicated pie baker and want the taste of the crust from before diagnosis, you can use your old recipes if you substitute the new Featherlight Mix for your old wheat-pastry flour and add xanthan gum. If you don't have a favorite, I've adapted one my aunt taught me: Featherlight Vinegar Pastry (page 242). If you haven't mixed up the Featherlight Mix, this will be a good excuse to do so or to use the old standby from *The Gluten-free Gourmet Cooks Fast and Healthy*: Donna Jo's Dream Pastry, which I repeat in this book (page 243).

For easier bottom crusts, the tastes here range from a low-fat crumb crust to a Nut Crust Supreme.

If you remember pies from other books in this series, I've included a list at the back of this chapter for easy reference.

Date and Walnut Pie

350°

Dates, walnuts, and brandy give an adult flavor twist to pecan pie. The recipe calls for cut-up dates. Because most packaged chopped dates are dusted with wheat flour to keep them separated, it is safer to cut your bits from whole dried dates.

Note: I prefer the Featherlight Vinegar Pastry for this crust (see page 242).

One unbaked pie shell, 9"
1 cup finely cut-up dates
2 tablespoons fruit brandy
⅔ cup brown sugar
2 tablespoons butter, melted

¾ teaspoon nutmeg
½ teaspoon salt
⅔ cup dark corn syrup
3 large eggs, beaten lightly
1¼ cups chopped walnuts

Preheat oven to 350°. Roll pastry dough to fit a 9" pie tin. Set aside.

In a small bowl, stir dates and brandy together. Set aside.

In a medium bowl, blend the brown sugar, butter, nutmeg, and salt. Whisk in the corn syrup and eggs. Add the nuts and the date mixture. Pour the filling into the crust.

Bake for 50–55 minutes or until a knife inserted in the center comes out clean. Cool before serving either plain or topped with whipped cream or nondairy whipped topping. *Makes 8 servings.*

Nutrients per serving: Calories 340, Fat 12g, Cholesterol 90mg, Sodium 220mg, Carbohydrates 56g, Protein 6g.

Chocolate Pecan Pie

350°

This is the pecan pie for true chocoholics. If you desire a sweeter version, use semi-sweet baking chocolate. For this pie, I prefer the Featherlight Vinegar Pastry (page 242) or Donna Jo's Dream Pastry (see page 243).

One unbaked pie shell, 9"
2 ounces unsweetened baking
  chocolate
⅓ cup (5½ tablespoons) margarine
  or butter
3 eggs or ¾ cup liquid egg
  substitute

½ cup sugar
1 cup corn syrup
3 tablespoons dark rum
1 cup coarsely chopped pecans
Whipped cream or nondairy
  whipped topping for garnish

Preheat oven to 350°. Have the crust prepared.

In a microwaveable bowl, melt the chocolate and margarine by microwaving on defrost for 3 minutes. Set aside to cool slightly.

In a medium bowl, beat together the eggs, sugar, corn syrup, and rum. Blend in the cooled chocolate-margarine mix. Place the pecans in the crust and pour the syrup batter gently over them. Bake for 40–50 minutes. The center will not be quite set but will set as it cools. Garnish with whipped cream around the outer edge of the pie, or top each piece with a dollop of the whipped cream or nondairy topping. This is a rich pie. *Makes 6 or 8 servings.*

Nutrients per serving: Calories 440, Fat 26g, Cholesterol 115mg,
Sodium 150mg, Carbohydrates 55g, Protein 5g.

Mock Oatmeal Pie

Rich with caramel flavor, coconut, and soy flakes, this pie should satisfy your sweet tooth. Use either Donna Jo's Dream Pastry (page 243) or the new Featherlight Vinegar Pastry (page 242) for the crust.

Note: Soy flakes are available at many health food stores. If unavailable, replace with crushed sliced almonds.

One unbaked pie shell, 9"
¾ cup sugar
¾ cup textured soy flakes
½ cup coconut flakes

¾ cup dark corn syrup
½ cup (1 stick) butter or
  margarine, melted
2 eggs, well beaten

Preheat oven to 350°.

In a medium bowl, mix together the sugar, soy flakes, coconut flakes, corn syrup, butter, and eggs. Pour into the prepared pie shell and bake for 45–50 minutes or until a knife inserted into the center comes out clean. Cool before serving. *Makes 6–8 servings.*

*Nutrients per serving: Calories 380, Fat 17g, Cholesterol 95mg,
Sodium 200mg, Carbohydrates 53g, Protein 6g.*

*T*o prevent a soggy bottom crust on your pie, be sure your oven is preheated to the correct temperature and cool the pie on a wire rack so the air circulates evenly around the baked pie.

Raisin Butterscotch Pie

350°

A smooth and rich butterscotch pie with the surprise of raisins to add to the taste. With sour cream in the filling and a meringue topping, this pie is extra special.

One baked pie shell, 9"
1 cup brown sugar
6 tablespoons cornstarch
½ teaspoon salt
1½ cups milk or nondairy
   substitute
3 eggs, separated

2 tablespoons butter
2 teaspoons vanilla
1 cup golden raisins
1 cup sour cream or nondairy
   sour cream
¼ teaspoon cream of tartar
6 tablespoons sugar

Preheat oven to 350°.

In a 2-quart saucepan, combine the sugar, cornstarch, and salt. Add the milk gradually; stir until smooth. Place the pan over medium heat and cook, stirring until slightly thickened.

Separate the eggs, placing the yolks in a small bowl and beating slightly with a fork. Place the whites in the bowl of your mixer.

Spoon some of the hot mixture from the pan into the egg yolks. Blend the yolks into the pan and continue cooking, stirring constantly for 5 minutes, until very thick. Remove from the heat. Add the butter, vanilla, and raisins. Stir in the sour cream and spoon into the baked pie shell.

Add the cream of tartar to the egg whites in the mixing bowl and beat until soft peaks form. With the mixer still going, gradually add the sugar. Spoon onto the top of the pie filling, making sure the meringue touches the crust all around. Bake for 10 minutes or until lightly browned. Cool before cutting and serving. *Makes 6–8 servings.*

*Nutrients per serving: Calories 350, Fat 12g,
Cholesterol 120mg, Sodium 260mg, Carbohydrates 57g, Protein 6g.*

Mud Pie

350°

You'll never feel deprived as a celiac when this pie is on the menu, for it's rich and satisfying. And for the cook, it's easy to make.

Pair this with the new Featherlight Vinegar Pastry (page 242).

One unbaked pie shell, 9"
½ cup (1 stick) butter, cut up
2 ounces unsweetened chocolate
1 ounce semisweet chocolate
1⅓ cups sugar
3 eggs

3 tablespoons corn syrup
2 tablespoons sour cream
1 teaspoon almond flavoring
Whipped cream or nondairy
   whipped topping

In a microwaveable bowl, melt the butter and the two chocolates on high (1–1½ minutes). Add the sugar, eggs, corn syrup, sour cream, and almond flavoring. Whisk until smooth. Pour the filling into the crust and bake for 50–55 minutes or until the center is set. Cool and garnish by piping the whipped cream around the edge where the crust and filling meet. *Makes 6–8 servings.*

*Nutrients per serving: Calories 400, Fat 22g, Cholesterol 130mg,
Sodium 170mg, Carbohydrates 50g, Protein 4g.*

---

*M*argarine can be used as a substitute for butter only if it contains 80 percent or more vegetable oil or fat. Many products that contain more liquid (such as soft or light margarines) can make your baked product soggy or hard.

Chocolate Tofu Pie

Quick and easy—and utterly delicious! No one will guess this smooth pie is both lactose and cholesterol free or that tofu is one of the main ingredients.

One baked pie shell, 9"
8 ounces medium tofu, squeezed
  dry between paper towels
2 squares semisweet chocolate,
  melted and cooled

⅓ cup sugar
1½ cups nondairy whipped
  topping

In the bowl of your mixer, combine the tofu, melted chocolate, and sugar. Beat until smooth. Fold in the whipped topping and spoon into your prepared crust. Cover loosely and chill for several hours or overnight. *Makes 8 servings.*

Nutrients per serving: Calories 130, Fat 7g, Cholesterol 0mg,
Sodium 15mg, Carbohydrates 16g, Protein 3g.

*F*or easy handling of our tender pie crusts, roll the dough on a piece of plastic wrap dusted with sweet rice flour and use the wrap to reverse the dough into the pie pan.

Glenda's Snickers Pie

This recipe, given to me by another celiac, really does taste like the Snickers bar. It's easy to make with a cookie crumb crust and can be frozen so it can be made ahead of that party.

CRUST:
1¾ cups GF cookie crumbs
¼ cup finely chopped pecans
¼ cup margarine or butter, melted

FILLING:
2 cups vanilla ice cream
¼ cup chunky-style peanut butter
One 3-ounce package instant chocolate pudding
One 8-ounce carton nondairy whipped topping

Prepare the crust with chocolate crumbs or add 1 tablespoon cocoa to other kinds of crumbs. Place the crumbs and pecans in a plastic bag. Pour in the margarine and blend. Press into the bottom and up the sides of a deep 9" pie tin.

For the filling, soften the ice cream and mix well with the peanut butter. Add the powdered pudding. Fold in the whipped topping and spoon into the crust. Cover with plastic wrap and freeze. To serve, remove from the freezer a few minutes ahead of time. Enjoy! *Makes 8 servings.*

Nutrients per serving: Calories 290, Fat 21g, Cholesterol 30mg, Sodium 240mg, Carbohydrates 26g, Protein 2g.

Orange Pie

Orange juice, zest, and 1 chopped orange make this a different and delightful taste treat. Add the coconut and whipped cream or nondairy topping and you have an easy dessert for any guests.

One GF baked pie shell, 9"
3 egg yolks
½ cup sugar
1 cup orange juice, divided
1 envelope unflavored gelatin
2 tablespoons grated orange rind
⅛ teaspoon salt

½ cup flaked coconut
1 orange, peeled and cubed, or one
   8-ounce can mandarin orange
   sections, chopped
1 cup whipping cream, whipped
   (plus sugar for sweetening) or 2
   cups nondairy whipped topping

In a medium saucepan, beat the yolks slightly. Add the sugar and ½ cup orange juice. Cook over low heat, stirring constantly, until the mixture reaches 160°. Remove from the heat.

Sprinkle the gelatin over the remaining ½ cup orange juice and grated rind. Add to the cooked egg mixture. Chill until the consistency of unbeaten egg white. Add the salt, coconut, and citrus sections. Fold in the whipped topping or whipped cream. Pour into the prepared pie shell. Chill. When set, this may be decorated with a piping of whipped topping or cream around the crust edge, or serve the slices with a twist of fresh orange and a sprig of mint. *Makes 8 servings.*

Nutrients per serving using whipping cream: Calories 320, Fat 23g, Cholesterol 150mg, Sodium 60mg, Carbohydrates 27g, Protein 4g.

Nutrients per serving using nondairy whipped topping: Calories 260, Fat 13g, Cholesterol 80mg, Sodium 200mg, Carbohydrates 53g, Protein 3g.

Pineapple Meringue Pie

Pineapple lovers beware! This pie with its mile-high meringue could become addictive. The recipe calls for 5 eggs; you can cut some cholesterol by using 4.

One baked pie shell, 9"
1⅓ cups sugar, divided
⅓ cup cornstarch
1⅔ cups canned pineapple juice

5 eggs, separated
2 tablespoons margarine or butter
½ teaspoon salt
½ teaspoon cream of tartar

Preheat oven to 350°.

In a large saucepan, blend ¾ cup sugar, the cornstarch, and the pineapple juice. Cook over medium heat, stirring constantly, until the mixture begins to thicken. Reduce heat to low and continue cooking until clear and very thick (about 10 minutes).

Beat the egg yolks and blend a little of the hot mixture into them. Add this to the pineapple mixture on the stove and cook for 2 minutes longer. Remove from the heat and beat in the margarine.

In the bowl of your mixer, place the egg whites, salt, and cream of tartar. Beat until soft peaks form. Gradually beat in the remaining sugar until stiff peaks form. Fold half the meringue into the pineapple custard. Pour into the pie shell. Top with the remaining meringue. Bake for about 15 minutes or until lightly browned. Cool before serving. *Makes 6–8 servings.*

Nutrients per serving (includes cereal crust): Calories 360, Fat 12g, Cholesterol 160mg, Sodium 350mg, Carbohydrates 58g, Protein 6g.

> *To* prevent the meringue from sticking to your knife when cutting a pie, dip your knife in water between cuts. Don't dry it.

Rhubarb Pie

375°–325°

A double-crusted pie sure to win raves. Combine this with Donna Jo's Dream Pastry (page 243) or the new Featherlight Vinegar Pastry (page 242) and you'll have everyone asking for the recipe.

Pastry for a 2-crust pie
2½ cups fresh or frozen sliced
  rhubarb
3 eggs
1¼ cups sugar, divided

¼ cup GF Mix
¼ cup margarine or butter
¼ teaspoon salt
2 teaspoons raspberry-flavored
  gelatin

Preheat oven to 375°. Prepare pastry and have the rhubarb cut or thawed.

Separate the eggs, placing the whites in medium bowl and the yolks in a large mixing bowl. Add ¼ cup sugar to the whites and beat with a handheld mixer until stiff. Set aside.

With the beater blend the yolks, remaining sugar, flour mix, margarine, salt, and gelatin. Fold in the rhubarb, then the meringue. Pour into the prepared pastry shell and top with a crust. Cut decorative holes on top for steam. Bake for 15 minutes at 375°; reduce heat to 325° and cook for 30 minutes longer. Cool. Serve at room temperature or chilled, as desired. *Makes 6 servings.*

Nutrients per serving: Calories 300, Fat 10g, Cholesterol 125mg,
Sodium 210mg, Carbohydrates 49g, Protein 5g.

---

*A*lways remember to vent a two-crust pie with several cuts in the top to allow the steam to escape.

Peach Praline Pie

425°

This fruit pie with the unusual praline-flavored topping is sure to be a hit with family and guests. And it's easy to make with the peaches given here or other fruit such as apricots, apples, or pears.

FILLING:

One unbaked GF pastry crust, 9"

3 cups sliced fresh, frozen, or canned peaches

¾ cup sugar (lower to ⅔ cup for canned fruit)

1½ tablespoons quick-cooking tapioca

1 teaspoon lemon juice

PRALINE TOPPING:

¼ cup sorghum flour (or rice flour)

3 tablespoons butter or margarine

½ cup brown sugar

½ cup pecans, chopped

Preheat oven to 425°.

In a large bowl, combine the peaches, sugar, tapioca, and lemon juice. Set aside.

For the topping, in a small bowl, combine the sorghum flour, butter, and brown sugar until the crumbs are the size of peas. Add the nuts.

Scatter one third of the topping onto the unbaked pie shell. Fill with the fruit mixture and sprinkle on the remaining topping. Bake for 45 minutes. Serve warm or at room temperature. *Makes 6 servings.*

Nutrients per serving: Calories 360, Fat 12g, Cholesterol 15mg,
Sodium 80mg, Carbohydrates 65g, Protein 2g.

Sour Cream–Pear Pie

A fruit pie fit for any company! This tasty pie needs only a bottom crust; the top is drizzled on and baked at the last half of the baking period. This filling blends well with the new Featherlight Vinegar Pastry (page 242).

One unbaked pie shell, 9"

FILLING:
2 cups peeled, cored, and diced
   pears (2 large pears)
½ cup sugar
1 egg, beaten
½ tablespoon cornstarch
1 cup sour cream or nondairy
   substitute

1 teaspoon vanilla
Dash salt

TOPPING:
½ cup sugar
⅓ cup Four Flour Bean Mix or
   GF Mix
3 tablespoons butter or margarine

Preheat oven to 350°.

In a medium bowl, combine the pears, sugar, egg, cornstarch, sour cream, vanilla, and salt. Blend gently. Spoon into the unbaked pie shell.

Bake for 25 minutes. Meanwhile, combine the topping ingredients until well mixed. Sprinkle the topping on the pie and return it to the oven for 30 minutes. *Makes 8 servings.*

Nutrients per serving: Calories 220, Fat 9g, Cholesterol 55mg,
Sodium 160mg, Carbohydrates 34g, Protein 2g.

Pumpkin Chiffon Pie

425°–350°

This pumpkin pie is as light as the name suggests which makes it a fine choice to end any holiday meal. You can use the low-fat version, which I suggest first, or the second version. Both are flavorful.

One deep unbaked pie shell, 9"

One 15-ounce can pumpkin

½ cup liquid egg substitute plus
   2 egg whites or 2 eggs plus 2 egg
   whites

¾ cup sugar

½ teaspoon salt

2 teaspoons pumpkin pie spice

1½ cups nondairy liquid or one
   12-ounce can nonfat (or regular)
   evaporated milk

Whipped cream or nondairy
   whipped topping for garnish

Preheat oven to 425°. Have the crust prepared.

In a large mixing bowl, place the pumpkin, liquid egg substitute (or the 2 whole eggs), sugar, salt, and spice. Whip slightly until the eggs are well mixed. Add the liquid and blend well.

In a metal or glass bowl (not plastic), beat the egg whites until they form soft peaks. Gently fold these into the pie mix. Pour into the prepared crust and bake for 15 minutes. Reduce the temperature to 350° and bake for another 45 minutes or until a knife inserted in the center comes out clean. Cool.

Serve cold with the whipped cream or nondairy whipped topping. *Makes 6–8 servings.*

*Nutrients per serving: Calories 170, Fat 2g, Cholesterol 65mg,
Sodium 270mg, Carbohydrates 33g, Protein 8g.*

Easy Lemon Tart

A lemon soufflé in a crust. This refreshingly light tart is easy to make; just beat the eggs, stir in the rest of the ingredients, and bake. I've even added a simple crust, but you can change it to any crust you prefer.

CRUST:

1½ cups GF cookie or graham cracker crumbs

3 tablespoons margarine or butter

¼ cup ground pecans or macadamia nuts (optional)

FILLING:

2 tablespoons GF Mix

1 cup sugar

4 eggs or 1 cup liquid egg substitute

1 tablespoon lemon zest

6 tablespoons lemon juice

½ cup (1 stick) margarine or butter, melted

½ teaspoon vanilla

½ teaspoon lemon flavoring

Preheat oven to 350°. Lightly grease a deep 9" pie tin or a 10" springform pan. Crush the cookie crumbs. Melt the margarine and stir into the crumbs. Add the nuts (if used). Press this into the prepared pan. Set aside.

For the filling, whisk together the flour mix and sugar. Break the eggs into a medium mixing bowl and add the flour-sugar mixture. Beat until light in color and slightly thickened (about 3 minutes). Stir in the lemon zest, lemon juice, melted butter, vanilla, and lemon flavoring. Pour into the prepared crust and bake for 20–25 minutes or until the filling is set and slightly browned.

Cool before serving, either cold or at room temperature. Refrigerate to keep more than 2 hours. *Makes 6–8 servings.*

Nutrients per serving: Calories 380, Fat 23g, Cholesterol 105mg, Sodium 330mg, Carbohydrates 40g, Protein 4g.

Almond Tart with Rhubarb

A rich almond-flavored dessert that's easy to put together, for the crust is patted into the tart or springform pan while the filling bubbles up over the fruit to create the illusion of a top crust. Use fresh or frozen rhubarb. This may be made the day of serving or 1 day before.

Note: *Try this also with peach or pear slices or plum halves.*

PASTRY:

1⅓ cups Featherlight Mix

¾ teaspoon xanthan gum

¼ cup sugar

½ cup (1 stick) margarine or butter

1 egg yolk

FILLING:

3 cups rhubarb cut into 1" slices

1 cup sugar, divided

¼ cup water

1 cup blanched almonds

6 tablespoons (¾ stick) margarine or butter

2 eggs

¼ teaspoon almond flavoring

Preheat oven to 300° degrees. Grease a 10" springform pan or tart pan with a removable rim.

In the bowl of your food processor (or in mixing bowl), combine the flour mix, xanthan gum, and sugar. Add the margarine and process (or work with fingers) until fine crumbs form. Add the egg yolk and whirl (or mix) until the dough holds together firmly. Form a ball and press the dough over the bottom and up the sides of the prepared pan. Bake for 20 minutes.

Meanwhile, for the filling, place the rhubarb in a 2-quart saucepan. Add 5 tablespoons of the sugar. Pour on the ¼ cup of water and let stand for 10 minutes. Then place on a medium burner and cook until the water boils, gently stirring once (do not break up the rhubarb pieces). Let boil for 2 minutes and remove from the heat.

In the bowl of your food processor, whirl the nuts to a fine powder (be careful not to overprocess to the butter stage). Add the remaining sugar, margarine, eggs, and almond flavoring. Beat until well blended. Pour into the baked crust. Top with the rhubarb pieces by lifting them from the syrup and laying them on the filling either randomly or in a pattern resembling the spokes of a wheel. Press them gently into the filling.

Bake at 350° for approximately 40 minutes. The filling, which will rise around the fruit, will turn golden brown. Cool for about 15 minutes before removing the ring. Serve warm or at room temperature. *Makes 9–12 servings.*

Nutrients per serving: Calories 360, Fat 22g, Cholesterol 100mg, Sodium 170mg, Carbohydrates 40g, Protein 4g.

You may substitute 1 tablespoon of flaxseed plus 2–3 tablespoons of water for 1 egg. You don't have to change the liquid formula.

Gingered Rhubarb Tart

400°

On the farm where I grew up we called rhubarb "the pie plant" and I always looked forward to this first fresh fruit pie of the early spring. A few years ago, I planted my own plants at our summer place. This year my rhubarb is old enough for picking and I adapted this recipe from the Seattle Times *and used my favorite cookie crumb crust to make it easy. A success!*

CRUST:
1½ cups cookie or cake crumbs
¼ cup finely chopped walnuts
3 tablespoons margarine or butter

FILLING:
3¼ cups (1 pound) rhubarb
2 tablespoons water
¾ cup sugar
¼ cup finely chopped candied
  ginger

3 egg yolks
1 teaspoon raspberry-flavored
  gelatin

MERINGUE:
3 egg whites
1 teaspoon lemon juice
⅛ teaspoon salt
½ cup sugar

Preheat oven to 400°.

For the crust, in a medium bowl, blend the crumbs and walnuts. Cut in the margarine and mix with a fork or fingers until all the crumbs are moistened. Pat into a 9" pie tin or springform pan. Bake for 10 minutes.

For the filling, place the rhubarb, water, sugar, and candied ginger in a medium saucepan and cook over medium high heat until the rhubarb is soft and beginning to lose shape. Remove from the heat and whisk in the egg yolks and gelatin. Pour into the partially baked crust. Bake for 10 minutes.

For the meringue, in a clean, dry mixing bowl, whip egg whites with the lemon juice and salt until they hold soft peaks. Gradually add the sugar and continue whipping until the meringue is stiff. Pile this on top of the rhubarb filling, making sure the meringue is spread to the edges. Bake for 6–8 minutes or until nicely browned. Cool tart completely before serving at room temperature or chilled. *Makes 6–8 servings.*

Nutrients per serving: Calories 320, Fat 12g, Cholesterol 105mg, Sodium 150mg, Carbohydrates 51g, Protein 5g.

---

*T*o make a never-fail meringue, beat 3 egg whites to soft peaks. Add 1 cup (7 ounces) marshmallow creme fluff and ¼ teaspoon salt and beat for 4 minutes. Spread on a baked or filled pie and bake at 350° for 15 minutes.

Upside-Down Cobbler
(Egg Free)

Sometimes called a "miracle pie," this is made with the batter on the bottom instead of the top so a crust bubbles up through the fruit as it bakes.

½ cup (1 stick) margarine or butter, melted

1 cup GF Mix or Four Flour Bean Mix

½ rounded teaspoon xanthan gum

1 tablespoon baking powder

¼ teaspoon salt

1¾ cups sugar (or to taste), divided

1 cup milk or nondairy substitute

4 cups peeled, pitted, and thinly sliced fruit (peaches, plums, nectarines, apples or 3 cups berries)

1 tablespoon lemon juice

Preheat oven to 375°. Use an ungreased 9" × 13" baking pan. Pour in the melted margarine.

In a medium bowl, whisk together the flour mix, xanthan gum, baking powder, salt, and ¾ cup sugar. Stir in the milk, mixing just to combine. Pour over the margarine but don't stir together.

Place the fruit with the lemon juice and remaining cup of sugar in a medium saucepan and bring to a boil. Pour over the batter. Bake for 40–45 minutes or until the top is lightly browned. Serve warm or cold. Top with ice cream, frozen yogurt, whipped cream, or nondairy topping if desired. *Makes 6–9 servings.*

Nutrients per serving: Calories 390, Fat 13g, Cholesterol 35mg, Sodium 340mg, Carbohydrates 68g, Protein 3g.

Cobblers and crisps can be baked in either glass or metal pans but those that are acidic (containing pineapple, citrus fruit, or cranberries) should not be stored in their metal pan because the acid can react with the metal.

Featherlight Vinegar Pastry

450°

This rivals Donna Jo's Dream Pastry for tenderness but is far easier to stir up. Just dig into your bin of Featherlight Mix and half the work is done. With this tender flour combination I have cut the fat by one third.

2¼ cups Featherlight Mix	1 tablespoon vinegar
1 rounded teaspoon xanthan gum	¼ cup liquid egg substitute or
½ teaspoon salt	1 egg
1 tablespoon sugar (or to taste)	4 tablespoons ice water
¾ cup shortening	Sweet rice for rolling

In a medium bowl, blend the flour mix, xanthan gum, salt, and sugar. Cut in the shortening until coarse crumbs form. In a small bowl, beat the vinegar and egg substitute together with a fork. Add the ice water.

Stir the wet ingredients into the dry ingredients with a fork and keep adding liquid until the dough forms a ball. Work a little with your hands to obtain a smooth texture. Cover and refrigerate for 30 minutes or more before rolling out.

Divide the dough in half and roll out on sweet rice flour–covered waxed paper or plastic wrap. Use as much of the sweet rice flour as needed to work easily. Place in a pie tin. If using plastic wrap for easier handling, remove it to the pie tin and invert the dough into the pan. Bake as directed for the filling used.

For a baked crust, prick the pastry with a fork on sides and bottom. Bake the crust in a preheated 450° oven for 10–12 minutes or until slightly browned. Cool before filling. *Makes enough pastry for a 2-crust 9" pie or 2 pastry shells.*

Nutrients per serving (⅙ crust): Calories 170, Fat 90g, Cholesterol 15mg, Sodium 105mg, Carbohydrates 19g, Protein 1g.

Donna Jo's Dream Pastry

450°

This crust is so good it had to be repeated in this dessert book. With a variety of flours, Donna Jo created a successful gluten-free pastry crust. For best results, follow the directions carefully and chill the dough for 1 hour or more before rolling out.

½ cup tapioca flour
½ cup cornstarch
¼ cup potato starch
1 cup sweet rice flour
1 rounded teaspoon xanthan gum
½ teaspoon salt
Dash sugar (optional)

½ cup (1 stick) margarine
½ cup Butter Flavor Crisco
1 egg, cold
1 tablespoon vinegar
4 tablespoons ice water
Sweet rice flour for rolling

Blend together the tapioca flour, cornstarch, potato starch, sweet rice flour, xanthan gum, salt, and sugar (if used). Cut in the margarine and Crisco in small dabs until you have shortening the size of lima beans (not cornmeal).

Beat the egg, using a fork; add the vinegar and ice water. Stir into the flour mixture, forming a ball. You may knead this a bit, since rice flour crusts can stand handling. Refrigerate the dough for 1 hour or more to chill.

Divide dough and roll out on a sweet rice–floured board (or on floured plastic wrap, for easier handling). Place in a pie tin. If using plastic wrap, remove it to the pie tin and invert the dough into the pan. Shape before removing the plastic. Bake as directed for the filling used.

For a baked crust, prick the pastry with a fork on sides and bottom. Bake the crust in a preheated 450° oven for 10–12 minutes, or until slightly browned. Cool before filling. *Makes enough pastry for a 2-crust 9" pie plus 1 pie shell.*

Nutrients per serving (⅙ crust of 2-crust pie): Calories 297, Fat 20g, Cholesterol 42mg, Sodium 209mg, Carbohydrates 27g, Protein 3g.

Cream Cheese Pastry

450°

Easy to handle with a wonderful flavor.

2¼ cups Featherlight Mix

⅓ cup (5 ½ tablespoons) margarine

1 rounded teaspoon xanthan gum

½ cup Butter Flavor Crisco

½ teaspoon salt

1 egg, cold

1 teaspoon sugar

1 tablespoon vinegar

4 ounces cream cheese

4 tablespoons ice water

In a medium bowl, blend the flour mix, xanthan gum, salt, and sugar. Cut in the cream cheese, margarine, and Crisco until coarse crumbs form. In a small bowl, beat the egg and vinegar. Add the ice water.

Stir the wet ingredients into the dry ingredients with a fork and keep adding liquid until the dough forms a ball. Work the dough a little with your hands to obtain a smooth texture. Cover and refrigerate for about 30 minutes before rolling out.

Divide the ball in half and roll on a sweet rice flour–covered board or on waxed paper or plastic wrap. Use as much of the sweet rice flour as needed to work easily. Place in a pie tin. If using plastic wrap for easier handling, remove it to the pie tin and invert the dough into the pan. Do not stretch while fitting it in. Bake as directed for the filling. For a baked crust, prick the pastry with a fork on the sides and bottom. Bake in a preheated 450° oven for 10–12 minutes or until slightly browned. Cool before filling. *Makes enough pastry for a 2-crust 9" pie or 2 pastry shells.*

Nutrients per serving (⅙ crust of 2-crust pie): Calories 293, Fat 20g, Cholesterol 33mg, Sodium 220mg, Carbohydrates 26g, Protein 3g.

> *F*or a glazed look to your pie crust, brush the top with milk and sprinkle with sugar before baking.

Simple Cereal Crust

This was the first crust I created after my diagnosis and, with the addition of the egg white, one I still use, for it's probably the easiest of all crusts to make. You simply shake in a bag and then press into the pie tin. This is best as the bottom crust on pies with fillings that will be baked with the crust, such as pumpkin pie, pecan pie, or a baked-custard pie.

For 9" pie crust

2 cups crushed GF rice and corn cereal (or 1 cup each)

1 tablespoon sugar

¼ cup finely ground almonds, pecans, or walnuts (optional)

2 tablespoons margarine or butter, melted

1 egg white beaten with a fork until frothy

In a plastic bag, combine the crushed cereal, sugar, ground nuts (if used), and melted butter. Knead the outside of the bag with your hands until well mixed. Add the beaten egg white and work that in. Pour the contents into a pie tin and pat into bottom and up sides with your fingers. Press in firmly. Pour in the filling and bake at the temperature called for in the filling recipe. *Makes one 9" pie crust. 8 servings.*

Nutrients per serving: Calories 80, Fat 5g, Cholesterol 0mg, Sodium 175mg, Carbohydrates 7g, Protein 2g.

Low-Fat Crumb Crust

450°

Usually a crumb crust, whether made with cookie crumbs, graham cracker crumbs, or with sweet bread crumbs, takes a lot of butter or margarine to stick together and become the tasty, tender crust we crave. The use of egg white can considerably lower the need for fat and still result in a tender crust.

TO 1–1½ CUPS CRUMBS ADD:

1 egg white whipped with a fork

1 tablespoon margarine or butter, melted

1 teaspoon water

OTHER ADDITIONS (IF NECESSARY):

1 tablespoon sugar if the crumbs are unsweetened

1 tablespoon cocoa powder if a chocolate crust is desired

¼ teaspoon cinnamon if using bread or cookie crumbs and you want the taste of graham crackers

Blend the crumbs with the egg white, melted margarine, and water and press into the desired pan. If a pie tin, press up the edges. If a springform pan, cover only the bottom unless the recipe calls for pressing up the sides. One cup of this recipe will cover the bottom of a 9" springform pan. You will need 1½ cups for a 9" deep pie tin, if pressing up the sides.

If pie is to be baked, just fill and bake at the temperature suggested for the pie. If the filling is already cooked or not to be baked, bake the shell in a preheated oven at 425° for 8–10 minutes or until slightly browned. Cool before filling.

Nutrients per crust: Calories 45, Fat 3g, Cholesterol 10mg, Sodium 55mg, Carbohydrates 4g, Protein 1g.

Almond Crust

Try this sweet and crunchy crust for cheesecake, tarts, or single-crust pies. My tasters loved it! This rolls as easily as the Featherlight Vinegar Pastry (page 242) but has an altogether different texture.

1 cup Light Bean Flour Mix
⅓ cup almond meal
3 tablespoons sugar
¼ teaspoon salt
6 tablespoons margarine, butter, or Butter Flavor Crisco

¾ teaspoon almond flavoring
2 tablespoons liquid egg substitute
2 tablespoons (more or less) ice water
Sweet rice flour for rolling

In a medium bowl, blend the flour mix, almond meal, sugar, and salt. Cut in the margarine until the mixture resembles coarse meal. Add the almond flavoring to the egg substitute and blend in, adding just enough of the ice water to form a firm dough ball. Knead gently on a firm surface and flatten into a disk shape. Wrap in plastic and refrigerate for at least 30 minutes or up to 10 hours.

For best results and easier handling, cover your rolling surface with plastic wrap and sprinkle with sweet rice flour. Place the dough disk on the surface and sprinkle with more sweet rice flour. Cover with another sheet of plastic wrap and roll to about ⅛" thickness. Uncover and, using the bottom plastic wrap to handle easily, flip the crust into your pie tin or springform pan. If making tartlets, cut circles to fit the shape of tartlet pans.

For a baked crust, prick the pastry with a fork on the sides and bottom. Bake in a preheated 400° oven for 10–12 minutes or until slightly browned. Cool before filling. If using a filling to be baked, pour the filling into the unbaked shell and bake at the temperature suggested for the filling. *Makes one 9" pie crust or one 10" springform pan bottom crust for cheesecake or 6 or more tartlet shells, depending on size. Makes 6 servings.*

Nutrients per serving: Calories 270, Fat 16g, Cholesterol 30mg, Sodium 230mg, Carbohydrates 30g, Protein 5g.

Nut Crust Supreme

425°

A very easy crust that pays huge dividends in taste. Use it for pies with creamy fillings to complement the nuts in the crust or for any cheesecake. This recipe will fill a low 9" pie tin or cover the bottom of a 9" or 10" springform pan. Vary the nuts to suit the filling. I've used macadamia, hazelnuts, pecans, walnuts, and coconut.

1 cup GF Mix
¼ teaspoon xanthan gum
¼ cup brown sugar

⅓ cup margarine or butter
½ cup finely chopped nuts

Preheat oven to 425°. Spray your pan lightly with vegetable oil spray.

In a medium bowl, stir together the flour mix, xanthan gum, and brown sugar. Cut in the margarine until fine crumbs form. Stir in the nuts and pat into your pan. Bake for 8–10 minutes for a pie with precooked filling.

For a pie to be baked with the shell, just pat into your pan and bake at the temperature required for the filling. *Makes 8 servings.*

Nutrients per serving: Calories 230, Fat 14g, Cholesterol 25mg,
Sodium 90mg, Carbohydrates 27g, Protein 2g.

As most pie recipes are only for the filling and allow a choice of crust (rice or bean), I have noted the base only on those pies that include the crust in the recipe. Under page numbers the first column for GFG is for the original; the second, the revised book. See page 92 for book title abbreviations.

PIE OR PASTRY	BASE	BOOK	PAGE	
Apple Cheese Crisp		GFG	197	171
Apple Crisp	rice	F&H	175	
Apple Pear Deluxe Pie		GFG	97	156
Apple Pie Imperial		More	153	169
Banana Cream Pie		GFG	94	152
Basic Cream Pie Filling		GFG	94	150
Berry Cobbler	rice	GFG	196	171
Blackberry Dumplings	rice	GFG	199	174
Boston Cream Pie	rice	GFG	95	154
Brownie Pie	rice	F&H	167	
Caribbean Lime Pie		More	155	
Chocolate Caramel Pie with Walnuts	rice/corn	F&H	167	
Claufoutis	rice	More	112	
Coconut Cream Pie		GFG	94	152
Cranberry-Apple Crisp	rice	More	161	
Crustless Coconut Pie		More	158	
Deep Dish Berry Pie with Cream Cheese Crust	rice	GFG	194	168
Easy Apple-Yogurt Pie	bean	F&H	166	
Egg-free Cheese Tart	rice/corn	F&H	180	
Fresh Strawberry Pie		More	150	
Fruit Dream Pie	rice	F&H	164	
Fruit Pizza	rice	F&H	190	
Impossible German Chocolate Pie	rice	More	157	
Key Lime Pie		F&H	170	

Lemon Buttermilk Pie		More	156	
Lemon Lemon Pie		GFG	95	153
Lemon Sponge Pie	rice	GFG	100	159
Lighter Basic Cream Pie Filling	rice	F&H	173	
Mock Apple Pie Filling		F&H	174	
Mock Mince Pie		GFG	213	203
Old-Fashioned Pumpkin Pie		GFG	213	195
Peach and Plum Crisp	GF mix	F&H	172	
Peach Cobbler	rice	F&H	187	
Peach Custard Pie		GFG	193	167
Peanut Butter Pie with Chocolate Crust	rice or corn	More	152	
Pear Torte		GFG	195	169
Pecan Pie		GFG	98	157
Pineapple Cheese Pie		F&H	170	
Pineapple Cream Pie		GFG	94	152
Pineapple Pie with Coconut Batter Topping	rice	F&H	168	
President's Day Cherry Cheese Pie		GFG	212	185
Quick Cranberry Pie		F&H	169	
Raisin–Sour Cream Pie		GFG	96	155
Raspberry-Rhubarb Tart with Ricotta Crust	rice	More	160	
Rhubarb Crumble	GF mix	GFG	198	172
Rum Pecan Pie		GFG	98	157
Sour Cream–Raisin Pie		F&H	171	
Swedish Apple Torte	rice	More	171	
Tropical Tofu Pie		GFG	99	158
Yogurt Peach Pie	rice/corn	F&H	165	
Walnut Cranberry Pie		More	159	

PIE CRUST RECIPES FROM OTHER BOOKS IN THE
GLUTEN-FREE GOURMET SERIES

Pie crusts can usually be your choice with most of the pie recipes in this and my other books, so I am listing ones you may remember have worked well in the past. Under page numbers the first column for GFG is for the original; the second, the revised book. See page 92 for book title abbreviations.

PIE CRUST	BASE	BOOK	PAGE	
Absolutely Sinful Cereal Crust	rice/corn	More	149	
Baker's Best Bean Pastry	bean	F&H	160	
Bean Flour Oil Crust	bean	F&H	161	
Cereal Crust	rice/corn	GFG	91	148
Chocolate Crust	rice/corn	More	152	
Cream Cheese Pastry	rice	F&H	162	
Crumb Crust	rice or bean	GFG	91	148
Ginger Cookie Crust	rice	GFG	92	148
Melt-in-the-Mouth Oil Crust	rice	More	147	
Mock Graham Cracker Crust	rice	More	148	
Ricotta Pastry	rice	More	148	
Very Best Cereal Crust	rice/corn	F&H	163	

Puddings

*P*uddings are an old-fashioned dessert that rival fruit in popularity for a treat at the end of the meal. Serve them often for they are filled with nutrition, require very little work, and can often be made a day ahead of time.

This is a very short chapter since we can buy many puddings on the grocery shelf—either already made or in quick-mix packages. The real problem with many of them is that they are not dairy free. The ones I've included here can be made with either a dairy or nondairy liquid.

There are also twelve pudding-type desserts in the "No Special Ingredients" chapter, as many of the puddings don't require any ingredients one must send away for. See the next page for a list of those special puddings.

If you remember a special pudding from another book, I've listed them at the end of the chapter to save you the trouble of searching the indexes.

Classic Bread Pudding

No dessert book would be complete without the old-fashioned bread pudding, now making a comeback on the American table. This basic recipe can be varied to suit many tastes. Save bread by cutting leftovers and odd slices into cubes and freezing, adding to the package whenever you have extra bread.

4 cups cubed GF bread (sweet, white, or lemon flavored)

⅔ cup chopped walnuts or pecans, toasted

2⅔ cups milk or nondairy substitute, divided

2 tablespoons margarine or butter

½ cup brown sugar

Dash salt

2 tablespoons rum (optional)

2 eggs plus 1 yolk

1½ teaspoons Vanilla, Butter, & Nut flavoring or vanilla

Preheat oven to 350°. Grease a shallow 2-quart casserole with margarine or butter.

Mix the bread cubes and nuts and place in the casserole.

In a medium saucepan, combine 1⅓ cups milk with the butter, brown sugar, and salt. Bring to a simmer and remove from the heat. Cool for 5 minutes.

Whisk the eggs and extra yolk with rum (if used), flavoring, and remaining 1⅓ cups milk. Add to the heated mixture and pour over the bread. Bake for 35–40 minutes or until set in the center. Serve warm topped with whipped cream or nondairy whipped topping. *Makes 8 servings.*

VARIATIONS:

CHOCOLATE-WALNUT BREAD PUDDING: Use walnuts for the nuts. Omit the rum and in its place add 3 ounces of chopped semisweet chocolate to the hot milk mix when you remove it from the stove.

CHERRY-PECAN BREAD PUDDING: Use pecans for the nuts. Use cherry flavoring and add ½ cup dried cherries to the hot milk when taken from the stove.

Nutrients per serving: Calories 230, Fat 13g, Cholesterol 110mg, Sodium 210mg, Carbohydrates 23g, Protein 8g.

*T*o avoid bubbles on the surface of a custard, beat the eggs just until the whites and yolks are blended, not foamy.

Apple Spoon Pudding

I remember this old-fashioned apple pudding from childhood, but it's still as tasty today made with our gluten-free flours. Serve it warm from the oven on a cold night and collect raves from the whole family.

1 cup Four Flour Bean Mix or
 Featherlight Mix
1 cup sugar
½ teaspoon salt
1 teaspoon baking soda
1 teaspoon cinnamon
¼ cup (½ stick) butter or
 margarine, melted

1 egg, well beaten
2½ cups peeled, cored, and
 chopped apple
1 tablespoon lemon juice
Whipped nondairy topping, ice
 cream, or whipped cream for
 topping

Preheat oven to 350°. Butter a 1½-quart casserole.

In a large bowl, whisk together the flour mix, sugar, salt, baking soda, and cinnamon. Add the melted butter, beaten egg, chopped apple, and lemon juice. Stir to blend into a soft dough. Spoon into the prepared casserole and bake for 35 minutes. The pudding should be soft, not cakelike, in texture. Serve warm with your chosen topping. *Makes 6 servings.*

*Nutrients per serving: Calories 320, Fat 9g, Cholesterol 55mg,
Sodium 480mg, Carbohydrates 59g, Protein 3g.*

Date-Nut Pudding

This old-fashioned cakelike pudding served in squares can be topped with whipped cream, a nondairy substitute, or ice cream. Remember to buy whole dried dates to avoid having them dusted with flour, as the cut pieces often are.

1 pound dates, chopped	½ teaspoon xanthan gum
½ cup hot water	1½ teaspoons baking powder
1 teaspoon baking soda	1 cup sugar
¾ cup boiling water	2 eggs, slightly beaten
1½ teaspoons butter or margarine	1 teaspoon vanilla
1½ cups Four Flour Bean Mix or Featherlight Mix	1 cup chopped walnuts or pecans

Preheat oven to 325°. Spray a 9" × 12" baking pan with vegetable oil spray.

In a 2-quart saucepan, place the dates and hot water. Bring to a boil. Add the baking soda, boiling water, and butter. Mix well, remove from heat, and cool.

Whisk together the flour mix, xanthan gum, and baking powder. Add to the date mixture. Stir in the sugar, beaten eggs, and vanilla. Mix well. Stir in the nuts. Spoon into the prepared pan and bake for 50–60 minutes. Cool. Cut into squares and serve at room temperature with your favorite topping. *Makes 12 servings.*

Nutrients per serving: Calories 290, Fat 6g, Cholesterol 35mg, Sodium 170mg, Carbohydrates 59g, Protein 5g.

Cranberry Trifle

Trifles are easy to put together but your guests will think you went to a lot of trouble. Try this colorful and tasty holiday trifle using leftover cake, canned cranberry sauce, and mandarin oranges with a quick-and-easy microwaved custard sauce.

CUSTARD SAUCE:
⅓ cup sugar
3 tablespoons cornstarch
2 cups milk or nondairy substitute
2 egg yolks
1½ teaspoons vanilla

TRIFLE:
3–4 cups torn leftover white or
   light (nonchocolate) GF cake

¼ cup rum
¼ cup orange juice
One 16-ounce can whole-berry
   cranberry sauce
Two 8½-ounce cans mandarin
   oranges, drained
Whipped cream or nondairy
   whipped topping

In a 4-cup glass measuring cup or bowl, combine the sugar and cornstarch. Add about ¼ cup of the milk and stir until the cornstarch is dissolved. Add the remaining milk and whisk smooth. Cover with waxed paper and cook on high for 5–7 minutes, stirring twice while the mixture comes to a boil and thickens. Whisk smooth.

In a small bowl, beat the egg yolks lightly. Whisk in about ½ cup of the hot mixture. Whisk this into the remaining milk mixture and return to the microwave. Cook uncovered for 1 minute on high. Blend in the vanilla.

To assemble the trifle, place half the cake pieces, torn into about 1" size, in a large clear bowl or trifle bowl. Mix the rum and orange juice and sprinkle half onto the cake. Top with half the cranberry sauce, 1 can of the oranges, and half the custard sauce. Repeat. Refrigerate for several hours (or overnight). Before serving, top with whipped cream or nondairy whipped topping to cover the trifle about 1" deep. *Makes 10–12 servings.*

*Nutrients per serving: Calories 390, Fat 6g, Cholesterol 160mg,
Sodium 130mg, Carbohydrates 76g, Protein 8g.*

PUDDINGS, TARTS, AND SIMILAR DESSERTS FROM OTHER BOOKS IN THE
GLUTEN-FREE GOURMET SERIES

See page 92 for book title abbreviations.

DESSERTS	BASE	BOOK	PAGE
A Lighter Plum Pudding	rice/bean	F&H	191
Apple Pudding	rice	More	179
Banana Bread Pudding with Caramel Sauce	rice/bean	Breads	268
Bavarian Cream with Fruit	none	GFG rev	166
Blackberry Dumplings	rice	GFG	174
Creamy Rice Pudding	rice	More	177
Double Dutch Treat	rice	More	111
Down-Under Trifle	rice/tapioca	More	176
Four-Layer Dessert	cereal	More	174
Fruit Cocktail Torte with Bean Flour	bean	F&H	128
Lemon Sauce Bread Pudding	rice	Breads	265
Lime Sponge Pudding	rice	GFG	198
Linzertorte	corn/rice	More	172
Maple Pecan Bread Pudding	rice/bean	Breads	264
Mother's Plum Pudding	rice/soy	GFG	216
No-Bake Fruitcake	rice/bean	F&H	129
Pam's Pavlova	corn	More	170
Pistachio Bars	rice	More	175
Prune Whip, Baked	none	F&H	188
Quick Bread Pudding	rice/bean	F&H	192
Quick Bread Pudding with Variations	rice/bean	Breads	267
Rhubarb Fool	corn	More	180
Spicy Bread Pudding	rice	More	178
Swedish Apple Torte	rice	More	171

Mixes, Butters, and Shortcuts

*E*very cook wants to learn shortcuts, and anyone who has to cook more than usual, as celiacs do, needs every time-saving suggestion possible.

Here are a few mixes to keep on hand to save time when baking, and some suggestions to keep you from running to the store for every recipe. Some of these are substitutes for expensive ingredients and have appeared in other books of mine, but are repeated here for your use in making desserts.

Basic Cake Mix
(with Variations)

I'll feel that celiac disease has come to be a household word when I can pick up a gluten-free cake mix at the corner grocery. Until that time, we are all going to have to send away or search the health food stores for our mixes.

But you can easily make your own and keep them handy at far less cost and trouble. You can also adjust the mixes so they won't contain ingredients that give you distress, such as guar gum, corn, or soy. The following mix will make 4 cakes and it can be doubled easily. Store the mix in a plastic bag or container. To make a cake, just add fresh eggs, shortening, and liquid.

5¼ cups GF Mix or Featherlight Mix

8 teaspoons baking powder

2 teaspoons baking soda

4 teaspoons powdered vanilla

2½ teaspoons xanthan gum

2 teaspoons salt

2⅔ cups sugar

2 tablespoons Egg Replacer

Whisk all ingredients together and store on pantry shelf.

VARIATIONS:

FEATHERLIGHT YELLOW CAKE: Preheat oven to 350°. In the bowl of your mixer, place 2 cups Basic Cake Mix. Add 1 egg plus 1 egg white (or ½ cup liquid egg substitute), ⅓ cup mayonnaise, and ⅔ cup nondairy sour cream. Beat for about 1 minute on medium and turn batter into a greased 8" square pan. Bake for 25–30 minutes.

LOW-FAT CAKE: Preheat oven to 350°. In the bowl of your mixer, place 2 cups Basic Cake Mix. Add 1 egg plus 1 egg white (or ½ cup liquid egg substitute), 2 tablespoons vegetable oil, 2 tablespoons pear or applesauce, and ½ cup low-fat milk or nondairy liquid. Beat for about 1 minute on medium and turn the batter into a greased 8" square pan. Bake for 25–30 minutes. This is excellent with the spiced ginger flavor.

LACTOSE-FREE, SOY-FREE CAKE: Preheat oven to 350°. In the bowl of your mixer, place 2 cups Basic Cake Mix. Add 1 egg plus 1 egg white, 4 tablespoons vegetable oil, and ⅓ cup citrus-flavored carbonated beverage. Beat for about 1 minute on medium and turn the batter into a greased 8" square pan. Bake for 25–30 minutes.

LOW-FAT CHOCOLATE CAKE: Preheat oven to 350°. In the bowl of your mixer, place 2 cups Basic Cake Mix. Whisk in 3 tablespoons cocoa powder. Add 1 egg plus 1 egg white, 2 tablespoons vegetable oil, one 2½-ounce jar baby pea puree, and ½ cup cherry cola. Beat for about 1 minute on medium and turn the batter into a greased 8" square pan. Bake for 25–30 minutes.

MOCHA FLAVOR: To any of the above recipes, add 1 tablespoon instant coffee granules plus 2½ tablespoons cocoa to the dry mix before adding any liquid.

ORANGE FLAVOR: To the Basic Cake Mix, add 1 tablespoon fresh orange zest before adding any of the liquids. This pairs especially well with the citrus-flavored carbonated beverage.

SPICE CAKE: To the Basic Cake Mix, add 1½ teaspoons cinnamon, 1 teaspoon cloves, and ¼ teaspoon allspice before adding the liquids.

SPICED GINGER FLAVOR: To the Basic Cake Mix, add 1 tablespoon finely chopped candied ginger before adding the egg and liquids.

Cobbler and Cupcake Mix

The bean flours adapt readily to this mix, which can top fruit or stand alone in a non-sweet lunch bag cupcake.

4 cups Four Flour Bean Mix
1½ teaspoons baking soda
4 teaspoons baking powder
2 teaspoons xanthan gum
1½ teaspoons salt

1 tablespoon Egg Replacer
2 cups sugar
2 teaspoons dried lemon peel
   or powdered vanilla

Whisk all ingredients together and store in a plastic bag or container on your pantry shelf.

TO TOP COBBLER: Preheat oven to 350°. Bring the fruit, sugar, lemon juice, and approximately 1 cup water to boil. Place in 8" × 10" or 9" square pan.

Measure 1¼ cup above mix into mixing bowl. In a small bowl, beat 2 eggs, 3 tablespoons oil or melted margarine, and ⅓ cup milk or nondairy liquid. Add to the flour mix and beat for 1 minute. Spoon in dollops onto the hot fruit. Bake 20–25 minutes or until the top is brown and springs back when gently pressed. Serve hot or cold with whipped topping or ice cream. *Makes 8 servings.*

FOR CUPCAKES: Preheat oven to 350°. Line 8 muffin tins with paper liners. Spray with vegetable oil shortening.

In mixer, beat 2 eggs until light and pale yellow. Add ¼ cup melted butter or oil. Add 1¼ cups mix alternately with ⅓ cup milk or nondairy liquid, beating well after each addition. Spoon into the prepared muffin cups. Bake for approximately 20 minutes or until the top springs back when gently pressed.

VARIATIONS: Use your imagination to vary these plain cakes by adding cocoa powder, cocoa and espresso powder, chopped candied ginger, cinnamon, cloves, and allspice to the flour mix before blending with the liquids.

Dream Pastry Mix

If you keep this mix on hand, you can make bases for cookies and bake your pies without all that mess of measuring and mixing. This is enough for 4 batches of pastry, each batch making one 2-crust pie plus an extra crust. Use it for many of the recipes in the Pies and Pastries section.

2 cups tapioca flour

2 cups cornstarch

1 cup potato starch

4 cups sweet rice flour

4 rounded teaspoons xanthan gum

2 teaspoons salt

2 teaspoons sugar

Combine all ingredients, mix well, and place in a plastic bag or closed container. Store it with your other flours. It does not need to be refrigerated.

TO MAKE DREAM PASTRY:

2¼ cups Dream Pastry Mix

½ cup (1 stick) margarine

½ cup Butter Flavor Crisco

1 egg, cold

1 tablespoon GF vinegar

¼ cup ice water (use bottled spring water)

Sweet rice flour, for rolling

Place the Dream Pastry Mix in a medium bowl. Cut in the margarine and Crisco in small pieces until you have shortening the size of lima beans (not cornmeal).

Beat the egg with a fork and add the vinegar and ice water. Stir into the flour mixture, forming a ball. You may knead this a bit since it can stand handling. Refrigerate the dough for 1 hour to chill.

Divide the dough and roll out on a board floured with sweet rice flour (or on floured plastic wrap for easier handling). Place in a pie tin. The plastic wrap can be used to invert the dough into the pan. Shape before removing the plastic. Bake as directed for the filling used.

For a baked shell, prick the pastry with a fork on the sides and bottom. Bake the crust in a preheated 450° oven for 10–12 minutes or until slightly browned. Cool before filling. *Makes enough pastry for a 2-crust 9" pie plus 1 pie shell.*

Nutrients per serving (⅙ of 2-crust pie): Calories 297, Fat 20g, Cholesterol 42mg, Sodium 209mg, Carbohydrates 27g, Protein 3g.

Nut Butters

Some of the recipes in this book call for nut butters, which can usually be purchased in the grocery store. But because it is sometimes difficult to find and we often don't need or use the amount in the jar we purchase, I've learned to make my own, fresh and inexpensively. Most grocery stores have nuts by the bulk. Suitable for butters are almonds, cashews, filberts (hazelnuts), macadamia nuts, and pecans.

Place the nuts in the bowl of a blender or food processor (using the measure called for in the recipe. For example: ⅔ cup nut butter—⅔ cup nuts). Cover and process until finely ground. Add 1 tablespoon margarine or butter for each ⅓ cup nuts. Process about 3 minutes more or until the mixture is smooth and spreadable. Scrape down the sides as necessary.

Almond Meal and Other Nut Meals

If you don't have store-bought almond meal or other nut meals that your recipe calls for, just pour your nuts into a food processor and process until the meal is the texture you wish. Be careful not to turn the meal to butter! It will take slightly more nuts by measure for the amount of meal that results.

Sweetened Condensed Milk

No sweetened condensed milk in the house? Here's a quick substitute you can stir up in a hurry if you have powdered milk handy. Noninstant milk is preferable but I have made this with regular instant powdered milk.

1 cup powdered milk
¾ cup sugar
⅓ cup boiling water

3 tablespoons butter or margarine, melted

Place the ingredients in your blender or in the small bowl of your food processor and blend at low speed. Scrape the sides and turn to high until the milk is smooth. *Makes equivalent of a 14-ounce can (approximately 1 cup).*

Diabetic Sugar Substitute

Use this easy-to-make sugar substitute in angel food cakes and frostings. Or use it to sprinkle on fruits or cereals. Your own taste will decide on the quantity of sugar replacement; some brands will taste bitter if too much is used.

2 cups nonfat dry milk powder or
   nondairy substitute
2 cups cornstarch

Replacement equivalent for
   1 cup granulated sugar

Measure all ingredients into a blender or food processor. Pulse for several seconds or until the texture resembles confectioners' sugar. *Makes 4 cups.*

Mock Mascarpone Cheese

Although this Italian-type dessert cheese is now more available in regular grocery stores, you still may have difficulty finding it in smaller stores. To save trouble, use this formula.

¾ cup ricotta cheese
2 tablespoons milk

2 tablespoons cream cheese,
   softened
¾ teaspoon lemon juice

Place all ingredients in a blender or food processor and puree until the mixture is smooth. *Makes 1 cup mascarpone cheese.*

Mock Raspberry Jam or Filling

No one will ever guess this marvelous raspberry-tasting filling is made with green tomatoes. Use it to fill one of the sponge rolls (pages 90 and 91), or as jam on toast or waffles. If you don't grow your own tomatoes (or it is winter), pick up some firm tomatoes at the market. Since they won't be ripe, they will work as well.

2½ cups peeled and diced green
    tomatoes (2–3)
2 cups sugar

Dash of salt
1 tablespoon lemon juice
One 3-ounce box raspberry gelatin

Place the tomatoes in a 2½-quart saucepan with the sugar and salt. Bring to a boil and cook for 10 minutes, stirring frequently. Remove from heat.

Add the lemon juice and stir in the gelatin. Return to stove and bring to a boil, stirring constantly. Boil 1 minute. Spoon into jars or refrigerator cups. Keeps refrigerated for up to 1 month. For longer storage, put in freezer containers and freeze. *Makes 3 cups.*

No Special Ingredients

*T*his chapter is dedicated to the beginning celiac who hasn't yet ordered the special flours and xanthan gum needed for most baking, and to the friends and relatives of celiacs who wonder what in the world they can make to top off a meal with something special.

Very early in my life as a celiac, a friend invited me to a gathering and assured me that she could easily make the basic dinner gluten free but asked, "What in the world can I serve as dessert? I don't have any of your flour."

Since she was a wonderful cook and took pride in her fabulous dinners, I suggested, "Meringues filled with fruit. They don't take any flour."

She served them filled with local fresh raspberries, and no one suspected they had joined me in eating gluten free.

That's why I start off this chapter with my original meringues. But over the years I've learned that, even without any of our special mail-order flours, one can make great cakes, tortes, cookies, cheesecakes and more to satisfy that desire for ending the meal with a mouth-watering, gluten-free dessert. The few flours I do use here (cornstarch, potato starch, and sweet rice flour) can all be found in the baking section of any grocery store.

Of course there are always gelatins and custards, along with fresh fruit, to end the meal. I didn't give recipes for those, except for a few of the fancier ones, like the flans (custards) and a mousse (gelatin).

Many of these recipes are so good you'll use them even if you do have the special gluten-free flours in your cupboard, but mainly you may want to recommend this chapter to a friend or relative who would like to invite you for dinner without asking you to bring the dessert.

Meringues

As these take no flour and can be filled with any fruit, fresh or frozen, they make a wonderfully easy GF dessert base. They can be made ahead of time and stored in a closed container for several days.

3 egg whites
¼ teaspoon cream of tartar

¾ cup sugar

Preheat oven to 275°. Line a baking sheet with brown wrapping paper.

In a metal or glass bowl, beat the egg whites and cream of tartar until frothy. Gradually beat in the sugar, a little at a time, until the mixture is very stiff and glossy.

Drop by spoonfuls in 3½" circles, 1½" thick, on the prepared baking sheet. With the back of a spoon, make a cuplike indentation for the fruit on each meringue. Bake for about 1 hour. Turn oven off and leave meringues in the oven until the oven has cooled.

To serve, fill with fresh or frozen and thawed berries and, if desired, top with whipped cream. *Makes 6 meringues.*

Nutrients per meringue: Calories 60, Fat 0g, Cholesterol 0mg,
Sodium 30mg, Carbohydrates 13g, Protein 2g.

Pecan Torte

Tender, flavorful, light—and no special ingredients! This is far easier to make than you would think, for it's spread in a jelly roll pan and cut into 4 layers, then filled with the Whipped Cream Frosting on page 130.

⅔ cup potato starch	4 eggs, separated
1 teaspoon baking powder	2 tablespoons water
½ teaspoon salt	1 teaspoon vanilla
1 cup pecan meal or ground pecans	½ cup sugar

Preheat oven to 350°. Grease a 10" × 15" jelly roll pan and line with waxed paper. Grease the paper.

In a medium bowl, whisk together the potato starch, baking powder, salt, and ground nuts. Set aside.

In the bowl of your mixer, beat the egg yolks, water, and vanilla on high until light. Gradually add half the sugar (¼ cup) and continue beating until thick and light (about 5 minutes). In another bowl, beat the egg whites and the remaining ¼ cup sugar until stiff peaks form.

Fold the dry ingredients into the egg yolk mixture in 4 portions. Fold in the meringue. Spread the batter evenly in the jelly roll pan. Bake for 25–30 minutes, or until a tester comes out clean. Cool for a few minutes and then turn out. Remove the waxed paper from the bottom.

Cool completely before assembling by cutting across the narrow width into 4 sections. Pile whipped cream frosting between the layers and on the top and sides of the torte. This will take 3 cups whipping cream. *Makes 10 servings.*

VARIATIONS:

CREAM-FILLED TORTE: Use the recipe on page 313, Microwave Custard Sauce, for the filling. You will only need 2 cups of whipping cream for frosting top and sides.

CREAM CHEESE FILLING: Blend 6 ounces of cream cheese with 1 cup of whipping cream and pile thickly between the layers.

JAM-FILLED TORTE: Use your favorite colorful jam as a filling (raspberry, apricot, pineapple).

Nutrients per serving: Calories 190, Fat 11g, Cholesterol 85mg,
Sodium 180mg, Carbohydrates 21g, Protein 4g.

Four-Layer Torte with Orange Cream Filling 400°–350°

This sinfully delicious dessert shows that gluten free doesn't have to be dull. Serve this and surprise any crowd. The cake can be baked ahead of time, and the orange curd made a day ahead. Assembling the torte doesn't take long. Decorate the torte by tucking a few fresh flowers along the base of the frosted cake.

CAKE:

9 eggs, separated
½ teaspoon salt
1 teaspoon cream of tartar
1½ cups white sugar
Grated rind of 1 orange
1 teaspoon apricot brandy
½ cup potato starch, sifted
½ cup cornstarch, sifted

FILLING:

½ cup (1 stick) butter or margarine
½ cup sugar
⅓ cup orange juice
1 tablespoon lemon juice
Zest from 1 orange
3 eggs
Nondairy whipped topping
One recipe Whipped Cream
    Frosting (page 130)

Preheat oven to 400°. Spray an 11" × 17" jelly roll pan with cooking spray. Line with waxed paper and grease well.

In a large bowl, beat the egg whites until peaks form. Add the salt and cream of tartar. Continue beating until stiff. With the beater running, add the sugar slowly and beat until thick. Set aside.

In another large bowl, beat the egg yolks until thick. Add the remaining sugar, orange rind, brandy, potato starch, and cornstarch. Continue to beat until thick. In 3 parts, fold the egg whites into the yolk mixture. Spoon into the prepared pan and bake for 10 minutes. Reduce the heat to 350° and bake for 10 more minutes.

Remove from the oven and turn out onto a cloth sprinkled with confectioners' sugar. Remove the waxed paper while still warm. Allow to cool flat.

For the orange filling, which can be made a day ahead, place the butter, sugar, orange juice, lemon juice, and orange zest in a 4-cup microwaveable bowl or measuring cup. Cook on high for 4 minutes. Stir.

In a small bowl, beat the eggs until blended. Gradually whisk about ⅓ cup of the hot lemon mixture into the eggs to warm them. Whisk this into the remaining orange mixture. Cook on high for 1½ minutes. Whisk until smooth. Continue to cook for 1–2 minutes until thickened. Again, whisk until smooth. Refrigerate to cool.

Mix the orange filling with almost equal parts whipped nondairy topping to form the orange cream.

Cut the cake into 4 sections. Place one section on the cake plate and cover with one third of the orange cream. Top with the next section and add another third of the filling. Add another section and repeat. Top with the last section.

Make up the Whipped Cream Frosting (page 130). Cover the top and sides of torte. Refrigerate after frosting. This will keep well for up to 2 days. *Makes 12 large servings.*

Nutrients per serving: Calories 330, Fat 13g, Cholesterol 235mg, Sodium 230mg, Carbohydrates 47g, Protein 7g.

Chocolate-Pecan Torte

A moist and not-too-sweet cake that can be topped with whipped cream or nondairy whipped topping, or served with ice cream or a fruit sauce. No one will believe that it contains no flour.

Note: *To toast the nuts, spread in an ovenproof pan and bake at 350° for 4–5 minutes.*

1 cup pecans, lightly toasted (see note)
3 tablespoons sugar
5 eggs, separated
½ cup sugar
2 tablespoons dark rum or 2 teaspoons vanilla

1 cup (about 6 ounces) finely chopped bittersweet or semisweet chocolate (use food processor for best results)
⅛ teaspoon salt

Preheat oven to 350°. Grease the sides and bottom of a 9" springform pan.

In the bowl of your food processor, grind the pecans with the 3 tablespoons sugar.

In the bowl of your mixer, beat the egg yolks with the ½ cup sugar until the mixture is thick and pale yellow (about 3 minutes). Beat in the rum. Stir in the pecan mixture and chocolate.

In another mixing bowl, use clean beaters to beat the egg whites and salt until peaks are stiff but not dry. Fold the beaten egg whites into the pecan-chocolate mixture in 3 additions. Spoon the batter into the prepared pan and bake until a tester comes out clean (about 40 minutes).

Cool in the pan. Run a knife around the sides to loosen the cake. Release the pan and transfer to a serving plate. Serve at room temperature plain or with any of the toppings suggested above. *Makes 6–8 servings.*

Nutrients per serving: Calories 300, Fat 17g, Cholesterol 135mg, Sodium 90mg, Carbohydrates 35g, Protein 6g.

Angel-Sponge Cake

300°–350°

When my cousin planned to serve her specialty (angel food cake) at a party, she baked this GF version for me, using easily found flour from the baking section of her grocery. It is light and tender when fresh but does dry out more rapidly than other recipes in this book. This may be served with fresh berries or iced with a light icing. An easy one is the Whipped Cream Frosting on page 130.

1¼ cups potato starch flour (measured after sifting)	3 tablespoons lemon juice
¼ teaspoon salt	6 eggs
1½ teaspoons fresh lemon zest	1½ cups white sugar
	¼ cup boiling water

Preheat oven to 300°. Have ready an ungreased 10" tube pan.

In a medium bowl, sift together the potato starch flour and the salt 3 times. Grate the lemon for zest and squeeze the lemon to get the juice.

Separate the eggs. Place the yolks in the bowl of your mixer and the whites in a grease-free bowl to be beaten later. Beat the yolks until light and fluffy. Add the sugar gradually, beating on medium. Add the lemon zest and the juice mixed with the boiling water. Remove the bowl from the mixer and fold in the dry ingredients.

Beat the egg whites until they form stiff peaks. Fold into the batter gently. Spoon into the tube pan and bake for 30 minutes at 300°. Increase the heat to 350° and bake for 40 minutes longer. Remove from the oven and invert the pan to cool. *Makes 10–12 servings.*

Nutrients per serving: Calories 220, Fat 3g, Cholesterol 115mg, Sodium 95mg, Carbohydrates 44g, Protein 5g.

Chocolate Mousse Cake

Rich and buttery tasting, this flourless cake may be served to any guest without apologies.

CAKE:
7 ounces semisweet chocolate
½ cup (1 stick) butter or margarine
7 eggs
1 cup sugar, divided
1 teaspoon vanilla
1 teaspoon cream of tartar

TOPPING:
1 cup whipping cream or 2 cups
  nondairy whipped topping
⅓ cup confectioners' sugar (for
  whipping cream)
1 teaspoon vanilla

Preheat oven to 325°. Have handy a 9" springform pan. Do not grease.

In a microwaveable bowl, combine the chocolate and butter. Melt in microwave on defrost or low. Separate the eggs, placing the yolks in one mixing bowl and the whites in another (not plastic). Add cream of tartar to the whites.

In the mixing bowl with the egg yolks, add ¾ cup of the sugar and beat until light and fluffy (about 5 minutes). Blend in the melted chocolate mix and vanilla.

Whip the egg whites until soft peaks form. Add the remaining sugar, 1 tablespoon at a time. Continue beating until stiff peaks form. Fold this into the chocolate mixture. Pour into the prepared pan and bake for approximately 35 minutes. Remove from the oven and let cool. Cake may drop as it cools.

Remove the springform rim. Refrigerate until cool and then spread with topping.

For the whipped cream topping, beat the cream until soft peaks form. Add the confectioners' sugar and vanilla. Beat until stiff.

For the nondairy whipped topping, add the vanilla to the already sweetened topping. *Makes 10–12 servings.*

*Nutrients per serving: Calories 390, Fat 28g, Cholesterol 190mg,
Sodium 130mg, Carbohydrates 32g, Protein 5g.*

Almond Cake

It's hard to believe that this delicious, springy, almond-filled cake contains no flour and very little sugar. With its zingy lemon tang, it's a sure winner. Serve it with ice cream, fruit, or nibble on it plain.

1⅓ cups (6 ounces) slivered almonds
8 tablespoons sugar, divided
4 eggs, separated

5 teaspoons fresh grated lemon peel (2 large lemons)
½ teaspoon Chinese five spice or apple pie spice
Pinch of salt

Preheat oven to 375°. Grease an 8" square cake pan with 1½" sides. Line the bottom with waxed paper and grease.

Place almonds and 2 tablespoons of the sugar in the bowl of your food processor and grind until fine.

Separate the eggs, placing the whites in the bowl of your mixer and the yolks in a mixing bowl. To the yolks add 2 tablespoons sugar, the lemon peel, spice, and salt. Using an electric mixer, beat until thick and smooth (about 2 minutes). Stir in the ground almonds.

Beat the egg whites until soft peaks form. Gradually add the remaining 4 tablespoons of sugar, beating until peaks are stiff but not dry. Gently fold one third of the whites into the almond-yolk mix. Add the rest in 2 more folds. Spoon the batter into the prepared pan. Bake for 35–40 minutes, or until a tester comes out clean. Cool for 10 minutes in the pan and then reverse onto a cake plate. Remove the waxed paper. *Makes 12 servings.*

Nutrients per serving: Calories 130, Fat 8g, Cholesterol 70mg, Sodium 40mg, Carbohydrates 12g, Protein 6g.

Almond Torte with Chocolate and Orange   350°

In Mexico, chocolate is often combined with ground almonds and flavored with cinnamon. This torte has these flavors combined with orange to make a dessert no one will guess is gluten free. This can be frosted with your favorite light and fluffy icing or served with whipped topping, frozen yogurt, or ice cream.

2 cups almond meal	6 eggs, separated
Zest of 3 oranges	½ cup sugar
3 ounces baking chocolate, grated	3 tablespoons orange juice
1½ teaspoons ground cinnamon	3 tablespoons apricot brandy

Preheat oven to 350°. Grease the bottom and sides of a 9" springform pan with vegetable spray. Line the pan with waxed paper and respray.

In a medium bowl, combine the almond meal, orange zest, grated chocolate, and cinnamon. Set aside.

In a mixing bowl, beat the egg yolks until light and lemon colored. Add the sugar, half at a time. In the bowl of your mixer, using clean beaters, beat the egg whites until stiff.

Beat the almond meal mixture, the orange juice, and one third of the egg whites with the egg yolks. Fold in the rest of the whites and spoon the batter into the prepared pan. Bake for 35–40 minutes or until the cake pulls away from the sides of the pan.

Loosen the sides of the pan and cool for 10 minutes before inverting onto a rack to cool. Remove the paper immediately and paint on the brandy with a pastry brush.

When cool, frost if desired or cut and serve with a whipped topping. *Makes 10–12 servings.*

Nutrients per serving: Calories 220, Fat 16g, Cholesterol 105mg, Sodium 35mg, Carbohydrates 15g, Protein 8g.

Chocolate Bean Cake

350°

The tasters wouldn't believe this was made with only 2 tablespoons of cornstarch. The taste and texture were as good, if not better, than many of my other chocolate cakes.

½ cup dried cherries, soaked
1 cup canned garbanzo beans, drained
1 cup canned fava (or northern) beans, drained
½ cup green or unripe tomato, pureed

4 eggs
1 teaspoon cherry flavoring
2 tablespoons cornstarch
1 cup brown sugar
3 tablespoons cocoa powder
1 teaspoon baking powder
½ teaspoon baking soda

Preheat oven to 350°. Grease an 8" square pan.

Place the cherries in a small bowl and cover with boiling water. Set aside. Separate the eggs, placing the whites in a large bowl to beat separately. (This step may be eliminated, but it makes a far lighter cake.) If you wish, add the eggs one at a time at the place I suggest adding the yolks. Beat after each addition.

In a food processor, puree the beans with the tomato puree until very smooth. Add the egg yolks and beat until smooth. Add cherry flavoring.

In a medium bowl, whisk together the cornstarch, brown sugar, cocoa, baking powder, and baking soda. Add to the egg mix and beat only until well blended. If whipping eggs separately, beat only until soft peaks form, and fold gently into batter.

Drain the cherries and stir in. Spoon into the prepared pan and bake for 50 minutes, or until a tester inserted in the center comes out clean.

Serve warm or cool, garnished with whipped topping, or frost with your favorite icing. *Makes 9 servings.*

Nutrients per serving: Calories 220, Fat 3g, Cholesterol 85mg,
Sodium 140mg, Carbohydrates 42g, Protein 7g.

Mini Sponge Cakes

Probably the one shortcut I miss the most is being able to pick up that package of sponge shortcakes featured at the grocery store during strawberry season. When a tester sent me this recipe I had to make it, even though it was February and strawberries were imported and expensive. It really does taste like those I remember from the package! And best of all, there are no special ingredients involved.

½ cup (1 stick) butter or margarine	1 teaspoon vanilla
1 cup confectioners' sugar	1 cup cornstarch
4 eggs	1¼ teaspoons baking powder

Preheat oven to 375°. Grease a 12-muffin pan for large 2½" muffins or a 15-muffin pan for smaller ones.

In the bowl of your mixer, cream the butter and sugar. Add the eggs and vanilla. Beat until light and fluffy. Mix the cornstarch and baking powder together and add slowly to the creamed mixture. (If added too quickly, it will fly about the kitchen.) Mix until well blended. Fill the muffin tins half full. Bake for 15 minutes. Remove from the pan while still warm. Serve topped with berries or Lemon Cream (page 316). *Makes 12–15 minicakes.*

*Nutrients per serving: Calories 180, Fat 9g, Cholesterol 90mg,
Sodium 140mg, Carbohydrates 20g, Protein 2g.*

Jelly Roll
(with Cornstarch)

375°

I was surprised when I tried this with cornstarch. The roll is just as tender as when made with rice flour and keeps just as well. For several variations see page 91 under Featherlight Sponge Roll.

⅔ cup cornstarch
1 teaspoon unflavored gelatin
¼ teaspoon salt
1 teaspoon baking powder
⅔ cup sugar
1 teaspoon dried lemon peel
4 eggs, separated

½ teaspoon cream of tartar
Confectioners' sugar for dusting
Lemon Curd (pages 314 and 315),
 berry jam, lemon cream, whipped
 cream, or nondairy whipped
 topping for filling

Preheat oven to 375°. Grease the bottom and sides of a 10" × 15" jelly roll pan. Line the bottom with waxed paper and spray with vegetable oil spray.

In a medium bowl, sift together the cornstarch, gelatin, salt, baking powder, and all but 1 tablespoon of the sugar. Whisk in the dried lemon peel. Set aside.

Separate the eggs, placing the yolks in a small bowl and the whites in the bowl of your mixer. Beat the egg yolks until thick and lemon colored. Set aside.

Beat the whites until frothy. Add the reserved tablespoon of sugar and the cream of tartar. Continue beating until glossy and stiff. Remove the beaters.

Gently fold the egg yolks into the whites. Fold in the dry ingredients in 3 parts. Pour the batter into the prepared pan and bake for 15–18 minutes, or until the top springs back after being lightly pressed.

Invert immediately onto a smooth cotton tea towel that has been dusted with confectioners' sugar. Remove the waxed paper. Immediately roll the warm sponge cake and tea towel, making sure the towel separates the sections of the cake. Let cool. Unroll and spread with the desired filling. Roll up again (without the towel) and dust the top with confectioners' sugar (if desired). Rewrap with foil. To serve, cut into 1½" slices. *Makes 8 servings.*

Nutrients per serving: Calories 120, Fat 25g, Cholesterol 110mg, Sodium 150mg, Carbohydrates 22g, Protein 3g.

Nut Butter Drops 350°

This was the first cookie I ate after my diagnosis. It was made with peanut butter and tasted so good, I couldn't believe it was gluten free. Now, with all the nut butters on the market, you can make it with many different flavors. If your nut butter isn't chunky, add a few finely chopped nuts to give it crunch. Try almond, cashew, hazelnut, or the new soynut butters.

Note: *Always use a processed nut butter such as Jif, not one of the natural or organic butters.*

2 eggs	1 cup sugar
1 cup nut butter, crunchy or smooth	1 teaspoon baking soda

Preheat oven to 350°.

Beat the eggs. Stir in the nut butter, sugar, and baking soda.

Drop by small spoonfuls on ungreased cookie sheets. Bake for 10–12 minutes. *Makes approximately 2½ dozen 2" cookies.*

Nutrients per cookie: Calories 80, Fat 4g, Cholesterol 5mg, Sodium 50mg, Carbohydrates 8g, Protein 3g.

Orange Shortbread

When an Australian friend invited us on a picnic in Sydney, she wanted to serve a dessert I could eat. She searched her cookbooks to find this gluten-free crowd pleaser with ingredients she could buy in her local grocery.

Note: *Look for sweet rice flour in small boxes next to the cornstarch and potato starch flours.*

½ cup (1 stick) butter or margarine   ½ cup sweet rice flour
½ cup cornstarch   1 teaspoon fresh grated orange zest
¼ cup sugar

Preheat oven to 350°.

Place the butter in a medium bowl. Sift the cornstarch and sugar over it and work in with a pastry blender (or your fingers). Add the sweet rice flour and orange zest. Work until the dough feels plastic-like.

Pat the dough onto an 8" square cake pan using a little flour on the fingers (if needed) to prevent them from sticking to the dough. Prick the sheet liberally with a fork. Bake for 12–15 minutes or until the batter starts to turn golden at the edges. Remove from the oven and cut immediately into 1¼" squares. Allow to cool in the pan before removing. *Makes 3 dozen squares.*

Nutrients per square: Calories 45, Fat 2½g, Cholesterol 5mg, Sodium 30mg, Carbohydrates 5g, Protein 0g.

---

*S*hortbread is preferably made with butter to retain its characteristic flavor and richness, but for the lactose intolerant it can be made with a good-quality margarine.

Lemon Melts

350°

This tiny frosted cookie absolutely melts in your mouth, leaving a zesty lemon taste. It's easy to blend together in a mixer, refrigerate in a roll, and then slice and bake. The frosting adds the final touch that makes this a fine dessert cookie to serve with fruit or mousse for any occasion.

COOKIES:

1½ cups cornstarch

One (2 teaspoons) envelope
  plain gelatin

⅓ cup confectioners' sugar

¾ cup (1½ sticks) butter, softened

1 teaspoon lemon zest

1 tablespoon lemon juice

FROSTING:

¾ cup confectioners' sugar

¼ cup (½ stick) butter

1 teaspoon lemon zest

1 teaspoon lemon juice

Place all of the cookie ingredients in the bowl of your mixer. Beat on low, scraping the sides of bowl often. Blend until it forms a firm dough. With your hands, shape half the dough into a 1" roll about 8" long. Wrap in plastic wrap. Repeat with the other half. Refrigerate until firm (1–2 hours).

Preheat oven to 350°. To form cookies, use a sharp knife and slice into ¼" rounds. Place about 1" apart on ungreased cookie sheets. Bake for 12 minutes or until slightly tinged with color. Cool completely before frosting.

For the frosting, combine all frosting ingredients in a small bowl. Beat on medium, scraping the bowl often. Frost the cookies and store in layers between plastic wrap in sealed tins. Refrigerate or freeze for serving later. *Makes 4 dozen cookies.*

*Nutrients per cookie: Calories 60, Fat 4g, Cholesterol 10mg,
Sodium 40mg, Carbohydrates 6g, Protein 0g.*

Marshmallow Krisp Bars

A light, crisp, no-bake bar. This is easy to make and not too sweet. Be sure the crisp rice cereal does not contain gluten.

¼ cup (½ stick) margarine or butter   6 cups GF crisp rice cereal
One 10-ounce package (about 40)
    regular size marshmallows or 4
    cups miniature marshmallows

Butter a 9" × 13" oblong cake pan.

Melt the margarine in a saucepan on low heat. Drop in the marshmallows, stirring often until melted. Remove from the heat and stir into the cereal. Press the mixture into the prepared pan. Cool before cutting into approximately 2" squares.

Microwave directions: Place the margarine and marshmallows in a microwave-safe bowl and microwave on high for 2 minutes. Stir and continue to microwave for another minute. Add to the cereal and continue from above. *Makes 24 bars.*

Nutrients per bar: Calories 80, Fat 2g, Cholesterol 5mg,
Sodium 75mg, Carbohydrates 16g, Protein 1g.

---

*T*o avoid scarring your baking pan when cutting bar cookies, line the pan with foil, leaving extra length on the sides to fold back as handles. Remove the fully baked cake to cut into desired shapes.

Mocha Puffs

A featherlight cookie with great taste. These meringues go well with puddings and Jell-O to make ordinary desserts into company ones.

1 teaspoon espresso powder	⅛ teaspoon salt
1½ teaspoons vanilla	¾ cup sugar
3 large egg whites at room temperature	2 tablespoons cocoa powder (Dutch processed)
⅛ teaspoon cream of tartar	

Preheat oven to 250°. Line 2 baking sheets with aluminum foil or parchment paper. In a small bowl, dissolve espresso powder in the vanilla. Set aside.

In the bowl of your mixer, combine the egg whites, cream of tartar, and salt. Beat on medium until foamy. With the beater going, gradually add the sugar and beat until medium-stiff peaks form. Add the coffee-vanilla liquid and whip until stiff peaks form. Remove the bowl from its stand and fold in the cocoa powder. (It doesn't matter if the batter is streaked. That adds interest to the finished look.)

With a spoon and rubber spatula, drop the mixture onto prepared sheets in balls with a diameter the size of a quarter. Leave 1" between cookies to allow for slight flattening.

Bake for 40–45 minutes. Remove from the oven and cool 5 minutes before removing from foil or parchment. *Makes about 40 cookies.*

Nutrients per cookie: Calories 20, Fat 0g, Cholesterol 0mg,
Sodium 10mg, Carbohydrates 4g, Protein 0g.

Date-Nut Kisses

An easy but elegant cookie to serve with fruit for that sweet at the end of the meal.

3 egg whites
⅛ teaspoon salt
1 cup sugar

½ cup chopped dates
½ cup chopped pecans or walnuts

Preheat oven to 375°. Line 2 cookie sheets with clean brown wrapping paper.

In a metal or glass mixing bowl (not plastic), whip the eggs with the salt until soft peaks form. Add the sugar gradually while still beating. Fold in the dates and nuts.

Drop the batter (like a meringue) from a spoon onto the paper, putting about 18 on a cookie sheet. Place in the oven. Wait until the heat has returned to 375° and turn the oven off. Leave in the oven for 1½ hours. To remove from brown paper, slide it onto a damp (not wet) counter and remove the cookies with a spatula. *Makes about 3 dozen.*

Nutrients per cookie: Calories 40, Fat 1g, Cholesterol 0mg,
Sodium 10mg, Carbohydrates 7g, Protein 0g.

Caramel-Pecan Kisses

325°

If you have pecans in the house, try this easy, tasty nibble that takes nothing but sugar and egg whites.

2 egg whites	1½ cups pecans, ground medium
1¼ cups brown sugar	fine with 1 tablespoon white
	sugar

Preheat oven to 325°. Line 2 baking sheets with Teflon liners or brown wrapping paper.

Using the egg-beater attachment in your mixer, beat the egg whites on high until stiff. Add the brown sugar slowly and continue beating until very thick (about 2 minutes). Fold in the ground pecans.

Drop by heaping teaspoonfuls onto the prepared sheets, spacing cookies about 2" apart. Bake for 12–14 minutes or until the cookies are slightly cracked. Let the cookies cool slightly before transferring them to a rack to cool. (If using brown paper, slide the paper to a damp counter surface for easy removal.) *Makes 3½ dozen cookies.*

Nutrients per cookie: Calories 50, Fat 2½g, Cholesterol 0mg, Sodium 5mg, Carbohydrates 7g, Protein 0g.

Coconut Macaroons

300°

A cookie for coconut lovers—and made without any special ingredients. These do not travel well, for they are brittle, but they can be made ahead and frozen for that special occasion.

Note: *If you don't have the fine macaroon coconut, put unsweetened shredded coconut in a food processor and chop to a finer texture.*

3 cups macaroon coconut (see note)	3 large egg whites
2 tablespoons cornstarch	1 cup sugar
	2 teaspoons vanilla

Preheat oven to 300°. Grease 2 large cookie sheets.

Combine the coconut and cornstarch in a medium bowl and set aside.

In the bowl of your mixer, beat the egg whites on medium to form soft peaks. Increase to medium high. Slowly pour the sugar in a very thin stream into the egg whites. Stir in the vanilla and coconut. Drop spoonfuls the size of very small eggs onto the prepared cookie sheets. These will not spread, so you may place them close together.

Bake for about 20 minutes or until slightly browned. *Makes 3½ dozen.*

Nutrients per macaroon: Calories 60, Fat 3g, Cholesterol 15mg, Sodium 25mg, Carbohydrates 9g, Protein 1g.

Raspberry Whispers

200°

The delicate taste of raspberry makes these meringues different and delicious.

4 egg whites	1 teaspoon almond flavoring
¼ teaspoon salt	1 cup sugar
¼ teaspoon cream of tartar	⅓ cup raspberry preserves

Preheat oven to 200°. Line 2 cookie sheets with foil. Have egg whites at room temperature.

In the bowl of your mixer, beat the egg whites until foamy. Add the salt, cream of tartar, and flavoring. Beat on medium until very soft peaks form. With mixer running slowly, add the sugar in a very thin stream. Beat until stiff peaks form. Beat in the preserves.

Drop by large teaspoonfuls onto the foil. Place these 1½" apart as they don't spread or swell much. Bake for 3½ hours. Turn off the heat without opening the oven and allow to stand for 3½ more hours. Remove from the foil and store in an airtight container. *Makes 3½ dozen cookies.*

Nutrients per cookie: Calories 25, Fat 0g, Cholesterol 0mg,
Sodium 15mg, Carbohydrates 6g, Protein 0g.

Haystacks

A very simple coconut drop calling for just 3 ingredients. Serve these with a bowl of Jell-O or plain pudding to dress up the dessert.

One 14-ounce package (4 cups) lightly packed coconut	½ cup sugar 3 eggs

Preheat oven to 350°. Grease 2 cookie sheets.

Chop the coconut slightly in the food processor. Place in a medium bowl and add the sugar. In a smaller bowl, beat the eggs until frothy. Combine the eggs with the coconut and mix thoroughly. Spoon out in 1" mounds on the prepared sheets. Bake for 12–15 minutes. Watch the oven. They should turn golden brown. Remove from the sheets while still warm. *Makes 3 dozen haystacks.*

*Nutrients per drop: Calories 70, Fat 4g, Cholesterol 20mg,
Sodium 45mg, Carbohydrates 7g, Protein 1g.*

Fruit and Nut Dessert Bars

A dessert for traveling! This sweet bar is a dessert that can be wrapped in plastic and carried in a lunch box, purse, or pocket. This keeps well.

1½ cups cut-up dried fruit (apricots, pineapple slices, dates, prunes, or raisins) or a combination

2 cups chopped nuts of choice
½ cup sweetened condensed milk

Preheat oven to 325°. Lay aluminum foil on the bottom of a 7" × 12" oblong pan so the ends extend up over the ends of the pan (for a handle to remove the foil in one lift). Lightly grease with margarine or butter.

Cut the fruit into tiny bits or chop with a food processor (do not overprocess).

In a large bowl, mix the fruit and nuts. Drizzle on the sweetened condensed milk and blend until it covers all the fruit and nuts (this will be sticky). Spoon into the prepared pan and pat smooth with greased hands. Bake for 25 minutes.

When slightly cool, remove from the pan using the foil handles. Cool before cutting into bars, approximately 1½" × 3". *Makes 16 bars.*

Nutrients per bar: Calories 180, Fat 11g, Cholesterol 5mg,
Sodium 140mg, Carbohydrates 20g, Protein 4g.

Rice Balls with Fruit and Nuts
(No-Bake)

So simple the children can help make these. So delicious the adults will keep eating them. If you buy chopped dates, be sure they aren't dusted with flour. It's safest to buy whole dates and chop them yourself.

1 cup (2 sticks) margarine or butter
1½ cups sugar
2 tablespoons milk or nondairy creamer
2 cups chopped dates

1 teaspoon salt
1 cup chopped walnuts or pecans
2 teaspoons vanilla
4½ cups GF crisped rice cereal
Flake coconut for rolling

In a medium saucepan, combine the margarine, sugar, milk, dates, and salt. Bring to a boil and cook for 2 minutes. Add the nuts, vanilla, and cereal.

Grease your hands and shape the mixture into balls of about 1¼" in diameter. Roll in coconut and set on waxed paper to cool and harden. Store in plastic containers with lids. *Makes approximately 6 dozen balls.*

*Nutrients per ball: Calories 70, Fat 4g, Cholesterol 0mg,
Sodium 80mg, Carbohydrates 10g, Protein 1g.*

---

*I*f you replace butter in a rolled cookie recipe with margarine, it will be softer, so you may need to chill the dough to make it more workable.

Pineapple Angel Pie

Fill the Meringue Pie Shell (page 301) or the Absolutely Sinful Cereal Crust (page 302) with this melt-in-your-mouth pie filling and listen to your guests rave.

¾ cup sugar	2 tablespoons lemon juice
¼ cup cornstarch	2 tablespoons butter or margarine
½ teaspoon salt	2 egg yolks, slightly beaten
One 20-ounce can crushed pineapple	1 cup whipping cream whipped or 2 cups nondairy whipped topping

Combine the sugar, cornstarch, and salt in a saucepan. Gradually stir in the pineapple and its juice, lemon juice, and butter. Cook over medium heat, stirring constantly, until thickened. Add a little of the hot pineapple to the egg yolks, then combine the egg yolk mixture with the hot liquids in the saucepan.

Cook for 1–2 minutes more, stirring constantly. Chill until cold. Fold the whipped cream or nondairy whipped topping into the cool pineapple mixture. Pour into the prepared shell. Refrigerate until serving time. *Makes 6 servings.*

VARIATIONS:

CRANBERRY-ORANGE PIE: Substitute one 12-ounce carton cranberry orange sauce plus ⅓ cup orange juice for the pineapple.

APRICOT ANGEL PIE: Substitute one 17-ounce can apricot halves, drained and pureed, plus ⅓ cup reserved juice for the pineapple.

*Nutrients per serving: Calories 350, Fat 18g, Cholesterol 125mg,
Sodium 270mg, Carbohydrates 47g, Protein 2g.*

Meringue Pie Shell

Even though I offered this in my first book, it is so good and easy that I had to include it in this collection. Use this sweet, frothy shell for light, fluffy pies like the Pineapple Angel Pie (page 300), or fill it with Lemon Cream (page 316).

2 egg whites	½ teaspoon vanilla
¼ teaspoon cream of tartar	½ cup sugar
¼ teaspoon salt	

Preheat oven to 275°. Grease a deep 9" pie pan.

Place the egg whites, cream of tartar, salt, and vanilla in the bowl of your mixer and beat until foamy. Then, beating constantly, add the sugar 1 tablespoon at a time. Beat until the peaks are very stiff and glossy. Spread the mixture on the sides and bottom of the prepared pan. Bake for 1 hour. Cool away from drafts before filling.

Nutrients per serving (⅙ of crust): Calories 70, Fat 0g, Cholesterol 0mg, Sodium 105mg, Carbohydrates 17g, Protein 1g.

Shiny metal pie pans work for cereal and crumb crusts, but for the best pastry baking, use glass or dull metal pans.

Absolutely Sinful Cereal Crust

This crust is so rich, it is truly sinful. It's also so special I had to repeat it in this book. Use it for any of your open-faced pies, whether they be fruit, pumpkin, or custard cream. But be prepared to cut the pieces smaller than usual, for this is a rich crust. Try this also for cheesecake.

Note: *If macaroon coconut (a fine grind) is not available in your store, use flaked or shredded coconut and chop it finer in a food processor.*

3 tablespoons butter or margarine, melted
⅔ cup brown sugar
1 cup GF rice flakes, crushed
1 cup GF cornflakes, crushed
⅔ cup macaroon coconut
⅔ cup finely ground walnuts

Stir together all the ingredients. Line a deep 9" greased pie tin with the mix, patting well up the sides, or pat into a 10" springform pan for cheesecake. Bake as directed for the filling used.

If the filling is already cooked, bake in a preheated 375° oven for 6 minutes, or until the crust is slightly browned. Cool before filling. *Makes 1 deep 9" pie crust or a 10" cheesecake crust.*

Nutrients per serving (⅛ of crust): Calories 220, Fat 11g, Cholesterol 10mg, Sodium 180mg, Carbohydrates 31g, Protein 3g.

Pineapple-Lemon Mousse
(with Substitutes for the Lactose Intolerant)

A flavorful, light dessert that takes no special ingredients. Make it for yourself or be sure your friends get a copy of the recipe so they can make a dessert you can have. This can be prepared a day ahead, to save time on party day.

Note: *The recipe below can easily be doubled.*

One 8-ounce can crushed pineapple
One 3-ounce package lemon-
  flavored gelatin
⅓ cup (about) pineapple juice
¼ cup water
1½ tablespoons lemon juice

1 tablespoon lemon zest
1 cup whipping cream or 1½ cups
  nondairy whipped topping
2 teaspoons vanilla (if using
  whipping cream)

Drain the pineapple in a sieve set over a measuring cup. Add enough juice to yield ¾ cup. Place the juice in a small saucepan and bring to a boil.

Place the gelatin in a large mixing bowl and pour the boiling juice over it. Stir until the gelatin dissolves. Mix in the drained pineapple, water, lemon juice, and lemon zest. Refrigerate until the mixture just begins to set, stirring occasionally.

If using whipping cream, beat it with the vanilla until stiff peaks form. Fold this or the whipped topping into the gelatin mixture. Transfer to a large serving bowl or spoon into serving dishes or goblets. Cover and refrigerate until well chilled, 4 hours to overnight. *Makes 5–6 servings.*

*Nutrients per serving: Calories 200, Fat 13g, Cholesterol 45mg,
Sodium 110mg, Carbohydrates 22g, Protein 1g.*

Chocolate Pots de Crème
(with Substitute for the Lactose Intolerant)

A smooth and flavorful baked chocolate pudding. All of my former Pots de Crème recipes did not cook the eggs, so there was the problem of possible salmonella. This easy recipe solves that problem.

1½ cups half-and-half or nondairy creamer
½ cup sugar
¾ cup semisweet chocolate chips or chopped chocolate

4 egg yolks
2 teaspoons vanilla
Whipped cream, sweetened, or nondairy whipped topping

Preheat oven to 350°. Have handy 6 custard cups or ramekins.

In a medium saucepan, bring the cream and sugar to a simmer, stirring occasionally. Remove from the heat and add the chocolate chips. Let stand about ½ minute before stirring, until the chocolate melts. Whisk in the yolks and vanilla.

Pour into the custard cups and place in a 9" × 13" pan. Pour hot water into the pan to come up 1" on the sides of the cups. Bake 25–30 minutes, or until almost set in the centers. Remove from the water to cool and serve warm or refrigerated, topped with whipped cream or nondairy topping. *Makes 6 servings.*

Nutrients per serving: Calories 304, Fat 19g, Cholesterol 164mg,
Sodium 33mg, Carbohydrates 33g, Protein 5g.

Maple Walnut Pudding

Dark brown sugar and maple flavoring make this tasty pudding good enough for any party.

Note: *This recipe may be halved for 4 servings.*

2 eggs	3 cups milk or nondairy liquid
⅔ cup dark brown sugar	2 teaspoons maple flavor
2 tablespoons cornstarch	⅓ cup chopped walnuts
¼ teaspoon salt	

Beat the eggs in a small bowl and set aside.

In a saucepan, combine the brown sugar, cornstarch, and salt. Stir in the milk to a thin paste and then add the rest, stirring until smooth. Cook over medium heat, stirring constantly, until bubbly. Cook and stir for 1 minute.

Remove from the heat and slowly stir about 1 cup of hot mixture into the beaten eggs. Gradually stir this mixture into the saucepan. Return to the heat and cook for 1 minute, stirring constantly. Remove and add the maple flavor.

Pour into 8 dessert dishes, top with the walnuts, and let cool, or stir in the walnuts and pour into a bowl to cool. Refrigerate or serve immediately. Spoon from this bowl to serve, topping with a dab of whipped topping or whipped cream. *Makes 8 servings.*

Nutrients per serving: Calories 180, Fat 6g, Cholesterol 65mg, Sodium 135mg, Carbohydrates 26g, Protein 5g.

Dairy-free Baked Custard

325°

When I first tried to make one of my favorite comfort desserts, a baked custard, I discovered that most nondairy milk substitutes would not firm up into that soft, smooth, jellylike consistency of the dairy custards. I kept trying until I found a soy beverage with the right combination of ingredients to bake in a custardlike milk or cream: plain Westsoy. You may use Lite to save calories; the flavor is still rich and creamy. Other nondairy liquids with the same combination of ingredients may work as well, but I have not experimented with them.

3 eggs, beaten	1 teaspoon vanilla
1½ cups nondairy substitute	Ground nutmeg or cinnamon
⅓ cup sugar	(optional)

Preheat oven to 325°. Place 4 custard cups or a 3½-cup soufflé dish in a square 9" pan or baking dish.

In a medium bowl, combine the eggs, nondairy liquid, sugar, and vanilla. Whisk until combined but not foamy (overbeating will leave bubbles on the surface). Pour the mixture into the prepared cups or dish. Sprinkle with cinnamon or nutmeg, if desired. Place the dish on a rack in the middle of the oven and pour boiling water into the dish around the cups to a depth of about 1".

Bake for 35–40 minute for the cups or 50–60 minutes for the soufflé dish, or until a knife inserted into the center comes out clean. Remove cups or dish from the water immediately to stop the cooking. Cool and serve at room temperature, or remove to refrigerator and cover. *Makes 4 servings.*

Nutrients per serving: Calories 160, Fat 6g, Cholesterol 160mg, Sodium 90mg, Carbohydrates 21g, Protein 5g.

Crème Brûlée 300°

This rich cream custard dessert, unlike the following flan recipe, is cooked on the top of the stove and poured into either custard cups or a large casserole and baked for a shorter time. This dessert can be made ahead, even to the final burnt sugar topping, and then refrigerated.

3 cups heavy cream or nondairy creamer
¼ cup sugar

3 eggs plus 3 egg yolks
1½ teaspoons vanilla
½ cup dark brown sugar

Preheat oven to 300°.

In the top of a double boiler over hot water, heat the cream and sugar until tiny bubbles form around the edge of the pan. Lower the heat and simmer for 1 minute. Remove from the heat.

In a medium bowl, beat the eggs and yolks. Pour the cream mixture into the beaten eggs in a thin stream, stirring constantly. Return the custard to the double boiler and cook over medium heat, stirring, until the custard coats the back of the spoon (3–4 minutes).

Add the vanilla and pour into 6 custard dishes or a 4–5 cup casserole. Set the cups (or casserole) in a large pan of hot water level with the custard and bake for 35–45 minutes, or until the center of the custard is set. Remove from water and cool. Refrigerate after cooling.

To serve, sift the brown sugar on top of the crème and place the dishes in pan of crushed ice. Broil at about 6 inches from the heat until the sugar carmelizes and forms a hard crust. Serve immediately or chill until serving time. *Makes 6–8 servings.*

*Nutrients per serving: Calories 560, Fat 49g, Cholesterol 375mg,
Sodium 85mg, Carbohydrates 24g, Protein 7g.*

Genevieve's Flan

350°

This custard dessert, served throughout Spain and Portugal, can be made easily in your own kitchen. The friend who sent it said that even if you choose the light cream cheese and low-fat milks, it will still turn out delicious.

4 eggs (or 3 eggs plus 2 yolks)

2 ounces regular or light cream cheese

One 14-ounce can regular or light sweetened condensed milk

One 12-ounce can regular or low-fat evaporated milk

1½ teaspoons vanilla

½–¾ cup white sugar

Preheat oven to 350°.

In a blender or mixer, whip the eggs, cream cheese, condensed milk, and evaporated milk for 7 minutes.

While those are blending, place the sugar in a heavy frying pan and cook over very low heat for about 7–10 minutes, until the sugar is melted and straw colored. Remove from the heat and pour into a Pyrex pie pan. Pour in the cream mix.

To bake, set the pie pan in another pan filled with about a ½" of hot water. Bake for 70 minutes. Invert on a large plate and spoon out the servings, including some of the caramel sauce for each. *Makes 8–10 servings.*

Nutrients per serving: Calories 350, Fat 13g, Cholesterol 145mg,
Sodium 160mg, Carbohydrates 51g, Protein 10g.

Coconut Flan

350°

Finally, a custard that will bake substituting some of our dairy-free milk for part of the recipe. And this is delicious.

One 14-ounce can sweetened
   condensed milk (no substitute)
1⅓ cups 4% milk or nondairy
   substitute

2 eggs plus 3 egg yolks, beaten
½ teaspoon vanilla
¾ cup angel flake coconut

Preheat oven to 350°.

In a medium bowl, whisk together the sweetened condensed milk, 4% milk, beaten eggs, and vanilla. Stir in the coconut.

Divide the mixture among 6 custard cups or large muffin cups and place in a 9" × 13" baking pan. Pour hot water into the pan to come about 1" up the sides of the cups. Bake for 30 minutes. Remove the cups from the water and cool. Refrigerate. To serve, top with a bit of coconut, whipped topping, or fruit. These can be made 1 to 2 days ahead. *Makes 6 servings.*

Nutrients per serving: Calories 360, Fat 15g, Cholesterol 210mg,
Sodium 135mg, Carbohydrates 44g, Protein 11g.

White Chocolate Rice Pudding

You won't have to apologize for serving a "common" rice pudding when you offer your guests this delicious version. Top it with a dab of whipped cream or nondairy topping with a piece of fruit on top (cherry, strawberry, or raspberry) or a dab of colorful jam. Or serve it with a sauce of mashed and sweetened fruit during fruit season.

4½ cups whole milk or nondairy substitute

⅔ cup white rice (not instant)

⅔ cup sugar

1 tablespoon vanilla

⅓ teaspoon salt

2 egg yolks

3 tablespoons rich cream or nondairy substitute

4 ounces white chocolate, chopped

Grated peel of 1 orange

¾ teaspoon cardamom

In a large saucepan, combine the milk, rice, sugar, vanilla, and salt. Cook over medium-low heat until thickened and the rice is tender (about 50 minutes). Stir occasionally.

Reduce heat to low. Whisk the egg yolks and cream in a small bowl until well blended. Add ½ cup of the rice mixture to this and add to the remaining rice. Cook for about 3 minutes, stirring until well blended. Remove from the heat and add the chocolate, stirring until melted. Add the orange peel and the cardamom. Transfer to a bowl. Cover and chill for several hours. Serve in dessert bowls or parfait glasses, and top as suggested above. *Makes 8 servings.*

Nutrients per serving: Calories 300, Fat 11g, Cholesterol 75mg, Sodium 580mg, Carbohydrates 44g, Protein 7g.

Lactose-free Mocha Pudding

The tofu combines beautifully with chocolate and coffee to make a real treat for those who can't have the usual chocolate puddings because of the dairy base.

3 egg yolks
3 tablespoons sugar
1 teaspoon vanilla
6 tablespoons sweet chocolate
   powder (I use Ghiradelli's)

Pinch salt
1 teaspoon espresso powder
1 cup silken tofu, blended smooth
1 cup nondairy whipped topping

In the top of a double boiler over hot water, whisk the yolks and sugar until light (about 3 minutes). Continue whisking over the simmering water until the mixture falls in ribbons when the whisk is lifted above the bowl.

Whisk in the vanilla, chocolate, salt, espresso powder, and tofu. Refrigerate to chill. Fold in the nondairy topping. Chill again before serving. *Makes 4 servings.*

Nutrients per serving: Calories 210, Fat 13g, Cholesterol 160mg, Sodium 160mg, Carbohydrates 20g, Protein 6g.

Lactose-free Tapioca Pudding

There are gluten-free tapioca puddings on most grocery shelves, but these are never lactose free. This is easy to make and delicious. The flavor can change with the different nondairy substitutes used. Try a nondairy creamer, thinned with half water, for a light pudding, or use a nut-based milk for a different flavor.

3 tablespoons quick-cooking tapioca

2 cups nondairy milk substitute

4 teaspoons pasteurized powdered egg whites

¼ cup water

6 tablespoons sugar, divided

2 egg yolks, beaten lightly

1 teaspoon vanilla

Nondairy whipped topping (optional)

Sprinkle the tapioca over the milk in a heavy saucepan. Let stand for 10 minutes to soften.

In a small bowl, sprinkle the egg white powder over the water. Beat until peaks form. Gradually add 3 tablespoons of the sugar and continue beating until stiff peaks form.

Bring the saucepan contents to a boil, stirring gently for about 6–8 minutes. Whisk the remaining sugar into the beaten yolks. Stir in a little of the hot tapioca mixture, and then stir this back into the saucepan. Cook for 4 minutes to thicken, stirring.

Remove from the stove. Add the vanilla and fold in the egg whites. Pour into a bowl. Refrigerate to chill. Serve in bowls topped with nondairy whipped topping. Add a maraschino cherry (if desired) for color. *Makes 6 servings.*

Nutrients per serving: Calories 300, Fat 13g, Cholesterol 110mg,
Sodium 180mg, Carbohydrates 33g, Protein 13g.

Microwave Custard Sauce

Use this quick-to-make custard sauce for a trifle or simple custard pudding, or mixed with bananas or coconut for a pie filling.

⅓ cup sugar	2 egg yolks
¼ cup cornstarch	1½ teaspoons vanilla
2 cups milk or nondairy substitute	

In a 4-cup microwave safe bowl, combine the sugar and cornstarch. Add about ¼ cup milk and stir until the cornstarch is dissolved and smooth. Whisk in the remaining milk. Cover with waxed paper and cook on high for 5–7 minutes, stirring twice, until the mixture comes to a boil and thickens. Whisk smooth.

In a small bowl, beat the egg yolks lightly. Gradually whisk in about ½ cup of the hot mixture. Whisk this into the milk mixture. Return the custard to the microwave oven to cook, uncovered, on high, for 1 minute more. Blend in the vanilla. *Makes 2 cups custard sauce.*

Nutrients per serving (½ cup): Calories 110, Fat 4g, Cholesterol 70mg, Sodium 35mg, Carbohydrates 16g, Protein 3g.

Microwave Lemon Curd

Microwave your lemon curd in about half the time and with a lot less work than cooking it on top of the stove.

½ cup (1 stick) butter or margarine   1½ teaspoons fresh lemon zest
½ cup sugar   3 eggs
⅓ cup lemon juice

In a 4-cup microwaveable bowl or measuring cup, place the butter, sugar, lemon juice, and lemon zest. Cook on high for 4 minutes. Stir.

In a small bowl, beat the eggs until blended. Gradually whisk about ⅓ cup of the hot lemon mixture into the eggs to warm them. Whisk this into the remaining lemon mixture. Cook on high for 1½ minutes. Whisk until smooth. Continue to cook for 1–2 minutes until thickened. Again, whisk until smooth. Cover and refrigerate for up to 3 days. *Makes 1½ cups.*

Nutrients per serving (2 tablespoons): Calories 140, Fat 9g, Cholesterol 75mg, Sodium 95mg, Carbohydrates 9g, Protein 1½g.

Top-of-the-Stove Lemon Curd

It's hard to find a gluten-free lemon curd in stores, so I've learned to make my own. Use this for the Lemon Cream (page 316) or in cake fillings, or in place of jam in making breakfast Danish. Or you may choose to fill tart shells or use the curd in a trifle (see page 259 for trifle suggestions).

⅔ cup sugar
½ cup lemon juice
Zest from 1 lemon

¼ cup (½ stick) margarine or butter
2 eggs, beaten

In a medium saucepan, blend all ingredients and cook over medium-low heat. Stir until thick enough to coat spoon, about 10 minutes. Do not let boil. Remove from the stove and pour into a bowl. Refrigerate for at least 2 hours. *Makes 1½ cups.*

Nutrients per serving (¼ cup): Calories 90, Fat 4½g, Cholesterol 35mg, Sodium 58mg, Carbohydrates 12g, Protein 1g.

Lemon Cream
(with Lemon Curd)

A marvelously easy but appealing lemon pudding. Serve this with a few gluten-free cookies (purchased or homemade), and you have company dessert. Or use this to fill tart shells, as a filling for cakes, or top the Mini Sponge Cakes (page 286).

Nondairy whipped topping or sweetened whipped cream
Top-of-the-Stove Lemon Curd (page 315)

Blend equal parts nondairy whipped topping (or sweetened whipped cream) and lemon curd.

Nutrients per serving (½ cup): Calories 180, Fat 12g, Cholesterol 35mg,
Sodium 60mg, Carbohydrates 19g, Protein 1g.

Million Dollar Cheesecake

This really lives up to its name, as both tasters and testers agree. It requires only a 6-minute baking of the crust and a few hours' chilling in the refrigerator. But it can be made ahead of a party (1 day or even 2), for it keeps well.

Note: *If you can't find macaroon coconut, put your coconut in a food processor and process to fine.*

CRUST:

3 tablespoons butter or margarine, melted
½ cup brown sugar
⅔ cup GF rice flakes, crushed
⅔ cup GF cornflakes, crushed
½ cup macaroon coconut (see note)
½ cup macadamia nuts, ground fine

FILLING:

⅓ cup lemon juice
One 14-ounce can sweetened condensed milk or fat-free sweetened condensed milk
One 20-ounce can crushed pineapple drained
One 9-ounce container nondairy whipped topping
1 cup chopped macadamia nuts (reserve ¼ for topping)
One 8-ounce package cream cheese or ⅓ fat-reduced cream cheese

Preheat oven to 375°.

To make the crust, in a medium bowl, stir together all the ingredients. Pat into the bottom of a 9" springform pan. Bake for 6 minutes, or until the crust is slightly browned. Cool before filling.

For the filling, in a large bowl, mix all the ingredients except ¼ cup of the macadamia nuts. Pour onto the crust in the springform pan. Top with the reserved nuts. Chill for several hours or overnight. Cut into small wedges. *Makes 12–16 servings.*

Nutrients per serving: Calories 360, Fat 25g, Cholesterol 30mg, Sodium 150mg, Carbohydrates 34g, Protein 5g.

Crustless Cheesecake #1 325°

This cheesecake is so delicious and fluffy, no one will miss the crust. Have all the ingredients at room temperature for easy mixing.

20 ounces cream cheese or light
   cream cheese
1⅓ cups sugar
Fresh zest from 1 orange
2 teaspoons vanilla

4 eggs
5 egg whites
Optional topping: sliced or crushed
   fruit, whipped cream, or
   nondairy whipped topping

Preheat oven to 325°. Butter a 10" springform pan and line the bottom of the pan with waxed paper. Butter the paper. Wrap the outside of the pan with foil.

Place the cream cheese and sugar in the bowl of your mixer and beat until smooth. Add the orange zest and vanilla. Turn speed to low and beat in the whole eggs, one at a time. In another bowl, beat the egg whites to soft peaks. Fold the whites into the cream cheese mixture in 2 additions.

Spoon the batter into the prepared pan. Set the pan in a larger baking pan. Pour enough hot water into the pan to come ½" up the sides of the springform pan. Bake for about 1 hour. Cool for 15 minutes and then, using a sharp knife, cut around the sides of the pan to loosen the cheesecake. Loosen the pan sides and cool cake completely before refrigerating for 4 hours or more. *Makes 12 servings.*

Nutrients per serving: Calories 290, Fat 18g, Cholesterol 125mg,
Sodium 190mg, Carbohydrates 25g, Protein 7g.

Crustless Cheesecake #2

A delicious cheesecake to make with either low-fat or regular cheeses. This can be made a day ahead or even 2 days, for this keeps well. Use an 8" springform pan or double the recipe and put it in a 9" × 13" oblong cake pan to serve up to 20 people.

Note: *If desired, add a crust by mixing 3 tablespoons melted butter and ¾ cup crushed sweetened GF cornflakes. Pat the mixture into the bottom of the pan.*

Crust (optional) (see note)
12 ounces cream cheese or ⅓ reduced-fat cream cheese
½ cup ricotta cheese
¾ cup sugar
4 eggs
2 tablespoons butter or margarine, melted and cooled

1½ tablespoons cornstarch
1½ tablespoons sweet rice flour
1½ tablespoons vanilla
1 cup sour cream or nondairy substitute (fat free okay)
Seasonal fresh fruit for topping

Preheat oven to 325°. Prepare an 8" springform pan by adding the crust (if using one), or spray with vegetable oil spray.

In the bowl of your mixer, beat the cream cheese, ricotta cheese, and sugar until smooth. Add the eggs, one at a time, beating after each addition. Add the butter, cornstarch, sweet rice flour, and vanilla. Beat until smooth. Fold in the sour cream (if using a nondairy substitute like IMO, thin slightly with nondairy liquid).

Pour into the prepared pan and bake, uncovered, for 1 hour. Do not open the oven door. Turn off the oven and let the cheesecake stand in the closed oven for 2 hours. Cool completely and then chill before serving. Top with fruit, if desired. *Makes 10 servings.*

Nutrients per serving: Calories 250, Fat 3g, Cholesterol 85mg, Sodium 140mg, Carbohydrates 42g, Protein 7g.

Egg-free Cheese Tart

375°

A quick and easy dessert that looks elegant when dressed up with any kind of fresh fruit or just decorated with a twist of orange slice. Use an 8" pie tin or springform pan and vary the taste of the crust with the nut of your choice.

Note: *Most grocery stores will have at least 1 corn or rice flake cereal that doesn't have malt flavoring or malt syrup.*

Note 2: *If the cereal is already sweetened, cut sugar to ½ cup.*

CRUST:

2 cups GF cereal flakes
⅔ cup brown sugar (see note 2)
¼ cup (½ stick) margarine or
   butter, melted
½ cup finely chopped nuts (cashew,
   pecan, or macadamia) or coconut

FILLING:

One 15-ounce carton ricotta cheese
   (2 cups)
3 tablespoons lime or lemon juice
½ cup confectioners' sugar
Fruit for topping

Preheat oven to 375°.

Place the cereal in a plastic bag and crush. Add the brown sugar, melted margarine, and nuts. Reserve 3 tablespoons for the topping, and pour the rest into the pie tin or springform pan. Pat into a crust. Bake for 6 minutes. Cool to room temperature before filling.

For the filling, with mixer or food processor, blend the ricotta cheese, juice, and confectioners' sugar until smooth. Spoon into the baked shell. Top with a sprinkle of the remaining crust mix.

Refrigerate. Just before serving, top with fresh, sweetened fruit (strawberries, raspberries, peaches, kiwi) or decorate with a twisted slice of lime or orange (including peel). *Makes 6–8 servings.*

Nutrients per serving: Calories 290, Fat 14g, Cholesterol 25mg, Sodium 210mg, Carbohydrates 39g, Protein 7g.

Meringue-Topped Coconut-Pecan Cheesecake   325°–350°
(with Variations)

So sinfully delicious no one will guess it's both gluten free and contains only ingredients from your local grocery store. Make any of the several variations shown below.

CRUST:

1½ cups shredded coconut

¼ cup chopped pecans

2 tablespoons margarine, melted

FILLING:

Two 8-ounce packages ⅓ reduced
   fat cream cheese

⅔ cup sugar

2 tablespoons water

1½ teaspoons vanilla

3 egg yolks

½ cup chopped pecans

MERINGUE:

3 egg whites

⅛ teaspoon salt

One 7-ounce jar marshmallow
   cream

Preheat oven to 325°. Grease a 9" springform pan on the bottom and sides.

In a small plastic bag, combine the coconut and ¼ cup pecans. Pour in the melted margarine and work with your hands until the margarine is distributed evenly. Pat into the prepared pan. Bake for 15 minutes. Remove and raise the oven temperature to 350°.

While the crust is baking, prepare the filling: Beat the cream cheese, sugar, water, and vanilla until smooth. Beat in the yolks until just combined. Pour over the baked crust. Place the springform pan on a baking sheet (in order to avoid overbaking the crust), and bake for 25 minutes or until the custard is nearly set. Remove and sprinkle with the ½ cup pecans and top with the meringue.

To prepare the meringue, in a clean bowl of your mixer beat the egg whites with the salt on medium until soft peaks form. Gradually add the marshmallow creme, beating on high for about 4 minutes or until the mixture forms stiff peaks. Spread over the hot cheesecake, carefully spreading it to the edges of the pan. Return to the oven and bake for 15 more minutes.

Cool for 1 hour before removing the sides of the pan. Refrigerate to chill before serving. *Makes 10–12 servings.*

VARIATIONS:

BUTTERSCOTCH: Use brown sugar in place of the white sugar.

MOCHA: Add 2 tablespoons cocoa powder and 1 teaspoon espresso powder to the filling.

CHOCOLATE: Add 3 tablespoons cocoa powder to the filling.

Nutrients per serving: Calories 320, Fat 19g, Cholesterol 75mg,
Sodium 360mg, Carbohydrates 33g, Protein 6g.

RECIPES FOR DESSERTS WITH NO SPECIAL INGREDIENTS IN OTHER BOOKS IN THE *GLUTEN-FREE GOURMET* SERIES

See page 92 for book title abbreviations.

RECIPE	BOOK	PAGE
Angel Food Cake	GFG	78
	GFG rev	105
Baked Apples with Nuts and Raisins	GFG	201
	GFG rev	176
Baked Prune Whip	F&H	188
Coconut Macaroons	GFG	52
	GFG rev	122
Creamy Rice Pudding	More	177
Forgotten Dreams	GFG	51
	GFG rev	122
Hawaiian Delight Meringues	GFG	192
	GFG rev	165
Linzertorte	More	172
No-Bake Peanut Butter Cookies	GFG	54
	GFG rev	128
Pam's Pavlova	More	170
Peanut Butter Drops	GFG	51
	GFG rev	121
Pecan Bites	GFG	52
	GFG rev	123
Rhubarb Fool	More	180
Shortbread	More	133
Tropical Fruitcake	GFG	214
	GFG rev	201

Companies That Sell
Gluten-free Products and Supplies

When I first started the *Gluten-free Gourmet* series almost two decades ago, we could count the suppliers for products without gluten on the fingers of one hand, and the products they carried were equally limited. So much has changed that today we can find over fifty large suppliers while more GF products are carried in health food stores and specialty markets. Many support groups sell the flours, mixes, and xanthan gum at their meetings or by mail order.

Even more exciting is the fact that in the last year or so, mixes for pancakes and waffles, cookies, cakes, and breads have appeared to join the GF cookies and crackers on grocery shelves, while Oriental stores carry fine white rice flour, tapioca flour, and potato starch. And the mail-order suppliers have branched out into more than just cookies and mixes. Some furnish main dishes either frozen or shelf stable to eat at home or while camping. Many others provide ready-baked full desserts in their local communities.

With these many suppliers specializing in gluten-free goods, you should find your baking needs close to home. But there are still a few flours and supplies used in this book that are so unusual that they will have to be special ordered until health food stores carry them on a regular basis.

ALPINEAIRE FOODS (shelf-stable dehydrated soups, meals for camping, hiking, and back-packing): 4031 Alvis Court, Rocklin, CA 95677; phone (800) 322-6325 or (916) 824-5000. Accepts orders by mail, phone, or fax. Some products can be found in sporting goods stores. Write or phone for a full product list.

AUTHENTIC FOODS (baking mixes for pancakes, bread, cakes, and veggie burgers; Gar-fava flour; Bette's Four Flour blend; brown and white rice flour; tapioca starch, potato flour, potato starch, and many other GF flours; xanthan gum; maple sugar; vanilla powder; and other flavorings): 1850 West 169th St., Suite B, Gardena, CA 90247; phone (800) 806-4737 or (310) 366-7612, fax (310) 366-6938. Internet Web site: http://www.authenticfoods.com or http://www.glutenfree-supermarket.com. Accepts orders by phone, mail, or fax. Write, call, or visit their Web site for complete product list. Some products can be found in health food stores.

BOB'S RED MILL NATURAL FOODS (bread and baking mix, cereals, GF flours, xanthan and guar gums, baking aids): 5209 S.E. International Way, Milwaukie, OR 97222; phone (800) 553-2258, fax (503) 653-1339. Web site: www.bobsredmill.com. Takes orders by mail, e-mail, phone, or fax. Write for an order form. Some products can be found in health food stores and in health sections of grocery stores.

'CAUSE YOU'RE SPECIAL CO. (mixes for cakes, cookies, bread, muffins, pancakes, pizza crusts, and pastry; plus rice, potato starch, and tapioca starch flours, xanthan gum): P.O. Box 316, Phillips, WI 54555; phone (815) 877-6722, fax (603) 754-0245; Web site: http://www.causeyourespecial.com. Accepts orders by mail, phone, or fax. Some products may be found in health food and specialty grocery stores.

CELIMIX PRODUCTS [Nelson David of Canada Ltd.] (baking mixes, soups, gravies, cookies, crackers, pastas, and more): 66 Higgins Ave., Winnipeg, Manitoba R3B 0A5; phone (866) 989-0379. Write or phone for full order form.

CYBROS, INC. (breads, rolls, cookies, white rice and tapioca flours): P.O. Box 851, Waukesha, WI 53187-0851; phone (800) 876-2253, fax (414) 547-8946. Accepts orders by mail, phone, or fax. Products can also be found in health food stores and are sold by some celiac organizations. Write or phone for their order form.

DE-RO-MA [Food Intolerance Centre] (gluten-free flours): 1118 Berlier, Laval, Quebec H7L 3R9, Canada; phone (514) 990-5694 or (800) 363-DIET, fax (450) 629-4781. Call, fax, or write for their full catalog.

DIETARY SPECIALTIES (baking mixes, dry pastas, snacks, and main dishes to heat and serve): 1248 Sussex Turnpike, Unit C-2, Randolph, NJ 07869; phone (888) 640-2800, fax (973) 895-3742. Write, phone, or fax for full product list or visit Web site: www.dietspec.com.

DIXIE LEGUMES PLUS, INC. (lentil soups, chili, casserole and salad mixes): P.O. Box 1969, Tomball, TX 77377; phone (800) 323-3668, fax (281) 516-3070. Web site: www. legumesplus.com. Accepts orders by phone, mail, or fax. Some products can be found in health food and gourmet stores and specialty supermarkets. Call for a free catalog.

EL PETO PRODUCTS LTD. (strictly gluten-free manufacturer and distributor of fresh-baked products, baking mixes, soups, pastas, gluten-free flours, cookbooks, snacks, and crackers; bean, rice, quinoa, millet, and other GF flours milled specially for them at The Mill Stone): 41 Shoemaker St., Kitchener, Ontario N2E 3G9; phone (800) 387-4064, fax (519) 743-8096, e-mail: elpeto@golden.net. Web site: www.elpeto.com. Order by phone, fax, mail, or e-mail. Some products can be found in specialty markets and health food stores.

ENER-G-FOODS, INC. (vacuum-packaged breads, rolls, buns, pizza shells, doughnuts, cookies, granola bars; dry mixes, cereals, and flours; xanthan gum; methocel; dough enhancer; almond meal; tapioca, bean, rice, and other gluten-free flours; and Bette Hagman's flour mixes; Egg Replacer; Lacto-Free; and cookbooks): P.O. Box 84487, Seattle, WA 98124; phone (800) 331-5222, fax (206) 764-3398; Web site: www. ener-g.com. Accepts orders by phone, mail, fax, or secure Web site. Phone for a catalog of their long list. Products can be found in some health food stores and specialty markets.

FOOD FOR LIFE BAKING COMPANY, INC. (baked bread and muffins, pastas): P.O. Box 1434, Corona, CA 91718-1434; phone (800) 797-5090, fax (909) 279-1784. Takes orders by mail. Write for their complete order form. Products can be found in the frozen food sections of specialty and natural food stores under Food For Life name.

THE FOOD MERCHANTS (polenta and polenta pastas): Quinoa Corporation, P.O. Box 279, Gardena, CA 90248; phone (310) 217-8125, fax (310) 217-8140. Accepts orders by mail. Some products can be found in health food stores and some groceries. Phone for full product list.

FOODS BY GEORGE (baked English muffins, pizza crusts, desserts, and main-meal items): 3 King St., Mahwah, NJ 07430; phone (201) 612-9700, fax (201) 684-0334. Items shipped frozen. Anyone interested should write or phone for an order form. Fresh items often sold at celiac meetings in New England area.

GLUTEN SOLUTIONS, INC. (offers 240 gluten-free products from 28 different manufacturers): 737 Manhattan Beach Blvd., Suite B, Manhattan Beach, CA 90266; phone (888) 845-8836, fax (810) 454-8277. Web site: www.glutensolutions.com. Phone for their order form or order on-line. Some products may be found in whole foods markets.

THE GLUTEN FREE COOKIE JAR (bread, bagels, pretzels, cakes, cookies, and baking mixes): P.O. Box 52, Trevose, PA 19053; phone (215) 355-9403 or (888) GLUTEN-0, fax (215) 355-7991. Web site: www.glutenfreecookiejar.com. Accepts orders by mail, phone, fax, or Web site. Anyone interested should write or phone for their order form. Some products may be found in health food stores.

THE GLUTEN-FREE PANTRY, INC. (gluten-free mixes, crackers, cookies, pastas, soups, and baking supplies such as xanthan gum, guar gum, dough enhancers; a long list of gluten-free flours including white, brown, and wild rice, garbanzo bean, several corn flours, and more): P.O. Box 840, Glastonbury, CT 06033; phone (800) 291-8386 or (860) 633-3826, fax (860) 633-6853. Web site: www.glutenfree.com. Write or phone for their free catalog. Accepts orders by Internet, phone, mail, or fax. Computer-savvy people can also shop on-line.

GLUTEN-FREE TRADING CO., LLC (a store with over 750 shelf-stable gluten-free items ranging from baking supplies and flours through condiments, cookies, and pastas): 604A W. Lincoln Avenue, Milwaukee, WI 53215; phone (888) 933-9933 or (414) 385-9950, fax (414) 385-9915. Web site: www.gluten-free.net. Phone, fax, e-mail, or write for their complete catalog.

GLUTINO (DE-RO-MA) (breads, bagels, pizzas, cookies, mixes, pastas, baked items, and gluten-free flours): 3750 Francis Hughes Ave., Laval, Quebec H7L 5A9, Canada; phone (450) 629-7689 or (800) 363-3438 (DIET), fax (450) 629-4781, e-mail: info@ glutino.com. Call, fax, e-mail, or write for their full catalog. Many items can be found in health food and grocery stores. Also sold through celiac organizations. Web site: www.glutino.com.

GRAIN PROCESS ENTERPRISES, LTD. (Romano, navy, chickpea, garbanzo-fava, and yellow pea flours, and other gluten-free flours including rice, buckwheat, millet, tapioca, potato, and arrowroot; xanthan and guar gums): 115 Commander Blvd., Scarborough, Ontario M1S 3M7, Canada; phone (416) 291-3226, fax (416) 291-2159, e-mail karen@grain-process.com. Write or phone for their list. Take orders by mail, phone, or fax. Some products can be found in health food stores. Web site: www.grainprocess.com.

KAYBEE GLUTEN-FREE PRODUCTS (mixes for bread, buns, muffins, cakes, cookies, pizza, and pyrogy): 629 Cudworth, Saskatchewan S0K 1B0, Canada; phone and fax (306) 256-3424. Phone or write for full order form.

THE KING ARTHUR FLOUR COMPANY, INC. (rice, tapioca, and potato starch flours; xanthan gum; baking tools and pans): P.O. Box 876, Norwich, VT 05055; phone (800) 827-6836, fax (800) 343-3002. Web site: www.KingArthurFlour.com. Accepts orders by phone, fax, mail, or Web site. Please request a free King Arthur Flour Baker's catalog.

KINNIKINNICK FOODS (breads, buns, bagels, doughnuts, cookies, pizza crusts, muffins, xanthan gum, guar gum; rice, corn, potato, bean, and soya flours; other baking supplies): 10306-112 St., Edmonton, Alberta T5K 1N1, Canada; phone (877) 503-4466, fax (780) 421-0456, toll free (877) 503-4466, e-mail: info@kinnikinnick.com. Web site: www.kinikinnick.com. Accepts orders via phone, mail, fax, or secure Web site. Offers home delivery of all products to most areas in North America. Some products may be found in health food stores and some in regular grocery stores in the alternative food section.

MRS. LEEPER'S PASTA (gluten-free corn and rice pastas): 12455 Kerran St. #200, Poway, CA 92064; phone (858) 486-1101, fax (858) 406-1770; Web site: m/pinc@pacbell.net or www.mrs.leeperspasta.com. Sold through health food stores and some gourmet sections in large grocery stores under the label Mrs. Leeper's Pasta. Write or phone to inquire where products are distributed in your area. Mail orders will be filled for those living too far from stores handling these products.

LEGUMES PLUS: See DIXIE LEGUMES PLUS, INC.

MENDOCINO GLUTEN-FREE PRODUCTS, INC. (cake mix, bread mixes, pancake and waffle mix, general-purpose flour): P.O. Box 277, Willits, CA 95490-0277; phone (800) 297-5399, fax (707) 459-1834, e-mail: sylvanfarm@pacific.net. Products marketed under Sylvan Border Farm label. Orders taken by phone, mail, fax, or e-mail. Write or phone for an order form. Some products may be found in health food and grocery stores.

NANA'S KITCHEN (Buttonelli Board for making easy spaetzle or pasta): P.O. Box 2640, Oroville, WN 98844 or RR1 Site 9, Comp 26, Chase, BC V0E 1M0, Canada; phone (866) 679-2818, fax (250) 679-2817, e-mail: hannelore@cookingwithnana.com. Web site for more information: www.cookingwithnana.com. Phone or e-mail for a brochure.

NANCY'S NATURAL FOODS (long list of GF flours including sorghum and bean, xanthan gum, guar gum, milk powders, and substitutes): 266 N.W. First Ave. Suite A, Canby, OR 97013; phone (877) 862-4457 or (503) 266-3306, fax (503) 266-3306; e-mail: nnfoods@teleport.com. Accepts orders by phone, mail, or e-mail. Ask for their long list of GF baking supplies.

THE REALLY GREAT FOOD CO. (mixes for breads, cakes, muffins, pizza, and more; cereal, snacks, soups, condiments, vitamins, and pasta; rice and tapioca flours; xanthan gum): P.O. Box 2239, St. James, NY 11780; phone (800) 593-5377, fax (631) 361-6920; e-mail: www.reallygreatfood.com. Accepts orders by mail, phone, or e-mail. Call or write for a full product list.

RED RIVER MILLING COMPANY [formerly Sam Pierce Plant] (sorghum [milo], mung, and garbanzo [chickpea] flours): 801 Cumberland Street, Vernon, TX 76384; phone (800) 419-9614 or (940) 553-1211, fax (940) 552-2772. Accepts orders by mail or phone. Products also sold through Miss Roben's and celiac organizations. Company mills only gluten-free products.

MISS ROBEN'S (over 500 GF products: baking mixes, ready-to-eat products, cookbooks, pastas, ingredients, and baking supplies, including sorghum, bean flours, Bette Hagman flour blends, xanthan and guar gums, personal-care items, plus free technical baking support): P.O. Box 1149, Frederick, MD 21702; phone (800) 891-0083, fax (301) 665-9584, e-mail: info@missroben.com. Web site: www.missroben.com. Accepts orders by mail, phone, e-mail, fax, or Web site. Phone or write for their full catalog.

SON'S MILLING (whole bean flour, sorghum, and other GF flours): 6820 Kirkpatrick Crescent, Victoria, BC V8M 1Z9, Canada; phone (250) 544-1733, fax (250) 544-1739. Accepts orders by phone, mail, or fax. Write or call for a complete list.

SPECIALTY FOOD SHOP (mixes, baked goods, pasta, crackers, soups, cookbooks, and a long line of gluten-free flours, xanthan gum, guar gum, rice and corn bran): Radio Centre Plaza, Upper Level, 875 Main Street West, Hamilton, Ontario L8S 4P9, Canada, or 555 University Ave., Toronto, Ontario, M5G 1X8; phone (800) SFS-7976 or (905) 528-4707 (Hamilton) or (416) 977-4360 (Toronto), fax (905) 528-5625 (Hamilton) or (416) 977-8394 (Toronto); e-mail: SFS@sickkids.on.ca (Hamilton). Web site: www.specialtyfoodshop.com. Hamilton takes orders by phone, mail, fax, or e-mail. Write for product list. Also has retail stores in Hamilton and Toronto.

STERK'S BAKERY (new French bread, dinner rolls, bagels, gluten-free flour, baking mixes, and more): 3866 23 Street, Jordan, Ontario, L0R 1S0, Canada, or 1402 Pine Ave. Suite 727, Niagara Falls, NY 14301; phone (905) 562-3086, fax (905) 562-3847. Accepts orders by mail or phone. Write for a free catalog.

TAD ENTERPRISES (rice, potato, and tapioca flours; xanthan and guar gums; bread mix, pizza crust, pasta): 9356 Pleasant, Tinley Park, IL 60477; phone (800) 438-6153, fax (708) 429-3954, e-mail: tadenterprise@aol.com. Accepts orders by mail, phone, e-mail, or fax. Write for order form for complete list of products

TAMARIND TREE (GF shelf stable, vegetarian, ready-to-heat-and-serve Indian entrees): 518 Justin Way, Neshanic Station, NJ 08853; phone (908) 369-6300, fax (908) 369-9300, e-mail: tamtree@bellatlantic.net; Web site: www.tamtree.com. Accepts orders by mail, phone, or e-mail. Products may be found in some health food stores. Check the Web site for list of products.

TWIN VALLEY MILLS, LLC (sorghum flour): RR1 Box 45, Ruskin, NE 68974; phone (402) 279-3965; e-mail: sorghumflour@hotmail.com. Anyone interested should write or phone for order form. Some of the flour may be found at health food stores. Check their Web site for more information at www.twinvalleymills.com.

This list, offered for the reader's convenience, was updated at the time of publication of this book. I regret I cannot be responsible for later changes in names, addresses, or phone numbers, or for a company's removing some products from its line.

Index

About the Author

BETTE HAGMAN, a.k.a. the Gluten-free Gourmet, was diagnosed as a celiac more than twenty-five years ago. Since then she has written four cookbooks, each offering a multitude of delicious wheat- and gluten-free recipes—what she calls a "prescription for living." She is a writer, lecturer, and a twenty-five-year member of the Gluten Intolerance Group (GIG). Bette Hagman lives in Seattle.